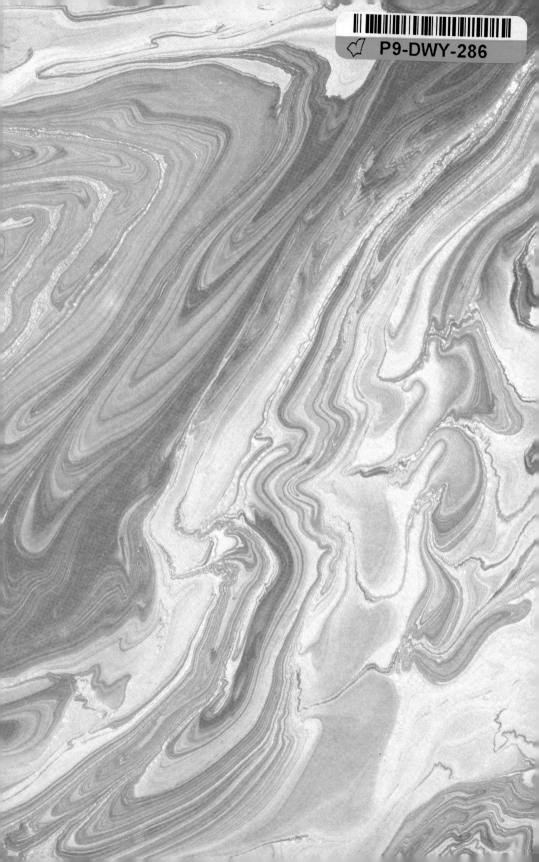

# THE WARS of PEGGY HULL

# THE WARS of PEGGY HULL

*The Life and Times of
a War Correspondent*

*Wilda M. Smith
Eleanor A. Bogart*

Texas Western Press
The University of Texas at El Paso

First Edition
Library of Congress Catalog Card No. 89-051841
ISBN 0-87404-215-1

All Texas Western Press books are printed on acid-free paper, meeting the guidelines for permanence and durability of the Committee on Production Guidelines for Book Longevity of the Council on Library Resources.

 — Permanence of Paper for Printed Library Materials, ANSI Z.39.48-1984.

# C O N T E N T S

# ACKNOWLEDGMENTS

Virtually hundreds of wonderful, helpful people aided us in our research for this biography. We are especially indebted to those who granted us interviews, loaned or gave us pictures, letters and other materials and whose names appear in the Notes and picture credit lines.

Peggy Hull's half sister, Alice Goodnough Reissig; nieces, Frances Goodnough Rankin, Josephine Goodnough Yakich, the late Eldora Goodnough Verburg; and cousin, Doris Haley Briney, shared family stories and/or loaned us family treasures.

Some people's help was crucial. Raymond A. Ruffino gave us permission to use Peggy Hull's papers. His sister, Eve Ruffino Burch, aided us in ways only she could have. George Griffin, then curator of the Kansas Collection at the University of Kansas Libraries, first introduced us to the Peggy Hull Deuell Collection; his successor, Sheryl Williams, has continued to do everything she could to help us. Professor James L. Forsythe, former chairman of the history department, now graduate dean at Fort Hays State University, and Marc Campbell, Esta Lou Riley, Mac Reed, and the other librarians at Fort Hays State helped by making either time or material available to us.

All of the following went above and beyond the call of duty for us: Fred S. Michener; Lt. Col. Theodore J. Crackel; Leslie Weirman Riley and the other librarians at the Cornwall (New York) Public Library; Lee Major, archivist, *Chicago Tribune;* Ken Rapp, archivist, West Point; David Len Jones; Adj. Gen. Beulah M. Cope, Ret., United Spanish War Veterans; James R. Fischl, veterans services officer, Veterans Administration; the staffs of the Kansas, Ohio, Minnesota, Hawaii, California, and Colorado state historical libraries, and the museum at Columbus, New Mexico; the librarians at the University of Kansas, Wichita State University and Bethel College; the public servants in the Ottawa and Saline county (Kansas) Register of Deeds and Clerk of the District Court offices; the dedicated workers at the New York Public Library (microfilm division), the Library of Congress, the *Cleveland Plain Dealer,* the El Paso Public Library, the library at Fort Bliss, and the *El Paso Times.*

In addition, we wish to acknowledge the assistance of the staffs of these public libraries: Deming, New Mexico; Cleveland and Columbus, Ohio; Hays, Salina, Wichita, Topeka, and Lawrence, Kansas; Monterey, Carmel, and Salinas, California; Chicago, Denver, and St. Paul.

We are especially grateful for the aid and support of the late Tom Mahoney who shared with us material he had collected with the help of Millard McKinney of El Paso and Adelaide Santonastase, librarian, *Editor & Publisher.*

Julia Edwards, author of *Women of the World,* has been unflagging in her encouragement and belief in the book; and our families and other friends have been understanding when we needed understanding and enthusiastic when we needed enthusiasm.

Dale L. Walker, director of Texas Western Press, has guided us through the publication process with wisdom, patience, and uncommon sensitivity. We are also grateful to Associate Director Nancy Hamilton, whose own interest in Peggy Hull predated her knowledge of our work, for her personal support as well as her expert editing. Our appreciation is also extended to Rebecca Quiñones for her outstanding work in designing the book.

Finally, each of us gives a special thanks to the other for we recognize that neither of us could have written this book by herself.

We dedicate *The Wars of Peggy Hull* to all of those who did not live to see the result of their help and who will never get to know the full story of Peggy Hull.

Portions of this book previously appeared in volume five of the *Prairie Scout,* published by the Kansas Corral of the Westerners.

# INTRODUCTION

Only a handful of friends attended the memorial service and her burial. The only public attention paid to her passing besides a death notice in the local newspaper was an article which appeared in the Overseas Press Club *Bulletin*. How could this have happened to a woman who had been as famous as Peggy Hull? After all, as the first woman to be accredited by the United States War Department as a war correspondent, she had been responsible for breaking down the barrier to official recognition of women in a profession jealously guarded by men.

She had been associated with the great and powerful, among them Gen. John J. Pershing and Robert R. McCormick. Her stories had been the leads in the *New York Daily News,* the *Cleveland Plain Dealer,* the *El Paso Morning Times,* the Army *Chicago Tribune.* Why then has she been deprived of her rightful place in the annals of notable American women? Is it because she was never an admitted feminist though she chafed, sometimes loudly, under sexist restrictions? Is it because she did not die a sudden and dramatic death like Ernie Pyle's which would have ensured her journalistic immortality? Or is it because she failed to find a publisher for her book, "Beyond This Post" (now lost)? Then there was the fundamental, sometimes crippling contradiction in her character, one side of which projected and promoted her image as a flamboyant, glamourous reporter, and another which longed for the traditional life of a dependent housewife, a role which in actuality bored her to tears, as well as to drink.

The split in her personality mirrored the general cultural ambivalence toward women in America during her early years (1889-1915). Technology brought electricity's bright lights, electric irons, washers, coffeepots, vacuum cleaners, as well as automobiles and telephones, within reach of the urban middle class; women's work became easier and less time consuming in a period when, perhaps even partly because of technology, women had finally fought their way close to being granted the vote.

That far-reaching changes were taking place in woman's sphere is evident in the magazines of the time. During the last decades of the nineteenth century, *Ladies' Home Journal* sent out mixed signals to women, "images of plucky, self sufficient women [competing] in the *Journal's* pages with maternal symbols of an earlier era."[1] It was inevitable that something had to give, and from the *Journal* and other magazines it was apparent that the image of independent woman was becoming the stronger. In 1905 the female form was corset-shaped and covered from neck to toenail. Then, year by year, hemlines crept up until by 1914 ankles showed, arms were bared, and filmy, insubstantial fabrics both loosely covered and coyly revealed the female figure, even to the "V" neckline's becoming fashionable.

In another radical development, by 1900 a lot of women were working outside the home for a paycheck, and during the first two decades of the twentieth century, fueled by such advances as the refinement of the typewriter, the number skyrocketed.[2] First operated by men, the typewriter soon became the province of a cheaper supply of efficient workers: women.[3] What's more, this symbol of the working woman, the typewriter, played a big part in Peggy Hull's career, for it invaded newspaper newsrooms with a vengeance. Extant examples of her copy indicate that she was not a particularly good typist, probably self-taught.

It is doubtful that she would have succeeded as a secretary; she was fortunate that standards for newspaper copy were not stringent and also that, by the time she decided on a journalistic career (1908), that field was fairly open to women, thanks to famous and glamourous pioneers like "Nellie Bly" and "Annie Laurie." Even so, most newspaperwomen were hired to handle "women's concerns" — society and homemaking-page editing. Although Peggy Hull did her share of it, this type of work did not appeal to her, even though, in the Midwestern middle-class culture from which she came, it was considered respectable, while "woman *reporter*" was held in low esteem; Peggy's mother, a poor one to throw social stones, self-righteously disapproved of her daughter's choice of career.

Peggy Hull's first direct contact with the Women's Rights Movement appears to have been when she was assigned to report on a woman suffrage meeting in Honolulu in 1912 when she was editing the woman's page in the *Pacific Commercial Advertiser*. Although this experience caused her to expand the scope of her column to include women's political and legal affairs and she often complained about sex-based restrictions, she never took an active part in the movement. In this way, she was typical of a large group of women achievers who enjoyed the fruits of the struggle for equal rights but did not directly involve themselves in that struggle. Her rationalization, that she spent all her time and energy on her profession and trying to get ahead in it and that when she succeeded it helped all women, was the typical one of a large segment of the working woman population then as it is even today. There is, of course, some truth in it. But the fact that feminists and suffragists were repeatedly attacked with the label "unwomanly" must also have played a big part in her reluctance to get involved. Having her "womanhood" questioned intimidated her as few other things did: She hardly flinched at gunfire, but, like most of us, she quailed before social scorn.

The opponents of the Women's Rights Movement knew what they were doing when they called the movement and those connected with it "unwomanly." This sneering attitude had a long history of effectiveness in keeping women in line. In 1917 Laurence Houseman wrote in an article for *Good Housekeeping* entitled "What is Womanly?":

> Every fresh effort of [the] social spirit to find itself and become effective in women has in the past been met either with contempt or reproof and has had to face at the beginning of each new phase in its activity the charge of unwomanliness.
>
> . . . Now compare that attack, fundamental in its nature, all-embracing in its condemnation, with the kind of attac [*sic*] leveled against the corresponding manifestations of the social or reforming spirit in man. In a man, new and unfamiliar indications of the stirring-up of the social conscience may earn such epithets of opprobrium as rash, hot-headed, ill-considered, pernicious, impracticable, Utopian, immoral — but we never label them unmanly. Initiative, fresh adventure of thought or action in man, has always been regarded as a natural concomitant of his nature. In a woman initiative has very generally been regarded (in so far as it breaks with the conventions of contemporary society) as unnatural, unwomanly. The accusation is fundamental. It does not concern itself with any unsoundness in the doctrines put forth but only with the fact that a woman has dared to become their mouth piece or their instrument. Go back to any period in the last two hundred years where a . . . new attempt was made by woman toward civic thought and action, and you will find that at the time the charge of unwomanliness was leveled against her.[4]

This was a charge, even implicit, that Peggy Hull could not bear; and, of course, with her military passion, she put herself in the way of it constantly. Still, she repeatedly recoiled from it. In fact, it sometimes seemed as if every other week she thrust her uniform to the back of the closet, draped herself in "pink filmy things," and played at being the Total Woman for twenty-four hours.

Although she was married three times, she had no children. There is no evidence to show whether this was from choice or an inability to bear children. Growing up under Victorian taboos, she no doubt learned that women were not supposed to have sexual feelings. And when the reaction against this came in the 1920s, it apparently did not affect her, at least outwardly. Whatever her attitudes were on this subject, she kept them to herself.

It may simply have been that her sexual drive was lower than her career ambitions. As far as can be ascertained, she did not write about her sexuality, and she did not talk about it, even to close friends or relatives; how she felt about it seems unknowable.

What is clear is that she was enthralled with "romantic" love. And throughout her life, there were men eager to take care of her.

The idea of "glamour" and projecting an image of it was of paramount importance to her as she admitted in a letter she wrote to her old friend, Minneapolis newspaperman Carroll Michener, in February 1945 from the Pacific war zone where she was reporting on World War II.

> Surely it is true that I was a born romantic — nothing was so important to me and I'm glad now that I did not try to stifle it as so many women of my generation did.[5]

But two pages later she continued:

> In spite of all the varied and exciting adventures I have had in the meantime that experience that afternoon [with you in Minnesota in 1915] made me realize what I wanted in life. I wanted a home and a woman's life — up until that particular Sunday afternoon when I . . . felt the warmth of a homelife, I had thought I wanted a career. That nothing else mattered. Success was my goal. It is odd then that I should have gone on for years striving for success when it was a domestic career that was my real desire.[6]

And that was not all. Behind the glamour girl and the frustrated homebody, "feminine as a kitten," this "kindest, most generous and compassionate human being,"[7] loomed that most "unfeminine," "unwomanly" of creatures, the War Lover.[8] She denied it, shocked by the mere idea, but that did not make it less true. In an interview for an article for *Park East Magazine,* she said:

> I had always been idealistic about the American Army and when other girls were sighing over love stories, I was stirred by reading of the great military campaigns. General Sherman was to me what the muscle bound matinee idols were to other girls.[9]

Despite Gen. Robert E. Lee's famous admission, "It is well that war is so terrible [or] we should grow too fond of it," it is a moral tenet of our culture that no one likes war. And Peggy Hull staunchly maintained, "I did not go to war because I liked the excitement or what my colleagues sometimes erroneously refer to as the glamor. I went because

I was not a man and could not carry a gun and do something for my country."[10] Protest as she might, it was obvious that she had always been really alive only in wartime in a war situation.

Peggy Hull's life was often painful, her happy endings turning into sad beginnings, relationships begun in hope and innocence often ending in heartbreak. Even her occupational character was not without blemish. But we believe that she would have agreed with Tolstoy's statement:

> I clearly realize that my biography, if it suppressed all the nastiness and criminality of my life — as they customarily write biographies — would be a lie, and that if one is going to write my biography one must write the whole truth.[11]

We have done our best to write the truth as we have found it.

*FROM* the sunflower-fringed cornfields of Kansas to the crimsoned battlefields of Europe, where the fate of civilization hangs in the balance; from the rollicking barn dances of the Middle West to the stately ballrooms of Paris; from the shy, sun-bonneted belle of a country village to the friend and confidant of heroes and statesmen . . .; from a raw cub reporter, hectored by dyspeptic rural editors, to an accredited war correspondent, chronicling the gripping events of the greatest armed struggle of right against might history has ever known — these are just a few of the triumphs achieved by Peggy Hull, who, not a dozen years ago, . . . was dreaming over a dog-eared geography and tracing the path to fame she meant to follow. And now she is telling the world she left behind how she made her dreams come true.

Peggy Hull,
"Plucky Yankee Girl Reporter"

## CHAPTER ONE

# Growing Up in Kansas

World War II, Pacific Theater of Operations, February 1945.

On a recently pacified island in the Marianas a middle-aged woman sat at a typewriter replying to a letter from an old friend, Minnesota newspaperman Carroll Michener.

> Just can't imagine that you are 59 — but then I can't even real-
> ize I'm 54. Never in all my life have I enjoyed each day as much
> as I do now. No one could ever have convinced me that such an
> age could possibly bring such sheer pleasure in living. And you
> should see how I'm living! In a hut in an army camp — sleeping
> on a canvas cot — running out of doors to a latrine and a shower
> shed quite a distance away — plowing through dust one day and
> mud the next.[1]

She had known Carroll Michener since they had worked on newspapers in Denver thirty-five years before. Denver was the first stop on his great adventure — working his way around the world. They had met again in Honolulu in 1912 and in Minneapolis in 1915. That was the last time. After that, he had settled down and her career had taken off.[2] Yet, she was the one who had longed for a traditional life, had tried for it three times between wars.

How had it happened that it was she who had become a war cor-respondent, and he was the long-time editor of the *Minneapolis Miller* and content to be? To him, he confessed, she had been a romantic figure.

> You were very nice and sweet — as you always were — to remem-
> ber me so glamorously—[3]

She had been glamourous. She had been aware of it, cultivated it, used it. Now, that glamour was almost lost in the too ample figure, the unflattering khaki skirt and blouse, the "sensible" shoes. In the old days, in those other wars, she had had glorious uniforms and shiny riding boots and a figure that had given new meaning to the term, military bearing.

She had not been raised for a "military" life. In fact, it would have been hard to find two more peaceful, civilian-oriented spots than Bennington, Kansas, and the tiny mortgaged farm eight miles east of it where Peggy Hull was born Henrietta Eleanor Goodnough on December 30, 1889.*

Although there were only 372 people living there,[5] Bennington was a lively little town. And it was not isolated. Twice a day the train puffed its way along the Solomon spur of the Union Pacific over the rolling prairie of north-central Kansas and entered the south part of the town with the noisy and exciting promise that The World was not far away; it was just down the tracks.[6]

Early on she had realized that boys had more freedom and fun than girls. One was supposed to accept it and be a good little girl. She did not accept it, and she was not a good little girl. From the time she was big enough to assert independence, she showed little interest in tea parties and dolls. Instead, she hung around with the boys, swimming, playing ball, even getting into fist fights with them. She was not, however, the tall slender athletic type. She was short and plump and developed early,[7] but she pushed her soft, feminine body to do whatever her mind willed it to do. Not given to introspection, she had no problems with her femininity. She never wished she had been born male. What she wanted was to do the things boys were allowed to do, and she was determined to do them, opposition or no. To that end, she played and fought with her boy friends, went on dates with her boyfriends, and seemed to have little trouble keeping the two types of relationship separate.

In her childhood she undoubtedly heard talk about the Spanish-American War and stories about the Civil War from her Grandfather Finn. She also read about war in her history books and Richard Harding Davis novels. But for the most part, to her war was as remote and as romantic as the moon. In those days, the eight-mile trip to Bennington, club dances, and town picnics were the exciting events of everyone's life. Bennington itself was a pretty little town, filled with trees; and Sand Creek meandered along its western edge. This setting gave an illusion of life at its most smooth and stable.

---

*After 1917 she usually gave 1890, and 1890 appeared on some of her passports and other legal documents.[4]

Henrietta's father, Edwy Goodnough, named for the ill-fated boy king of England who died in 959 at the age of nineteen,[8] was born on the Oneida Indian reservation in Wisconsin on May 19, 1862. His father, the Reverend Edward Augustus Goodnough, was the Episcopal missionary there. Edwy's mother, Ellen Saxton Goodnough, "naturally bright and cheerful, attracted the Oneida women as visitors to the Mission House, giving them kindly welcome and often entertaining them with a practical lesson in housekeeping."[9] She was the ideal missionary's wife, almost as well-loved by the Indians she served as by her husband and six children.

In the happy times of Edwy's early childhood on the reservation, the Indians had given each of the Goodnoughs an Indian name. Edwy's earliest was "Ah-re-we-ost-oni" which meant "a good word." When he was six, he was renamed "This-ta-rak" (grasshopper), because he was such a frisky little boy. When he was eight, his mother, Ellen Saxton Goodnough, who in her thirty-three years had survived childbirth, forest fires, and a smallpox epidemic, died of pneumonia.[10] When Edwy's world had changed, so had he. Gone forever was the happy little "grasshopper," and when his father was married again, to a woman not eager to care for another woman's children, the children, except for Alice who was crippled, were farmed out to various relatives, Edwy going to live with a paternal aunt in Massachusetts.[11]

As soon as he finished his schooling and was old enough to be on his own, around 1879, he left for eastern Kansas where his Saxton grandparents had moved in 1859. Later, visiting his great uncle 140 miles to the west in Bennington, he decided to settle down and take up farming.[12]

As an adult, Edwy Goodnough was a quiet, reflective man, a reader and a thinker and, unfortunately, not by nature the farmer he tried to be. He seemed not to have the knack for coaxing a living out of the sometimes reluctant land.

Henrietta's mother, Minnie Finn Goodnough, whom Edwy married in 1882, was the daughter of pioneers Sidney and Henrietta Finn. In earlier times Sidney Finn had been a merchant who, during the Civil War, operated a wagon train, selling supplies to the soldiers. In 1874 the family traveled from Wisconsin to Kansas in a covered wagon and homesteaded near Bennington, eventually acquiring another 160 acres of land under the Timber Culture Act. Under this law the national government deeded land to settlers to encourage the cultivation of trees on the relatively treeless prairie. The Finns also tried to raise blackberries commercially. Though everybody worked, including the young children, they did not always make enough to live on, and they had to mortgage the farm land.[13]

The farm that Minnie and her husband Edwy and their son Edward and their daughter Henrietta lived on was only a mile and a half from the Finn farmstead, a closeness which created problems for the Goodnoughs, for Minnie was emotionally tied to her parents. Unhappily, she was *not* emotionally tied to her husband; though she frequently played the organ at local dances for pay and otherwise tried to contribute financially to the family, in her relationship with her husband, she was willful and independent, two traits which she passed on to her only daughter.

So it was little Henrietta who was the curious, rebellious one, Edward who was the tractable little child who never went beyond the post which their mother designated as the limit of safety.[14]

But for them there was no safety. When Henrietta was five and Edward, eleven, their world fell apart: Their parents were divorced. The divorce was a messy one, their mother charging their father with abandoning her, refusing to live with her, and refusing to support her,[15] their father countercharging that their mother was "carrying on" with the owner of the local drug store, neglecting their home, and generally creating a scandal.

Further, their father contended that when he took Minnie and the children to Bennington to a picnic on June 23, 1892, when it came time, around six in the evening, for him to take care of his farm chores, Minnie would not go home with him but "stayed in Bennington until a late hour spending most of her time with [the druggist], and there conducted herself in a way unbecoming of a married woman." In what must have been a humiliating accusation for him, he alleged, even pinpointing a date, that she "frequently told [him] that she cared nothing for [him], and on the 5th of July, 1892 [she] told [him] that she married when she was so young that she did not then know what it was to love and that she could no longer be true to him."

Finally, in his petition he asked for custody of both children, charging that Minnie was "utterly unfit to have the care and custody" of Henrietta and Edward,[16] and it did seem at times that Minnie was, at the very least, a "careless" mother. There was, for instance, that cold, dark night that Minnie and a woman friend had been driving home in the wagon across a heavily rutted field with baby Henrietta and seven-year-old Edward. He had bounced out of the wagon, had been knocked unconscious, and a rear wheel had run over his throat. When he regained consciousness, he was still in the field, lying on the cold ground. Badly injured, he staggered home alone, to find that his mother had not even missed him yet. Edward had stammered ever after and became painfully shy.[17]

Since Kansas law at the time made it difficult to obtain a divorce unless adultery, abandonment, or worse could be shown, most of the charges

Henrietta Eleanor Goodnough as a child, about 1896. *(Courtesy of Alice Goodnough Reissig)*

may have been more a matter of usefulness than truthfulness, though there was probably truth in the most mutually painful of them. Whatever the truth, divorce, though not uncommon, was regarded with grave social disapproval; a stigma attached to those involved, even the innocent. In a small town, the social memory was elephant-like, and a family of divorce, especially a scandalous one, never quite regained its complete respectability.

While Edward was permitted to stay with his father, the court granted the divorce and custody of Henrietta to her mother.[18] They moved in with her parents, Sidney and Henrietta Finn, and their twins, little Henrietta's ten-year-old Aunt Myrtle and Uncle John.[19]

Although Henrietta, a sad little child, was too small to understand all of the implications of her broken home, she realized that hers was not the same family life that most of her friends and relatives had, and she desperately missed Edward and her father.

When the Finns moved to Marysville in 1896, Henrietta and her mother moved with them. Marysville represented a new start to them all: Grandfather Finn operated a livery stable; Grandmother Finn, with Minnie's help, ran a boarding house; and Henrietta went to school.[20] The next spring Minnie married Henry William Hoerath, a house painter by profession;[21] Henrietta had a second father, whom fortunately she liked, and a new home, which she did not because it was on "the wrong side of the tracks." Years later with the wisdom of hindsight, she realized that there had been "rather nice people on our side of the tracks."[22]

But Marysville was not any more sheltered for her than Bennington had been, for her playmate, Trixie Pulleine, smothered to death when a sand bank collapsed on her;[23] later, when Henrietta was nine, the family dentist, a long-time friend of her kin, made sexual advances to her. She never forgot Trixie — or the dentist. He had been so afraid she would tell, he had nearly died with fear. She did not tell. If she had, it would only, she thought, have made a lot of people — her mother, her grandmother and grandfather, her aunts and uncles, and the dentist's wife — unhappy and caused her a great deal of trouble, so, like most children to whom it happens, she kept it a secret. But it had a permanent effect on her.[24]

Many years later she came to believe that this childhood experience had not been a totally negative one, that when the old dentist had

> laid a heavy hand upon [her] thigh and squeezed it, [it might even have been] an act of Providence . . . for [she] had [her] living to earn in a day when "nice" girls didn't go out to work unless they were school teachers or music teachers — otherwise they remained

8

at home in pitiful states of poverty being the ladies which society of that age demanded. Young women in those days who became telephone operators, salesladies, clerks or office workers, or seamstresses were considered fair target for the prowling male — and this [she] was to know at a tender age.[25]

In 1900 the Hoerath family moved from Marysville to Bennington where Will made a fairly good living doing carpentry work, paperhanging, bricklaying, furniture upholstering, sign painting, and odd jobs. He also worked in towns around Bennington which meant that he was away from home sometimes for several days — and nights.[26] Minnie, with good reason, suspected that during these absences he was sometimes unfaithful to her.[27] This was not, of course, without a certain poetic justice, considering Minnie's own past reputation.

In 1902 Minnie and Will went to Colorado to run the boarding car for a Union Pacific bridge gang. Twelve-year-old Henrietta stayed behind and moved in with her Aunt Ella Haley's family so she could finish the school term.[28]

In the early years of the twentieth century automobiles were few and expensive, especially in rural America. Trains were a major means of transportation, and those who lived in communities on the railroad line found it easy and relatively inexpensive to go to nearby towns to shop or visit. Also, the railroads employed a lot of labor, and men willing to work hard for long hours could earn a good amount of money. Fixing meals for railroad work gangs was well paying, and it could have been a very good thing economically for Will and Minnie Hoerath, but only four months after they left for Colorado, they returned to Bennington because Minnie was homesick.[29]

At this time it was difficult for Will to find enough steady work around Bennington; so after a series of minor moves, the family settled in Nebraska. In March 1905, like a cat with her kittens, Minnie, ever pining for Bennington, moved them back.[30]

This move was a happy one for fifteen-year-old Henrietta. Edward, almost twenty-two, spent much of his nonworking time with them (their father had remarried and moved to Arkansas); he and Henrietta became very close. Will Hoerath, appointed city marshal with orders to arrest drunks and users of "profanity or indecent language on the streets" at one dollar a head, built a new house for them on the *right* side of the tracks, and they all entered into the social life of the community. Henrietta went to the Bennington school, and because she had a talent for playing the mandolin, she was very popular at parties.[31]

A great deal was happening in Bennington in 1905, much of it chronicled by the *Ottawa County Democrat,* a typical weekly newspaper: Lots of people were going lots of places on the train, enough rain fell in early

Henrietta at fifteen with basketball teammates in 1905. She is second from the right on front row. *(Courtesy of Nell Partridge)*

July to lay the dust, Chris McConnell was frequently tardy or absent from school, Esther Hathaway had a painful chin boil, and in August a band of Gypsies camped in the area for a week, making their talent for foretelling available to anyone willing to pay for a glimpse of the future. Most important, a girls' basketball team was organized, and Henrietta won the position of first center. Her dearest friend and the star player, tall, slender Viola Hathaway, was right forward. Despite the fact that the team repeatedly went down to defeat, it was still a focus of community pride because it was the first basketball team little Bennington had ever had.

Henrietta also had a part in the school play, "Tempest and Sunshine," acting her role to the hilt, for even then she never did anything by halves. And she spent much of her leisure time with the boys. Not surprisingly, most girls were jealous of her freedom.[32]

Short and well developed with big brown eyes, brown hair, and a soft, clear complexion, she was an irrepressible, self-reliant girl determined

10

"to be somebody." She was an omnivorous reader, and she thrilled to the exploits of Nellie Bly, the first woman to achieve fame as an investigative reporter, and Richard Harding Davis, the famous war correspondent and novelist; the wail of the Union Pacific set her to dreaming of far places and exciting adventures. Very bright, she always had an answer for everything. She was also physically intrepid, which led her to jump right into the thick of it when the boys got into fights on the school ground. This "shocked" most of the other girls, who already envied her, and she was the target of gossip.[33] Like her mother, she was willful and independent; like her natural father, a reader and ponderer; and like her "Dad" Hoerath, restless and a dreamer. The townspeople saw some of these qualities in a less than positive light, and there were those who even felt that she was being permitted to "run wild."

But when Minnie did try to control Henrietta, it sometimes resulted in an "unseemly" public display. The town, like most, loved a little excitement, and on these occasions Minnie and Henrietta supplied it, like the time Minnie humiliated her in front of her boyfriend. Henrietta was usually much too busy to take care of her clothes, especially her underthings, a situation that infuriated Minnie who finally decided to do something drastic about it. When Henrietta came home from school one evening, accompanied by her boyfriend, items of her underwear, washed and arranged on the bushes in front of the house, greeted them. Henrietta, mortified, could never face the boy again.[34]

The truth was that, far from being the tough, uncaring, even defiant young woman she sometimes appeared to be and which a lot of people thought her, Henrietta was terribly vulnerable. Though she was often able to use this vulnerability to her advantage, it also led her into dangerous situations, and many times she did not see the danger until it was much too late.

Henrietta was by nature and nurture independent and intelligent, and the constant moves the family made, the continual uprooting, made her restless and adaptable. It also made schooling so difficult that, although she was a good student, she did not graduate from high school. Eager to become self-supporting, in August 1907 she moved to Oketo to stay with her grandparents who had recently moved there from Marysville. She was going to study pharmacy, considered by the family to be a suitably respectable occupation for her, under the tutelage of her Aunt Myrtle's husband, John Wright, owner and operator of the Oketo drug store.[35] Her special affection for and closeness to her Aunt Myrtle no doubt helped to make her uncharacteristically compliant.

It was soon obvious to everyone, however, that her heart was not in pharmacology; in December, she followed her mother, stepfather, and brother to Junction City.[36] Only four miles from Fort Riley where the

Henrietta Eleanor Goodnough with her mother, Minnie Finn Hoerath, "Betty" (face blacked out), and a parrot, about 1907. *(Peggy Hull Deuell Collection, Kansas Collection, University of Kansas Libraries)*

two battalions of troops which constituted the U.S. Mounted Cavalry School were garrisoned, Junction City was a military town. Soldiers were everywhere: in the shops, in the cafés, in the streets.

If times had been different, adventuresome Henrietta, whose schoolgirl hero had been General Sherman, might have thought about joining the army to see the world. As it was, another career opportunity right there in Junction City also presented a chance for a restless young woman to travel "around the world and up and down and every place [she] wanted to go,"[37] a career in journalism; Henrietta decided to become a newspaper reporter. Her mother was less than delighted with her decision. In fact, she was horrified. As far as she was concerned, Henrietta might as well have joined a burlesque troop.[38]

Her mother's opposition to her going into newspaper work had no observable effect on her. She wanted to do newspaper work and she was going to. However, even though she was bound and determined to have a career, and one of her own choosing, she took it for granted that she would get married — sometime. And she would have children — probably. And having gotten the yearning for excitement and travel out of her system, she would settle down and be content — enough, anyway.

For her career ambitions the times were on her side. There was growing freedom for women. Skirts were getting shorter, showing some leg; bathing suits, finally designed for swimming, revealed that there were real and discernible bodies underneath them. Society still saw women primarily as mates and homebodies, but the women's rights movement was changing things, even for the women who did not support it. As a result, lower and middle economic class women were beginning to see possibilities they had never seen before, dream dreams long denied by convention and economic necessity.

Since journalism was one of those career possibilities increasingly open to women, when Henrietta applied for a reporting job at the *Junction City Sentinel,* she had a reasonable expectation of being hired. A.D. Colby, the editor, told her "he needed only one reporter and he already had one. But, . . . if she wasn't worried about her finger nails and was willing to set type, she could have [that] job" if she wanted it.[39] Of course she wanted it; it was a "foot in the door." She even collected overdue bills for the paper. Soon she was given the chance to do some reporting, and she had, by being patient and willing, the job she had hoped for in the first place.

During the year and a half that she lived in Junction City, Henrietta not only worked on the *Sentinel,* but also occasionally clerked in a department store to supplement her income. The meager wages she earned for her newspaper work were not enough to pay for her clothes and her travels to Bennington and Marysville and Oketo or to Leavenworth and Kansas City. Some of her trips were simply to visit school friends like Viola Hathaway or relatives like her Aunt Myrtle Wright, but other trips were to look for a better job, for she had great plans for her future.[40]

*O Powers that be . . .* teach me to know and to observe the rules of the Game. Give me to mind my own business . . . and to . . . [hold] my tongue. Let me never lack proper pride or a due sense of humor. Preserve me . . . from growing stodgy and unimaginative. Help me not to cry for the moon or over spilled milk; . . . Grant me neither to proffer nor welcome cheap praise; to distinguish sharply between sentiment and sentimentality. . . . When it is appointed me to suffer, let me . . . take example from the well-bred beasts, and go away quietly to bear my suffering by myself. . . . Give me nevertheless to be always a good comrade, and to view the passing show with an eye constantly growing keener, charity broadening and deepening day by day. Help me to win, if win I may, but . . . if I may not win always, make me at least a good loser. Vouchsafe me not to estrange the other me at my elbow . . . and grant that I may carry my cup, brimming, yet unspilled to the last—

"A Prayer" [author unknown]

## CHAPTER TWO

# Go West,
# Young Woman

When Henrietta decided she had gone as far as she could on the *Sentinel* and felt it was time to move on as well as up (she hoped), editor Colby offered to help get her a job on a Kansas City paper. However, she had made up her mind to go west. The West was Opportunity. The West was Excitement. The West was Romance.

"You'll starve to death," Colby prophesied darkly.[1]

But she was determined. She wrote to every newspaper in Colorado and finally got a job as advertising manager at the *Chronicle-News* in Trinidad.[2] In August 1909 she and her brother took the train west, Edward going along to help her get settled.[3]

The *Chronicle-News* turned out to be merely a stepping-stone to the *Denver Republican,* for in Trinidad she met the brother of one of the owners of the *Republican,* and he got her a job there virtually overnight. The job was not reporter; it was telephone operator, but it was a start at a big metropolitan daily, and before long she was promoted to reporter which was how she met George Hull.[4]

Peggy's idea of the ideal man was one who was tall and blond. George Hull was not tall (five feet, five and three-fourths inches), and he was not blond. But he was a reporter (for the *Denver Times*), a Spanish-American War veteran, and the nephew of the mayor of Denver, all of which made this thirty-two-year-old widower a fairly "good catch" in the eyes of a twenty-year-old newspaperwoman from Kansas.[5]

From the first, she knew George was attracted to her — not unusual, a lot of men were — her small soft body, her huge brown eyes, eyes which produced a remarkable effect when she turned them on some-one. However, marriage would mean a commitment that she was not

Henrietta in 1910 at the age of twenty at the time of her marriage to George Hull. *(Courtesy of Alice Goodnough Reissig)*

ready to make, so when the job editing the *Salina Daily Union's* society section opened up, she went home to Kansas.

George came after her, and because she was not very happy in Salina (her mother, now living there, and she were having their usual problems), being married was looking better to her. After all, twelve years' age difference was not so much when she considered they would be in the same profession. Ideal, really. Not only that, George was successful. His short stories had been published in national magazines. And if he was not quite as successful as her own society-column report made out, and she was not quite as famous a feature writer — "one of the most brilliant women writers in the West"[6] as she described herself — still, she might have been forgiven for heaping it on, rubbing it in the noses of all those hometown know-it-alls who had thought she would never amount to anything, anything respectable, anyway.[7] The nephew of the mayor of Denver wanted her; the nephew of the mayor of Denver was going to have her.

On a Thursday evening in October 1910, Henrietta Eleanor Goodnough and George Charles Hull were married in her mother and stepfather's house on North Ninth Street in Salina, after which the newlyweds traveled on the 10:40 Union Pacific to Denver[8] where they settled into an apartment and went to work on the *Republican.*[9]

One reason Henrietta was eager to go back to Denver was that she had friends like Carroll Michener there. Perceptive, considerate, and fun, Carroll was one of those disarming people to whom others gravitated. He and Henrietta renewed their easy friendship; when he went west to work on the *San Francisco Chronicle,* it was not long before the Hulls followed. Soon, Henrietta had good reason to reflect on A. D. Colby's ominous warning, for they did nearly starve in a succession of low-paying jobs on various publications. Eventually, George worked his way up to city editor of the *San Francisco Post,* but Henrietta was still writing only occasional feature stories, and there was a lot of competition for newspaper jobs.[10]

In the meantime, Carroll moved on to Honolulu to work on the *Pacific Commercial Advertiser,* and he wrote enthusiastically of opportunities there, so Henrietta and George got Hawaii fever. With his work record, George had no trouble getting the guarantee of a job on the *Hawaiian Star;* he set sail for Honolulu in the middle of April 1912. Henrietta stayed in San Francisco until the end of May and arrived in Honolulu just in time to see Carroll off for his next destination, Shanghai.[11] This time the Hulls did not follow him because Hawaii turned out to be the land of opportunity for them.

The Honolulu of 1912 was a bustling port of 59,000 made up of native Hawaiians, Japanese, Chinese, Koreans, Filipinos, Portuguese, English, and Americans with a few Germans, Frenchmen, Scandinavians, Puerto Ricans, Spaniards, and natives of the Azores and Madeiras all mixed up with 80,000 American servicemen, most of them stationed around Pearl Harbor.

For most "haoles" (Caucasians), the life of sun-drenched streets, swaying palms, white-sand beaches, exotic orchids, anthuriums, and hibiscus, was relaxed and pleasant. But the surface tranquility was belied by seething social undercurrents. Drug use was rampant, the military hospital primarily concerned with treating spaced-out soldiers and sailors. Passenger ships were regularly searched, and opium and cocaine were regularly found hidden on them. Political scandal was common; assault and battery was the most frequently prosecuted crime, followed by "smoking and having opium in possession" and "furious and heedless driving, including auto speeding."[12] Automobile accidents were commonplace.

The sugar and pineapple industries were thriving. The Mutual Telephone Company had in operation an automated dial system. There were twenty foreign-language newspapers, three major English ones. The ominous events just prior to World War I in Europe and the continuing revolution in Mexico were front-page news.

On the lighter side, Monte Carter and His Dancing Chicks presented broad farces at the Bijou, following the run of Graham's Rats, forty trained rats that marched onto the stage and did "clownish stunts and acrobatic feats" on little "paraphernalia";[13] at the Hawaii and Popular theaters, they were showing such feature movies as "The Last Days of Pompeii," the three-reel "Gun Men of New York," and white hunter Paul Rainey's six-reel "Wild Animal Hunt in Africa," which was accompanied by a well-prepared lecture. Opera star Lillian Nordica and famous Irish tenor John McCormack appeared at the Opera House just across King Street from Iolani Palace. Miss Alice Teddy, the performing bear, was giving children's matinees at Ye Liberty Theater and holding "receptions" afterward to meet her tiny fans.

It was not the most healthful place on earth. Leprosy was not uncommon, the colony on Molokai world famous due to the earlier work of Father Damien there. Tuberculosis was epidemic, and the health service launched a major campaign through the schools and newspapers to familiarize people with the symptoms and the importance of early diagnosis and treatment. In 1913, during one two-week period in October, thirteen people died from contagious diseases, twelve of them from tuberculosis. The White Plague was feared as cancer came to be feared later.

Divorce could also have been considered epidemic. Since Hawaii had become a territory of the United States thirteen years before, there had been 5,000 divorce suits brought in the Island courts. At Pearl Harbor an airplane climbed to a remarkable 400 feet. Queen Liliuokalani celebrated her seventy-fifth birthday, Duke Kahanamoku was the champion swimmer of the world, and it took six days to sail the 2,400 miles from Honolulu to San Francisco.

Even though she had grown up in a land of white, culturally homogeneous people, Henrietta had no trouble adjusting to the heterogeneous, polyglot society of Hawaii. She seemed to identify with the native Hawaiian as one outsider identifies with another, for she did feel herself an outsider, and she could never forget the whispers, the gossip of her adolescence. Not one to shoot the wrong snake, she knew exactly where the blame belonged; she despised gossips, bigots, and talebearers. So anyone who was different, especially different and defenseless, could count on her as a friend and defender.

In 1912 the native Hawaiians needed all the friends and defenders they could get. Honolulu belonged to the haole, and not only as a result of main strength. The Hawaiian culture was not fashionable, even among native Hawaiians; unlike the large Oriental population which had been better able to resist the temptation of Occidental culture, many of the native Hawaiians admired the trappings of western civilization too much and were too eager to adopt haole manners, dress, and customs.

Henrietta considered the Polynesian physique the most beautiful she had ever seen and regretted that interbreeding was changing it.[14] Nevertheless, whatever her esthetic preferences, she took people as they came. "Haole" or "hapa-haole," half-breed, whole-breed, pure-breed, mixed-breed, if they were her friends, they were her friends; if not, not, whatever their pedigree.

Her first great career opportunity in Hawaii came when she was hired as editor of the woman's page of the *Pacific Commercial Advertiser.* "Of Interest to Maid and Matron" appeared in the Sunday edition, and soon it bore her byline.[15] She also wrote little tales ("If I Had Lots of Money" and "Paul Had a Way with Him" were two) for the "Children's Corner."

On October 27, though the Hulls' marriage had become a shaky affair, partly because George had a serious drinking problem, they had a public celebration of their second anniversary.[16]

In November she started a free service which became one of her specialties, making Christmas purchases for "out-of-town readers and shut-in women."[17]

Henrietta's first reporting assignment was to cover a meeting of Hawaiian suffragettes. As she recounted the experience in the *Advertiser,* she entered Hirano Hall calm and confident. Forty-five minutes later she left "a nervous wreck."[18]

The native women were suspicious of her from the first. On her way to a seat, she was confronted by one of the leaders. "You think you will find anything of interest at this meeting?" the leader asked warily. It dawned on Henrietta that "they thought she had come to laugh, to make fun of their efforts." She needed to get this story. Resorting to subterfuge in an effort to allay their mistrust, she said, "I am deeply interested in the ballot for women; I have but recently come here from the Coast where I worked in behalf of the vote for women. I read of your meeting and wished to ascertain what success the women of Hawaii were having and to help them if I could."

She thought her little fiction had gotten her off the hook. She was wrong. Now they were eager to hear about the movement on the Mainland and expected her to tell them about it. One deception gone wrong, she tried another. "My throat is bad," she said. "I cannot talk today. [However], I will write a speech for you. You can translate it in your own language and all the members of your association will get the benefit of it."

At that, they gave in, and Charles "Soapbox" Barron, the scheduled speaker, took the floor. His remarks addressed a class conflict in the ranks. This situation, he warned them, hampered the movement. "What difference does it make if a society woman gives a suffragette tea at Waikiki, let them have it; you have your teas and meetings, you are all working for the same goal and if you don't meet at the same place it doesn't make any difference, it will all help to get what you are after in the long run — the right for women to vote."[19]

Although Henrietta had never worked in the suffrage movement, she believed that, by example, she had made a real contribution to the women's cause. Certainly, she of all people was familiar with the limitations imposed by discrimination, and though she wanted the love of men, she needed, in fact craved, the admiration of other women. Probably as a result of this suffrage meeting, she started including women's rights articles and items on the woman's page, pieces like "China's New Woman" and "Woman's Rights in the Territory Today" and "Suffragists Stir Washington with Preparations for 'Cavalry' Parade."

Even so, it seems surprising that a woman who was struggling so hard in a man's world, trying to break away from the stereotype of the kind of job women could do on newspapers, would not have been radically involved in the women's movement of the time, for in reality, under the frivolousness and flirtatiousness, she was independence personified, a career-centered, hard-driving loner, determined to find fame and fortune or die trying.

It was not that she was unsociable; quite the contrary. She loved to be with other people, adored parties and get-togethers. And she went with the crowd in any group of which she considered herself a member. Indeed, she tried to make herself believe that she was the most average of middle American women, wanting nothing so much as a conventional life, the security of a home and family. Further, it did not help that most people of the time viewed women newspaper reporters the way her mother did. On the surface uncaring, even defiant, underneath she was unsure and easily embarrassed. As a result, every so often Henrietta was overcome by the need to overcompensate for her natural self-sufficiency, looked on then not as a strength, but a weakness.

Another consideration tending to make her reticent was that suffragettes had to endure ridicule, taunts, and aspersions on their womanliness. Henrietta could not bear to have her femininity questioned.

Philosophically, she might have been in trouble, but financially she was doing very well. For the times, she was making a very good salary,[20] and as her income increased, she could even afford to send exotic presents to her relatives in Kansas and to her half sisters Alice and Eleanor, her father's daughters by his second wife, in Arkansas.[21] Evidence not only of her generous nature, it also showed them all that she was somebody they could be proud of, important and well paid.

Though she was not a "joiner," she did become a founding member and later secretary of the Women's Press Club of Honolulu. The club, proving to be her kind of organization, held few meetings and very soon came to nothing.[22]

In addition to her other jobs, she wrote articles on her impressions of the Islands and notable Islanders such as humane society worker Rose Davison and leprosy researcher Dr. James Wayson which were published in magazines like *Sunset* and *Ocean Travel*.

When the *Evening Bulletin* and the *Hawaiian Star* had merged on July 1, 1912, George had been one of the lucky reporters hired on to the staff of the new *Honolulu Star-Bulletin* by editor Riley Allen,[23] evidence that he was a competent journalist, despite his drinking.

On the other hand, Henrietta's success was often less the result of journalistic skill than of sheer energy and passion, energy and passion which were reflected in her writing. Though sometimes that writing tended to be excessive, her loyal readers, and she had many, never doubted her sincerity. The *Sunday Advertiser* of December 22 carried her Christmas "Greetings to the Readers of the Woman's Page." They referred to features of the page and contained a disarming example of her genuine eagerness to please, journalistically.

A wisp of the holiday spirit flitted in from the
open window
And lingered a moment on my desk. It recalled to
me the proximity

Of Christmas Day when all the world teems with
good fellowship,
With tenderness and with love. It is a
propitious occasion on
Which to greet the readers of this page and to
wish them all the
Good things of the holiday season.

At this particular time there is a kindred
feeling of good will:
Therefore; if you fail to find just what you
wanted in "Things Worth
Knowing"; if that recipe you have been looking
for so long doesn't
Appear in "Good Things to Eat"; if "Health and
Beauty" fail to bring
You either of these; if "Dress" does not improve
your appearance and
Is sometimes beyond your pocketbook; if "Society
from the Mainland"
Is about people you have never heard of . . .; if
the
"Honolulu Junior" story isn't as clever as you
could have written — —
Have patience and grant, with the broad sympathy
and sisterhood
Of the Christmas season, peace to, and
forbearance with, my humble efforts.

H.G.H.

In April 1913 she went home to the Mainland, reportedly to visit her relatives in Kansas; it was the middle of September before she returned to Hawaii. By then George was no longer at the *Star-Bulletin,* but had moved to the *Advertiser.* Henrietta did not return to her regular job at the *Advertiser.* More and more the Hulls' paths seemed to be crossing less and less. Hers took a more lucrative turn when, two weeks after her return, she established the Trans-Pacific Steamer Letter Service and set herself up in the public relations business.[24]

Before long she "had a monopoly on all the press agent jobs, public relations work, advertising campaigns, was assistant manager of the Opera House"[25] where she met celebrities like Irish tenor John McCormack and movie star Fatty Arbuckle. She even wrote an occasional article for the *Star-Bulletin*. She "lived luxuriously in a lovely bungalow on the side of a mountain and had a Chinese cook."[26]

By ordinary standards she was making a lot of money, but the move to public relations was not a smart one for a passionate newspaper reporter. A lot of "real" reporters resented public relations work and considered it second-rate, the more so because it paid more than reporting. Now her newspaper work was in great part limited to hypes of entertainment features and advertisements. Even though it was the training ground for her later newspaper advertising columns, which she reverted to to support herself when regular reporting jobs did not materialize, she found she was not taken as seriously by many members of the hard-news reporting fraternity; it hurt her that she was considered a journalistic lightweight.

In addition, it was becoming obvious that her marriage to George Hull was not going to survive. Even though George was not a "mean drunk," Henrietta finally concluded that she could not put up with his drinking any longer. (She later told friends that the last straw had been "the night he climbed naked to the top of a flag pole.")[27] Desperately unhappy, guilt ridden because she wanted out, she poured her feelings into a poem, "The Poet's Death."

Sweet Death, I see thee before me now, all white
And Crystal in the clinging shadows of my study,
tenderly
Clothed in woodland flowers, breathing music of
the skies.
It has been dark — midnight to me for many years,
thy
Presence brings the light of eternal peace,
wooing me
From a world of crime, of sham, of misery, of
weariness,
Guiding my feet out upon the white path to Divine
Rest.

Didst thou speak? Ah Yes, I heard thee say the
magic
Word "Come." Goodbye vain world! Vain world of
dead dreams—
Of wearied hopes, of sterile quests, of false
desires—
Vain world, depraved, debauched, reeking in thine
own
Uncleanliness — I leave thee, gladly!

It appeared in the *Advertiser* on November 16, 1913.

On December 13, 1913, George sailed alone for the Mainland on the *Sierra*.[28]

For the next three months Henrietta threw herself into her work. She rode the interisland steamers, stopping to drum up business and sightsee on the other islands. On Hawaii she stayed at the Volcano House and went up to view Kilauea. She hired a car and chauffeur to take her from Hilo to Laupahoehoe just because the name appealed to her. Though she was nervous about staying alone in the hotel there, it did not deter her. The fact that there was no electricity in the village (the hotel was lit with lamps), was not only intimidating, it was exciting.[29]

Back in "civilized" Honolulu, the "thés dansant" (tea dances) struck Hawaiian society, the first ones held on Tuesdays on the roof garden of the Young Hotel and lasting from four to seven o'clock with an intermission for tea. Already popular on the Mainland, the new dances were considered dissolute and degenerate by the more "moral" elements of the population, a positive obstacle to "clean living." In the course of the Tango or the One-Step, people touched, even rubbed, and everyone knew where that kind of thing led; red-blooded men could hardly be expected to control themselves at such close quarters. Worse, the evil penetrated right into the home, prompting an editorial writer to note: "If you do anything in your own home, it will not be without cost, and you are quite liable to be called 'peculiar'"; he went on to ask, "Can you stand the pressure?" The *Journal of the American Medical Association* condemned the dances, contending that they posed a threat to the morals of the young and the cardiovascular systems of the old.[30]

Henrietta was not intimidated by this kind of pressure, and she loved to dance. In fact, she had belonged to the Trinidad Club, a "jolly" dancing group, when she had worked on the *Chronicle-News;* the tea dances with their Turkey Trots and Bostons held no terrors for her.

In spite of all these lovely distractions, however, the Islands had lost their charm for her. At first, though mosquitoes, house lizards, and flies had kept Hawaii from being Paradise, it had been close enough. Now "too much money and too much native beauty palled," and she announced that she was leaving to rejoin George who was living in Los Angeles. She returned to the Pacific coast in March 1914.[31]

Their reunion, if there was one, was short-lived, and their separation proved to be permanent.

As usual Henrietta was able to promote work for herself, this time in the Imperial Valley in south-central California. There she and two other reporters were sent to Calexico, where a contingent of American soldiers was stationed just across the border from the Mexican fort at

Mexicali, to investigate the unrest there, especially reports that Americans who ventured into Mexicali were disappearing — forever.[32]

With this as a background, she later wrote an account of a hair-raising adventure she said she had had there, only narrowly escaping death at the hands of Mexican bandits. Since, in the account, her rescue was effected in a National Highway Twelve automobile and the column where the story appeared was advertising Nationals, her actual experience was probably much less exciting than her description of it. Her press agent work had had its effect: Some of her most breathtaking stories were either highly doctored fact or outright fiction, dreamed up to illustrate the advantage of one brand of product over another.

Along this same line, an ambitious project which she proposed in connection with the San Diego Exposition which was being planned for 1915 was outlined in the *San Diego Daily Union* of October 7, 1914. The story, typical of what became her special style, combined advertising and excitement. It bore the bold headline,

WOMAN TO DARE DEATH WITH BIRDMEN;

a box-caption, "Henrietta Goodnough Hull, who will make transcontinental Air Journey to Boost San Diego Exposition," over three pictures of her; and a subhead, "Fascinating Thrilling, Flirtation with Oblivion Holds Irresistible Charm Which Lures Volunteer Aviatrix Into Novel Above-Earth Journey." The story with her byline followed. Though the purple style of the day, it was also vintage Henrietta Goodnough Hull.

On or about December 15, a French Morane-Saulnier monoplane will leave New York for San Diego. I hope to be a passenger and the first woman to cross the continent in an aeroplane. W. Ralph Apperman, an aviator of several years' experience, and Bernard J. Lange, his business manager, . . . will make the flight for the purpose of widely advertising the San Diego Exposition and to establish a new record for cross country flights.

. . . Members of the Imperial Valley Chamber of Commerce made a wager with me that I would be afraid to undertake the trip.

. . . Flying is not the dangerous game it once was, although an aerial trip across the United States in the dead of winter will not be as comfortable or as safe as riding a Pullman, but there will be vastly more glory in it.

. . . After the first swift fear of death is over you don't think about the horror of getting killed and I don't feel a bit nervous about it. I am just anxious to be off.

27

On my way to New York, I will stop in all the important cities and write articles concerning the "San Diego Aerial Pathfinder" flight and the Exposition, contributing in this way my share to the publicity end.

. . . I do not expect the first day's flight will find me just as calm as I am when I get home from church, but it will teach me a lot in controlling my nerves and steeling myself to a few hardships.

My friends call me the "Little Gambler" because when I make a wager even on some inconsequential thing, I like to put everything I have on it and I guess it was this spirit that made me go in for this trip.

I like to feel when thinking of the flight that I stand on a ridge which one might call the Ridge of Either Way. On one side is a valley of life, success, happiness, on the other death and oblivion, and whichever way I fall will be complete.

If Lange and Appermann [sic] grant this opportunity I shall always feel very grateful to them for giving me a chance, or, as the dramatic stars say, my "Big moment," and if we all "go out" together, I shall be proud to share the fate of two such fearless and daring men.

In the end, this grand project did not get off the ground. She had succeeded in selling a story with her byline to the major newspaper in San Diego and in getting publicity to help her career along, but that accomplished, she found herself once more at loose ends. The problem was that, having no real plan, she was not sure where she wanted her career to go or how to get it there. One thing she did have was the Micawberish philosophy that something would turn up; it always had.

What turned up was a reporting job at the *Denver Times*. It was lucky for her that the trip had not materialized because it would have locked Henrietta into several weeks of publicity and public relations, and even though she was good at it, the work did not satisfy her. What did was the excitement of a big, busy newsroom: typewriters clattering, telephones ringing shrilly and incessantly, rewrite men barking questions into phone mouthpieces, everyone yelling for the copy boys, the copy boys running from desk to desk, the "ribald laughter . . . [and the] occasional clinking of glasses."[33] That was what got her blood flowing. The atmosphere of the newsroom — "part seminary, part abattoir" — was what had thrilled her about newspaper work right from the start.

On the other hand, to Harvey Deuell, also a reporter and copyreader at the *Times,* there was very little glamour in journalism. It was a business, a business of selling, and "reporter" was just one rung on the ladder up. "The good reporter [was] always a good salesman. . . . First he [had to] sell himself to those from whom he [wished] information. He [had to] show them that, even if he [did not] speak their vernacular, he at least [understood] their point of view." And "after obtaining the news, he [had to] turn salesman again and sell it to the public."[34]

It was inevitable that, working on the same paper, they would meet. What was not so inevitable was that they would fall in love; like George Hull, Harvey was not Henrietta's blond Adonis. However, he was tall and, she thought, handsome.

Harvey Vail Deuell, born on November 20, 1890, in Brooklyn, New York, was the only child of a prominent family. He graduated from Erasmus Hall High School there, studied further under tutors, then in 1909 moved with his parents to Colorado. During his first two years in Denver, he worked as a stove salesman, a mechanic, a law clerk, a construction job timekeeper, and a bank employee. In 1912 his father, George Jasper Deuell, an insurance actuary, died; suddenly twenty-two-year-old Harvey was the "man of the family." Realizing he had to have something more permanent and wanting an occupation more challenging than the ones he had had, he began to see the possibilities in the world of newspaper work.[35]

Harvey got his first newspaper job on the *Denver Republican* by pretending to be an experienced reporter. It did not take the city editor long to find out that he was not. Since dissembling and even outright pretense were not capital crimes in newspaper circles, he was not fired, but his salary was immediately cut to $9.40 a week, probably less as a punishment for his dishonesty than as the penalty for his inexperience.[36] After he had gotten some experience at the *Republican,* he moved on to the *Rocky Mountain News* where he covered Colorado's notorious Ludlow coal mine massacre of 1914 which claimed forty-five lives and stands out as one of the bloodiest chapters in the history of American labor. His stories, forerunners of modern investigative reporting, were a major factor in bringing about investigations of the whole terrible situation by the U.S. Commission on Industrial Relations and the Colorado legislature.[37]

That Henrietta and Harvey viewed newspaper work in totally different ways mattered less than that they were in love. But what mattered a great deal more was that Harvey was the sole support of his mother, a responsibility his mother and he both took very seriously. Added to that was the fact that, to Mrs. Deuell, any woman who interested Harvey was a threat; the idea of the not-yet-divorced Henrietta as a daughter-in-law was especially repugnant to her. It looked as if things were permanently stalemated for them.[38]

Still, Henrietta did have one tiny spark of hope. Despite the fact that she liked Colorado and the State House beat to which she was assigned and enjoyed working with reporters she liked and respected, especially DeLos Walker, who often shared stories with her,[39] she was receptive to the suggestion that the way to get Harvey to make a commitment was to flee as heroines did in romantic novels. According to the plot, he would come after her, she would be divorced, they would be married and Live Happily Ever After.[40]

Experience suggested it worked. George Hull had come after her when she had left Denver the first time. Though they had not lived happily ever after, they had gotten married. Where she "fled" to this time was Minneapolis, Minnesota, which was far, but not too far, and where she had a major newspaper contact in Carroll Michener, returned from his round-the-world jaunt to newspaper life at home.

Peggy Hull, about 1915. (In authors' possession, courtesy of Raymond A. Ruffino)

In Minneapolis, Henrietta worked on the Daily News and waited for Harvey to leave his mother and come after her. She soon saw that it was going to be a long wait.

From the beginning of her newspaper career to 1914, Henrietta had written under the name she had been christened in honor of her grandmother Finn; in her opinion, the name had been satisfactory. But when she went to work in Minneapolis, her editor, saying he "wouldn't be caught dead putting at the head of any column in his newspaper a name such as Henrietta Goodnough Hull," encouraged her to come up with a new one. The new one they agreed on was "Peggy Hull."[41]

Unfortunately, his concern at that point proved to be largely academic since most of her work for the Daily News bore no byline, but her human interest stories and trial reporting appeared regularly under headlines like "Barred from Room of Dying Husband Mrs. Rogers Says," "She Had only Five Pennies But She wanted the Fur: Slum Child Gets Life's First Disillusionment in Big Department Store," and "Auto Gives Clue to Murderer of Taxi-Cab Driver."[42]

In the meantime, waiting for Harvey, she renewed her friendship with Carroll. It afforded her a restful, enjoyable escape from her recent difficulties and unhappiness. They went for rides in the fall woods when the leaves were their most glorious reds and yellows. He introduced her into his circle of friends, where she was immediately accepted. In the homes of Carroll's friends, she saw a pleasant, secure kind of life, the best, the most desirable kind of life, she was sure.[43] She thought she was ready for that kind of life now, but she knew that Harvey was not, probably never would be.

The realization that she might as well forget Harvey, combined with the fact that she had never liked trial reporting and most of her assignments continued to involve crime and courtrooms, strengthened her feeling that it was time to move on.

Where she moved on to was Cleveland, and it was there that the whole course of her life changed.

*I'm a soldier now!* Monday night I joined the Women's Auxiliary of the Ohio National Guard's Training School and I'm going to learn to shoot a rifle and to do Red Cross work.

Peggy Hull,
*Cleveland Plain Dealer*

## CHAPTER THREE

# "I'm a Soldier Now!"

In February 1916 Henrietta Hull, now Peggy Hull, took the train to Cleveland, Ohio, where she was to begin her new job, writing an advertising column for the *Cleveland Press*. All of the advertising experience she had had in Hawaii was about to pay off.

She really preferred to do reporting, of course, but her experience had been that the money in newspaper work was in advertising, and at this time especially, the amount and variety of newspaper advertising was increasing at an astonishing rate. Only fifty years before, it had been taken for granted that most women were not interested in anything but their homes and families; newspapers were filled with "men's concerns": business reports, politics, hard news. In fact, most editors assumed that women simply did not read newspapers. Toward the end of the nineteenth century, however, suddenly newspapers began to actively woo women readers with short stories, recipes, and beauty hints.[1]

The change was partly the result of the growing clamor for suffrage, the increasing and visible militancy of feminists, and the general "recognition that a status revolution, elevating wives and daughters from their role as household pets to something approaching equal place in society, was almost won."[2] Economic forces were at work also, forces made apparent by "the growth of department store advertising. Such advertisements were directed chiefly to women in the home, and therefore newspapers — especially in their evening and Sunday editions — had to be made to appeal to women readers."[3] Soon "discovering" that women had wider interests than they had previously supposed, editors began hiring women reporters to cover and write about general news from the "woman's point of view" to capture and keep women as readers.

It did not take long for merchants like A. T. Stewart in New York City and John Wanamaker in Philadelphia to see the potential in the situation. Buying newspaper space in which to run ads of their merchandise, they succeeded in persuading women to forsake the small shops in their neighborhoods, which each carried only a few items, for giant, centrally-located department stores. Full-page ads promising cheaper prices and greater selection in return for the inconvenience of a trip into the center of the city started appearing in the late 1870s and had such an impact that the ratio of commercial to editorial space soared, ad revenues soon replacing subscriptions and newsstand sales as the chief source of a newspaper's income. By 1910 roughly 60 percent of many large newspapers' earnings came from advertising fees, and during the next twenty years the percentage continued to rise.[4]   It was hardly surprising then that journalists who offered something innovative in the way of advertising were rarely without jobs. Columns which had less the look of a professional ad and more that of a regular feature, incorporating descriptions of items for sale in area stores, were becoming popular. It was this kind of column that Peggy Hull hired on to do at the *Press*. Her gimmick was to concoct little tales, most of them almost totally fictitious, to give her pieces human interest and make the ads seem personal — one friend writing to another recounting an adventure — and in the process telling him or her about a wonderful buy, play, or stay. Not unexpectedly, each business she mentioned paid a fee for her journalistic attention. The pattern of the column, "When Peggy Goes a-Shopping," was always roughly the same, only the "events" described and the advertisers involved in them changed.

In one of her first pieces, she claimed to have lost her baggage claim check when she had traveled from Minneapolis to Cleveland. Since her good clothes were in her trunk, and she was temporarily without access to them, she was forced to buy a new outfit for a party she was giving. She proceeded to describe the (beautiful, reasonably priced) clothing she had found at her sponsors' stores to get her through the crisis.

That she did not intend to deceive her readers as to the real nature of her pieces was evident from a note at the bottom of her column:

P.S. — When articles are mentioned in my column together with the prices and the places they are for sale, such reference is advertising. The proprietors of the various shops invite me to come to their places and tell in my own way about attractive novelties or bargains as they appeal to me. The addresses of the firms so advertising this week are listed above.[5]

She even combined celebrity interviews with her advertising in such a way that she was able to use the names of well-known people without

36

their actual endorsement of her sponsors' products, as in her column, "Peggy Plays Pinochle with John McCormack." McCormack was the famous tenor whom she had first met in Honolulu; and when he was performing in Cleveland, he agreed to give Peggy an interview:

> We sat in a big blue divan in the Statler hotel and chatted about music and people and commonplace things until we almost ran out of conversation. Finally we decided to play pinochle because it was a nasty day out doors and he couldn't go for his usual ride. . . . After Mr. McCormack had won one game I told him I would buy him a necktie to wear on St Patrick's day if he could win the second. And he did![6]

She went on to describe shopping for the tie at one of her clients' stores.

Of course, as far as the advertisers themselves were concerned, it did not hurt that Peggy had a magnetic personality and a talent for attracting attention to herself. As a result, it was not long until she moved over to the larger *Cleveland Plain Dealer* where she perfected this bread-and-butter writing. Under the headline "Girl Writes Clever Stories: 'Peggy' Hull Puts Facts in the Form of Interesting Fiction" and a picture with the caption "Miss Henrietta G. Hull," the *Editor & Publisher and The Journalist* reported on the "unique advertising stunt . . . being run twice a week by the Cleveland *Plain Dealer*. It consists," the article continued,

> of a story, in fiction form, of happenings in the high-class retail establishments of the city. Retail stores, banks, mercantile establishments, and any enterprise that wants to advertise in an unusual way, figure in these stories.
>
> Miss Henrietta Goodnough Hull is the originator of the scheme. She handles the proposition from lining up the prospects to writing the story. Her chief stunt, however, is to "have things happen to her" as she puts it, in order to make the interest keen. The series of stories usually carries a two- or three-column head, with picture, and always carries the name "Peggy," under which name Miss Hull writes.
>
> An example of one of her "happenings" was to have herself held up by a masked bandit, which story was used to advertise a bank.
>
> Although the plan is not new in other cities, the novelty appeals immensely to advertisers here.[7]

The "masked bandit" story involved her "only brother Roland." As this story went, she was walking alone at night when suddenly she was confronted by a masked man who, after he had frightened her into resolving to put all her money into a First National Bank account, revealed that he was not a robber after all but that lovable rascal, Roland, in disguise, teaching her a lesson. The audacious Roland was completely unlike her actual only brother, sweet shy Edward, now married, whom she rarely saw but still adored.

She invented other hair-raisers, like a breath-taking automotive escape from Mexican bandits to advertise the National Highway Twelve automobile company, and developed stock semi-fictional and wholly fictional situations, fabricated other relatives and friends who "visited" her in her new "home" at the Statler Hotel, and whom she involved in adventures or whom she took shopping in her advertisers' stores.

Peggy Hull's brother, Edward S. Goodnough. *(Courtesy of Josephine Goodnough Yakich)*

Soon she expanded her activities and her income as she had earlier in Honolulu by offering a personal shopping service. Under a column title "Let Peggy Shop for You," she wrote, "You mustn't forget to call me up or write to me if you want any shopping done. I can buy men's things just as well as women's and I'd like to try to please you all."[8]

In a column titled, "There's No Such Thing As Lonely Sunday," she told about discovering a little magazine which offered, to all boys under eighteen who made three purchases in a local shop, membership in something called the Beta Kappa Beta fraternity. "Of course I'm not a boy and I'm over eighteen," she confessed,

> but I thought it would be lots of fun to join, so I went to Mr. Dolan, the manager, and asked him if he couldn't break the rule just once for me. You see I had qualified for a senior membership, having made eight purchases. Mr. Dolan laughed at me at first and then agreed when I showed him my picture taken in one of their smart junior suits. Don't you think I look like a boy? Now, I envy the Beta Kappa Beta boys because they can wear those comfortable suits all the time.[9]

No one seeing this column or the accompanying picture of her in one of the suits could have been surprised by her subsequent passion for uniforms.

Whether or not hers was truly a split personality, the different sides of Peggy Hull's nature could have lived quite happily together had it not been for the social disapproval one of them generated. To counter it, she made a great point of the comfort and practicality of male attire; though the clothes were undoubtedly more comfortable than those considered fashionable for women, the most important thing about them to her may have been that they symbolized the power of the ruling sex.

In this same column, granting equal time to the other, more conventional, side of her nature, she rhapsodized over the gothic romances available in the Statler Hotel library.

> Before I had even realized the magic of that room it was filled with the characters of the play. Marion De Lorma, beautiful, clever and gorgeously arrayed, rustled by me to tell the Cardinal of the most recent conspiracy. Chevalier de Mauprat, courteous and sincere, spoke in low tones to me of his love for Julie, the Cardinal's ward. One by one they passed before me — they fought their duels and conspired against their leaders and I, lost in a whirlpool of emotions, sat unaware of time or place until I reached the last line.[10]

The times were right for a florid kind of journalism, and Peggy obviously had a flair for it. In a day of "Forbidden Fruit," "Sin," and "Birth of a Nation"; of the KisselKar, Locomobile, and Verlie Six; of Radway's Ready Relief, Hostetter's Stomach Bitters, and Dr. Kilmer's Swamp-Root — a day of fierce and elemental commercial competition, of shameless ham and hype — Peggy was free to exploit her considerable talent for marketplace puffery. In fact, she was so successful as an advertiser that, when a group of Cleveland businessmen, wholesale merchants, and manufacturers who constituted the "Gyro Club," an organization designed "to stimulate and encourage personality in business and to keep civic and industrial welfare always in the foreground," decided to hold an exhibition at the armory, they asked her to edit their exhibition publication, the *Gyro Scoop*. Attracted by her pragmatism, they considered her their business equal, almost; and made arrangements for her to attend the affair as their special guest.[11]

Her job as editor of the *Scoop* was to describe the exhibition booths and write straight-arrow, jingoistic editorials devoid of any controversial themes. She had early learned that advertisers did not mind exhibitionism, some even admired it, but they did not like controversy, particularly political controversy. It was bad for business. If she held any unpopular opinions, she knew enough to keep them to herself and out of her columns and editorials.

Despite the business-as-usual surface of the exhibition reflected in the commerce-promoting contests and competitions, an ominous military note was sounded with the announcement that there would also be exhibits intended to promote the country's preparedness, contests for soldiers of the Ohio National Guard, and a military parade. This military concern was not spontaneous. Cleveland had been the first city in the nation to establish a National Guard Training Course for Citizens, part of the program which President Woodrow Wilson was pushing as civilian preparation for "any emergency" which might confront the country. The obvious "emergency" was World War I which had been raging in Europe for a year and a half. Playing up stories of European women taking military responsibility when they were needed ("Women Soldiers Now on the Firing Line," "Makes Women Soldiers: France Calls on Them for Garrison Duty"), the press was helping to get American women in the frame of mind to accept the idea that they should be ready and willing to serve in at least quasi-military or support positions.

This notion required no great mental leap for Peggy Hull. Now, in Cleveland it was all coming together for her: events of the time, her natural inclination toward the military, and soon, the opportunity to become involved in it all.

This opportunity was the result of the political turmoil in Mexico which grew out of the revolution that had begun against dictator Porfirio Díaz's regime in 1910. One of several guerrilla leaders who supported Francisco Madero in forcing Díaz to resign and leave Mexico was Pancho Villa, who had in his youth been little more than a common bandit robbing trains, looting banks, and raiding mines.

As Mexico suffered through a series of brief presidential administrations during the next six years, Villa's personal ambitions grew. From a position of military leadership in Chihuahua in northern Mexico, he claimed he was speaking for the entire nation. However, when he was defeated at the crucial First Battle of Celaya by Gen. Alvaro Obregón in April 1915, his hopes of gaining national support seemed dim. The final blow came when President Wilson extended de facto recognition to the regime of Venustiano Carranza in October 1915.

"Pancho Villa, who had courted the United States for years and who had not even criticized the invasion of Veracruz [April 1914], was incensed. Determined not to turn the other cheek, he began to take his vengeance on private United States civilians."[12]

On January 9, 1916, a group of United States mining engineers and technicians left by train for Mexico from El Paso, Texas. Setting out to reopen a mine in Chihuahua, they were "assured of a safe conduct and Mexican government protection."[13] At Santa Isabel the train was stopped by a band of Villistas, and seventeen Americans were murdered while one escaped to tell about it.

Just two months later, on the morning of March 9, 1916, the Villistas carried out their notorious raid on Columbus, New Mexico, when 485 men attacked and terrorized the town's 400 inhabitants, leaving 18 Americans dead and many wounded.[14]

Public opinion was aroused to such an extent that President Wilson was forced to act, and Brig. Gen. John J. Pershing was ordered to head a punitive expedition to pursue and break up Villa's band or bands.[15] Pershing's troops crossed the border on March 15, 1916.

Peggy was caught up in it when the training of civilians was extended to women with the formation of the Women's Auxiliary of the Ohio National Guard. She was, of course, one of the first to join.

"I'm a soldier now!" she proclaimed ecstatically in her column.

Monday night I joined the Women's Auxiliary . . . and I'm going to learn to shoot a rifle and to do Red Cross work. The drills and exercises are splendid from a health standpoint and the military training teaches self control, a good thing for the majority of us because we are so apt to lose our heads in an emergency. There were over two hundred women present at drill Monday night and I am glad to see so many interested in preparing themselves for any need of the future.[16]

Then, feeling that she must assure her readers (and herself) that she was, even so, still a very feminine woman, she continued:

When Roland heard of my enlistment and knew I was taking it seriously he went across the street . . . and bought me a wonderful pink azalea plant, all in full bloom. It was a gorgeous sight.[17]

Two weeks later she announced, facetiously,

I'm studying very hard to be an officer — I think I'd like to be a Brigadier General, or something like that, and of course it will take a lot of work and self-sacrifice.[18]

The article included a picture of her in uniform: shirt, pants, high boots, holding a campaign hat ("I just thought I'd dress up and show you how I'm going to look when I'm promoted"). This was followed by her usual advertising of Cleveland stores which gave her a chance for another ultrafeminine apologia.

It may look like a long jump from a uniform to lace and soft frilly things, but I've been preparing for Easter just as much as you have, in spite of the fact that I've been training every day.[19]

In June 1916, President Wilson called up the National Guard to be sent down to patrol the border while Pershing's force was pursuing Villa. The Ohio National Guard was to be a substantial part of the patrol.

Her military fever coming to a boil, Peggy made up her mind that she was going to go along to the Southwest when the Ohio troops were sent. Regarding herself as a de facto, if not a de jure, member of the Ohio National Guard,

[she] just went to the managing editor [of the *Plain Dealer*] and said, "I'm going down to the border with the Ohio National Guard!" He said he wouldn't be a party to sending a girl to an army camp![20]

Unsuccessful in her attempt to get financial backing from the *Plain Dealer* but determined to go anyway, Peggy announced her intention to become a free-lancer and send her stories about the activities of Ohio's sons and sweethearts from the border to any newspaper which would buy them. She did win a partial victory with the *Plain Dealer*'s agreement to buy articles from her as long as they contained advertising for Cleveland businesses.

She did not leave right away because the Cleveland troops did not immediately go to the border. Instead, they were sent to Camp Willis, four miles north of Columbus, Ohio, for further training and to get them used to camp life. When the first contingent was ready to leave Cleveland, their mascot, a goat labeled "Villa" and draped in a yellow blanket, was hoisted "resisting violently" onto the troop train.[21] Later, its reluctance seemed a foreshadowing.

On July 4, Peggy went down to the camp to see for herself what was going on there. It was her first experience in a military camp and, feeling the need of moral support of a friendly face, she decided to try to find a captain she knew, Robert Norton. When she had not found anyone from Cleveland Troop A after two hours of looking, tired and hungry, she sat down to rest on a hayrick not far from the mess tent. Before long a soldier emerged with a plate of food. Prompted by her empty stomach, she greeted him and said, with more than a trace of coyness, "If you were a newspaper woman . . . and you just had to get a story and you were two miles from the nearest restaurant, what would you do?"[22]

The soldier, quite equal to the "challenge," answered good-naturedly, "I'd ask some fellow with a pan of stew to divide with me!" It was her first taste of army camp food.

She got her first taste of the army camp attitude toward woman's place from Maj. Harold Bush, commander of the artillery camp, who told her, "A military camp is a matter of war — not friendship — and it's no place for a woman."

But she found Col. C. X. Zimmerman either more tolerant of her presence or more susceptible to her charm, for five minutes after they had met, the initially gruff Zimmerman was calling her "Peggy" and inviting her to the officers' mess.

Later, she was entertained in the tent of Capt. F. T. Mudge of Battery A in an unmilitary-like fashion, reminiscent of the style of Gen. George Custer. There was a white linen table cloth, a complete set of white china, and at the close of the meal, when the captain brought out a "box of bonbons, [she] couldn't help but think Sherman must have made some mistake about war."

But the real thrill for her, a thrill she came to crave, she experienced that evening when

> [she] stood at attention, one lone woman, among 12,000 men and saluted the flag as Major Fanning's band played the Star Spangled Banner — and just for a second [she] forgot that [her] place was behind the firing lines, for [her] spirit touched that invisible force which makes the learned and the illiterate lay down their pens and tools to fight for a common cause — honor![23]

In fact, her whole life changed that night at Camp Willis. This seemed to her to be what she had been born for, and she felt that fate had been cruel to deny it to her. There appeared to be nothing she could do about it immediately. So, having written several articles describing her experiences at Camp Willis, she returned to Cleveland. While she completed final preparations for her trip to the border, she resumed her advertising column with a vengeance, trying to get together a little extra money to tide her over until she got settled in Texas.

It was at this inopportune moment that her mother arrived with the expressed intention of moving in with her.[24] There seemed no point in fighting a situation which would soon resolve itself; despite her devotion to the Statler, to placate her mother, Peggy moved them into an apartment. This was only one of several occasions when her mother, leaving her second husband because she suspected him of being unfaithful to her, tried to establish a permanent home with her. Minnie Finn Goodnough Hoerath frequently made it plain that she felt she and her daughter could live together to their mutual advantage. To her some-times bitter disappointment, Peggy never let it happen.

It was not only that they found it impossible to get along very well for very long or that her mother loudly disapproved of her life style, feeling that her daughter was much too "friendly" with some of her men friends. The most decisive obstacle to their living together was that Peggy was always on the move, always looking for a better job or more excite-ment. Living out of her trunk, she packed up and took off whenever she was ready. Another person, a mother, even a husband, complicated an otherwise simple operation. In this case especially, dragging her mother along with her to Texas was out of the question because on top of everything else, Minnie was not a "trooper"; living out of a suitcase did not, she made it clear, appeal to her as the proper way for respecta-ble people to operate. Peggy did feel an obligation to her mother, and when Minnie was back with her husband or living with other family members, she sent money to her regularly.[25]

Resolving that when the time came, she was leaving — alone — Peggy went on with her plans, confident that time would take care of the latest problem with her mother, who would probably go back to Hoerath as she usually did. Because Peggy had to hustle if she was going to be ready for the big trip financially, her columns were jam-packed with advertis-ing. Typical was one titled "Peggy Will Go to Mexico to Write War News" which said, in part:

> Here I am ready to leave for the border with the . . . Guard. Yes, I'm really going and I'm going to write you lots of letters all about your friends and relatives who have responded to the call to arms. It has been a strenuous and exciting week for us all — a bit tear-ful one too — especially for the brides who have seen their hus-bands leave.
>
> The first thing I investigated when I learned I was going was my baggage. One can't go to war with the same equipment one would go on a summer vacation. In the London Leather Shoppe . . . I found a splendid Indestructible trunk and a small compact traveling bag. The bag is thoroughly fitted out with toilet articles and an emergency medicine case. These bags will be almost indispensable if you expect to go to Mexico and I advise you to look at them before you purchase any luggage.[26]

Technology and mass production were transforming the United States into a consumer-oriented, gadget-loving society, and the accessibility of products like simple, inexpensive cameras was revolutionizing social history.

This going to the front or any place in fact without a Kodak would certainly be losing a chance to get snap shot pictures, not only of interest at the present moment but pictures which will be of great value in the years to come.

The Chilcote-Sargent Photo Supply Co., . . . where I bought my Kodak, has a complete stock of special small size Kodaks which were purchased especially for the soldiers going away. They are so made that good sharp pictures can easily be taken by anyone as they are immediately ready for use at any distance and the films can be mailed back to the Chilcote-Sargent Co., to be finished at a slight expense.

Before this time wrist watches had been considered effeminate, but as always happens in a war atmosphere, necessity and convenience were changing many attitudes considered socially useful in peacetime but counterproductive in wartime. Peggy was doing her part in this process. Her motivation was more self-interested commercialism than social altruism, however.

At last the men who have so consistently scorned the wrist watch are going to find how absolutely indispensable these misjudged timepieces are. Officers and their subordinates will have plenty of use for a wrist watch, and by the time they come back from the war they will have forgotten how their friends smiled when they first appeared with one strapped to their wrists. . . . Webb C. Ball [has] . . . a great number of . . . watches and I should think they would be fine for the officers and boys of the guard. They are firmly fastened in leather straps and range in price from $3.50 to $10.

Then her usual "ultra-feminine" affirmation —

The hardest part about leaving Cleveland will be to put away my thin, dainty summer dresses and the pumps I have purchased at various times in Chisholm's Boot Shop to go with them. Having spent a summer on the Mexican border as a "war" correspondent, I know how useless they would be, so I'm starting away next week with four pairs of comfortable, broad toed, flat heeled shoes. . . . You see, you have to change your shoes at least twice a day there — no matter how comfortable they are — so I bought two pair of tans and two of canvas.[27]

She went on to tell about a farewell dinner she had given for some friends at the Statler, describing the outdoor café, the orchestra, the great service and good food, and saying that she expected to miss the Statler "more than any other of [her] Cleveland haunts." She also wrote a lengthy account of a shopping trip to the Euclid Market, concluding with, "Please watch for my stories while I'm gone because I'm going to find lots of interesting things to write to you."

Already she was mentally attuned to the cycles of soldiering: The soldier got ready, marched off, did his job, and if he survived, came home to a hero's welcome. Psychologically as much a soldier as any guardsman going to the border, she ended with, "When I come back I want to feel that you are all here waiting for me and that you have not forgotten me."[28]

And that July, when she finally boarded the train bound for Texas, she was, at last, a soldier going off to war. The yearning was over. Ahead lay the adventure and excitement she had, as a child, dreamed about.

*My train was late* — of course — and I didn't arrive until after midnight. I was scared too — because I had heard such terrible things about bandits making surprise attacks under the cover of night — and I was all alone and didn't know a soul. But I climbed into a big taxi and the driver whisked me away to the Paso del Norte Hotel.

When I walked into the lobby my first impulse was to drop into one of the big chairs and have a good cry. But by the time I had reached the desk all that feeling vanished. There was the nicest young man smiling at me and he said "Good Evening" just as though I had been living at the Paso del Norte all my life. It chased away that awful homesick feeling and perked me up a lot.

Peggy Hull,
*El Paso Herald*

# CHAPTER FOUR

# With Pershing on the Mexican Border

When Peggy climbed aboard the train for Texas, she thought that the Ohio troops would be right behind her, but it seemed that every time orders came through to start their southward movement, those orders were immediately cancelled. It looked as if they might be off around August 16, but a sudden rail crisis immobilized them once more.

In El Paso she settled into the Paso del Norte Hotel and, writing her column for the *Plain Dealer* in the form of letters describing conditions and events in El Paso, she cleverly worked her Cleveland advertisers into her stories. In an early column she wrote that on her way to El Paso she saw several girls in St. Louis wearing "white hightopped kid shoes with orange colored vamps,"[1] a style which Stanley Chisholm of Cleveland had told her about before her departure; more closely related to her new "assignment," she reported that

> a great many of the trucks used by the government at this point are made by the White Motor company in Cleveland, and of course, it being one of my own home town industries, I was interested in learning how they were holding up under the terrific strain. The highways they have to travel cannot be called roads — they are gulleys. Long, tortuous gulleys — filled with rocks and deep holes burrowed out by an occasional sweeping rain and it is over such roads that American trucks are getting the first crucial test of their efficiency. I asked the captain of the train in which the White trucks are used if he had found them satisfactory, and I thought you would like to know that a Cleveland industry has made good on the Mexican border, for he was unstinted in his praise of their sturdiness and efficiency.[2]

Peggy Hull in her first uniform, borrowed from the Ohio National Guard, 1916. *(Peggy Hull Deuell Collection, Kansas Collection, University of Kansas Libraries)*

This claim is supported by Haldeen Braddy in his *Pershing's Mission in Mexico*. M. Sgt. Herbert W. Conklin with the Fifth Cavalry of the Expedition told him that "every truck manufacturer in the country sent down trucks; the best was the White."[3]

In spite of an earlier announcement that she was giving up such frills, Peggy was glad she had brought her "party frocks and afternoon gowns" because as usual she was invited to many parties and dances. She concluded one column with, "The Ohio militia will be here in a few days now — probably by the time you read this letter. If you have any relatives or friends I can look up for you [or] if there is anything I can do for you — down here among the cactuses, don't hesitate to write me."[4] Included was a picture of her in guard uniform. This picture often accompanied her reports from the border while chiefly social and advertising columns carried a picture of her in a long-sleeved dress, making a slight curtsy, with her hands holding out the sides of her skirt.

Denied permission to cross the border into Mexico to report on the activities of Pershing's troops who were searching for Villa, Peggy countered with another even wilder proposal: an airplane flight along the Mexican border, over to Vera Cruz and on to Mexico City where she would interview President Carranza. Admitting that it was a "regular Richard Harding Davis assignment," she contended that "with Russian girls of 16 fighting in the army alongside their brothers and fathers . . ., a girl these days has as much right to attempt the daring as has a man."[5] The proposed flight, "one of the most original advertising campaigns that any company has every launched," was to be made "in a steady, reliable, air-going craft, to demonstrate the adaptability of the airplane to commercial purposes." Her prediction that "these little jaunts by air will before long be as common as a trip to the mountains by auto"[6] was more than commercial hype; it was also her vision of the future. Although it all proved to be another of her grandiose schemes which never got off the ground, her dreaming about flying once again demonstrated her frustration at not being permitted to do what the male reporters were allowed to do and on the practical side gave her the opportunity to advertise the International Aircraft Company of Detroit which she claimed was manufacturing a special plane for the adventure.

She had been in El Paso four weeks when the Ohio troops finally arrived.

They are here at last! . . . Sunday — flanked by two majors of the United States army — I had the honor to welcome Col. C. X. Zimerman [*sic*] and the Fifth regiment to El Paso. Believe me, I was a happy girl when Capt. C. C. Chambers leaned out of the window of the Pullman as it went by our car and yelled, "Hello, Peggy!"[7]

She vowed publicly that she would stay in Texas until the militia was recalled, even though that would mean she could not get back to Cleveland to buy her fall wardrobe from her favorite stores.

In fact, nothing could have dragged her away. From early childhood she had lived in a world of fantasy in which soldiers were her heroes. Now she was in a position to share their experiences in "fighting on the side of right."[8] She was at last in her natural element, and she threw herself into it.

Wherever the army was there was Peggy. When reviews were held at Fort Bliss, Peggy was there on the friskiest mount in the corrals. When General Murgia [Francisco Murguía] entertained General [J. Franklin] Bell in the hippodrome in Juarez toasts were drunk to Senorita Peggy, the pride of the Americans present. She was the friend of every soldier in the American army.[9]

Exhilarated by the romantic military atmosphere, she wrote:

I've been completely overwhelmed with generals, colonels, majors and captains. And somebody may even introduce you to Private Nobody and the first thing you know you'll find out he is a Philadelphia millionaire or a Harvard Professor![10]

One of the officers most important to her future was Col. Peyton C. March of the Eighth Field Artillery whom she met later as a general at an artillery training camp in France and finally as army chief of staff in Washington, D.C., when she received her first accreditation as a war correspondent.

The glamour of military life did not blind her to some of its harsher realities, like prostitution and the problems that accompanied it. Great believers in the "leveling down" effect of the army, that "as a rule the coarser element . . . creates the atmosphere of the group,"[11] most of the commanding officers of the camps in and around El Paso were indifferent to its presence, feeling that in every military situation prostitution was inevitable. Even Pershing, bowing to "military necessity," approved a restricted quarter for prostitution near the big camp at Colonia Dublán in Mexico.[12] Commanding officers tried to control the attendant venereal disease by requiring men who had had sexual contact with prostitutes to present themselves at infirmaries for "prophylactic treatment" in an effort to keep them from transmitting syphilis, gonorrhea, or other "social" disease. Most medical personnel felt that this was the most effective approach, but it required the cooperation of the affected soldiers, many of whom simply did not report their sexual activities to authorities; and since in most situations it was impossible for the army to keep track of the movements of thousands of military personnel, many evaded the health care network. So, much disease went untreated.

The remarkable thing was that it was not worse than it was because prostitution was rampant around almost all of the camps. M. J. Exner, a doctor who went to the border to study the situation, found that many Mexican and black women as well as white were doing a land-office business. At many of the houses, shacks, or "crib" buildings, there were long lines of soldiers waiting their turn. One woman, "below average in attractiveness," [13] told him that on a good night she had fifty clients, and another who was found to have active syphilis had "serviced" 120 men in two days.

At two of the more remote camps, the commanders had decided not just to contain the effects of prostitution but to banish it altogether. In Exner's view this approach had been a complete success. But what was possible at the remote desert camps where comings and goings could be controlled was not possible in the cities, and in addition, lost in the whole question seemed to be any real concern for the women caught up in the life.

Since Peggy had suffered from the hostile military attitude toward most women and especially those who hung around army encampments, her sensibilities were aroused by one of the "exorcisms" carried out by the commander of the camp at Columbus, New Mexico. Eight women whom he had labeled "undesirables" were "escorted" out of town. Peggy, empathizing with them, came to their defense in an article entitled "The Undesirables."

Eight little girls, pitiful, defiant, and shabbily independent. . . . Eight girls — still in their teens, their childish cheeks flagrantly painted — their little red satin middy blouses a mute appeal for admiration. . . .

Last week in Columbus a soda fountain shop was doing a rushing business. Soldiers flocked there in preference to places of lesser respectability. Probably eight little girls were responsible for it — they were pretty and they weren't stingy with their smiles. They could dance, too. And every time they danced the generous boys in khaki didn't forget to leave a dime or quarter for them. In fact, things were going very well. Josephine found times so prosperous that she invested in a pair of puttee-topped boots.

"Gee, but they were swell," so her seven little companions said.

In the meantime the medical officers of the district began to scratch their heads and note with annoyance the ever mounting "lack of health" figures. Something had to be done. They conferred with the provost marshal. The segregated district was rigidly inspected and then some one thought of the eight little girls. Seven dollars a week is hardly enough to live on and what with puttee-topped boots and red satin blouses — well, it looked bad for the eight little girls and they were called before the military authorities.

And the verdict you know. There was a great scurrying in Columbus yesterday morning in a certain part of the town and a lot of ceremony in another. The provost marshal was awfully busy. He had eight passengers to put on the eastbound train and there wasn't much time.

Down the main street of the little border town came the Twelfth cavalry band, escorting the commander of the southern department to the station. The provost marshal was mounted on a large horse giving a fine imitation of Paul Revere — one of the eight little girls was missing. The train whistled — long and warningly. Then he found her back of a freight car saying good-by . . . to a soldier.

But Marty wasn't much concerned or maybe she hid it under her defiance.

"Well," she said as she watched the oncoming band and the military cortege, "the old town isn't doin' so bad by us after all — We gotta band to play us off an' a major general as an escort," and she raised a short, pert nose ever so slightly at the provost marshal.

They are here [El Paso]. Eight little girls in red satin middy blouses — the first cankerous hate in their hearts for the law that sends them — hopelessly wandering and with a stigma that marks them "undesirables."[14]

Peggy seemed to be the busiest person on the border — attending the "hops" put on by the people of El Paso for the officers and their friends and families, visiting camps Bliss and Pershing[15] where she often took gifts of food and soft drinks, expanding her circle of army friends in guard units and the regular army, and still finding time to write her letters to the *Plain Dealer* from the Paso del Norte, the favorite hang-out of soldiers on short leave.

Just as important as her contacts with future generals were the contacts she made with male newspaper correspondents. In particular, Floyd Gibbons, who had spent four months traveling over northern Mexico with Villa in 1915 and whom she later called "The Richard Harding Davis of World War I"; Webb Miller, who took her under his wing and was the first war correspondent to die in World War II; and Nicholas McDonald, a movie newsreel photographer from Chicago, "inspired" her to do things she hardly realized she was capable of. Their "inspiration" took the form of daring her to do something and then suggesting she did not have the nerve.[16]

She really proved herself in their eyes and in the eyes of at least some of the officers when she persuaded Brig. Gen. Charles G. Morton, commander of the Tenth Division, to let her go along with the 20,000 soldiers from the camps near El Paso on a fifteen-day hike into New Mexico.

> I had a terrible time convincing him I could stand the hardships. When I finally gained his consent, I knew my military career depended upon [that] hike.[17]

It turned out to be a more grueling experience than she had anticipated, she wrote in her "colorful" account of the experience;[18] but when her wake-up call came at four o'clock that first morning, she was "wide awake and out of bed instantly." Slipping out of her pink crepe de Chine night gown, she quickly pulled on her uniform — "pearl gray woolen skirt and flannel shirt, a heavy pair of rubber soled shoes and a campaign hat." She hesitated for a moment, loath to leave the comfort of her room. Then she heard the sound she loved most, "the faint echo of a bugle," and she was out the door and on her way.

At Fort Bliss she fell into line with the troops who had already started to move out. She was a great deal more excited about the adventure than most of the real soldiers.

> I mentally pictured all women of my profession envying me the trip — I glowed with pride at the privilege of marching away into the setting sun with the protectors of the nation's honor — I saw myself the center of admiring groups of my own sex — I could see myself walking into the office of the largest newspaper in New York City and the managing editor saying: "Oh, yes, you're the young woman —"
>
> Ouch! My imagination had taken me too far. I stumbled over a miniature boulder and went sprawling into a mesquite bush at the side of the road.

Two privates came to her rescue and helped her back to her place in the ranks.

From then on she gave up day-dreaming and concentrated on keeping up with the march. There was no singing and very little talking. Most of the time the only sounds were of "shuffling feet and the thud . . . of equipment as it swayed from the shoulders of soldiers." They were not even out of the city before her feet started to hurt. The hurt became excruciating and shot through her whole body. Unused to fighting this kind of pain, she could not keep up and soon started to lag behind. She was not the only one. A very young soldier limped along beside her, and another man dropped back to join them. They hobbled along together, keeping each other's spirits up enough to struggle on.

Luckily, that first day they made camp early. Even though it was October, the sun beat down on them "maliciously." As far as the eye could see the land was desolate and depressing, a waste of sand, creosote bush, and mesquite. The barren slopes and "haughty" peaks of the Franklin Mountains "followed the sky line from east to west." To the south the river,

> stretching . . . like a lazy, lonely snake, threw off a steaming . . . stench and its murky currents belied the cognomen "Silvery Rio Grande."
>
> The air [was] heavy with the smell of sweating men, shedding horses, stables and straw.

It was evident from a conversation she overheard that not all of the soldiers were filled with the military fervor that Peggy had.

> "Soldierin's h-----" said a deep voice. . . .
> "Dontcha like it? . . . Well, you were wild to come!" . . .
> "You hated the idea, didn't you?" The deep voice was growing heated.
> "I was enlisted. Had to come. You're a volunteer."
> "I'm a fool!"
> "Granted — Looked good from up North, didn't it?"
> "Ya-ah! . . . Your country needs you. Get Villa — the colors are calling — Star Spangled Banner! Brave boys! Bah! All rot! Cactus! Sagebrush[!] Sand! Sun! Flies! Stink!" . . .
> "You're a patriot! Ain't that enough? Your country needed you."
> "Needed me — needed me for what? To eat out of tin pans and polish a ribbon clerk's shoes?"[19]

She gave up her eavesdropping and, aching and exhausted to the point of illness, limped to her tent where she "dropped in a heap on the hard pallet." She fell asleep immediately and slept through supper and the campfire camaraderie after it. The next thing she was conscious of was a young man's voice at her tent doorway saying, "I've brought you some breakfast." He was the one she had marched with the day before. She started to get up, but her body hurt so she lay back down. The young man knelt and held a cup of coffee to her lips. "Better take it easy as you get up — you won't hurt so much," he said.

After he had left, she struggled with getting her shoes on over her swollen feet, but she was flagging and next to abandoning the march and looking for a ride back to El Paso. Again the one sound that always saved her throughout her "military" life saved her now: the rallying notes of a bugle. Soon she was tramping along again with her comrades.

That day turned out to be worse than the first one even though she did not have to endure so much painful marching, for a fierce sandstorm blew up suddenly.

Units became separated. Minor commands were lost. Water wagons were overturned in the desert or else lost their way and wandered from the main column. The wind raged and blinded us all with fine white sand. We had no luncheon and no dinner. About one o'clock in the morning after the storm had spent itself, our weary field kitchen staggered into camp and the First Kentucky Field Hospital — I was traveling with them — turned out for food — and such food. Sanded bacon — sanded bread — sanded coffee sweetened with sanded sugar.

I felt as though I had never had a bath. My hair was bristling and hard to sleep on. I didn't want a military career then, but I had convinced the general I did want one and I couldn't quit.[20]

By determination alone, she stuck it out for the four more days to Las Cruces, the turn-around destination of the march. As she was standing in the chow line at the field kitchen, a "pleasing masculine voice" behind her said, "Private Hull, you have been promoted to the rank of first lieutenant. Report at Kentucky field hospital No. 1 at once." The voice belonged to Capt. S. S. Creighton, U.S. Medical Corps. After ordering her to "crack your heels together, stick out your chest — hold up your head — chin — now salute!" he led her to the officers' mess tent to eat with "the brass."

This "promotion" was not the only welcome attention she received as a result of her perseverance on the march.

When I came through like [a] hardened veteran — well, I will always count as one of the triumphant moments of my life the reception which [Brigadier] General [Charles] Morton gave in my honor — five hundred officers and several of them generals. It definitely marked my embarkation as a field correspondent.[21]

In fact, General Morton was so impressed with her spunk and staying power that he saw to it that she got a ride most of the way back to El Paso. At the conclusion of this experience, Peggy reverted to her ultra-feminine side, writing, "I'm home now — and over on the bed there's a shimmering heap of pink silk. Tomorrow I'm going to buy all the pink things I can afford — and let the men — be the soldiers."[22] Of course, it was only a temporary resolve.

When the Ohio troops had arrived in El Paso, they had been accompanied by the *Plain Dealer*'s official staff correspondent, James Lanyon; so Peggy could no longer count on the Cleveland paper's buying any of her army stories. Further, she was coming to the end of her advertising column in the *Plain Dealer* because of her distance from her advertisers. It was not long until, in her usual enterprising way, she landed a job on an El Paso paper.

She started in late September 1916 at the *El Paso Herald* with a column under the familiar heading "When Peggy Goes A-Shopping." In the first column was the announcement that

> Herald readers are offered the advantage of its new Shopping service and Information Bureau. Miss Peggy will purchase for you — free of charge — any article mentioned in her columns or elsewhere in The Herald and will gladly give you any information regarding theatres, hotels, shops, railroads mentioned below. If you wish to use this service, phone, wire, or write Miss Peggy, care El Paso Herald — telephone 5050. There is No Charge To Either Customers or Advertisers for this Service.[23]

She did not stay with the *Herald* for long, but moved to the *El Paso Morning Times.* How simple it was for her to adapt her Cleveland advertising tales to El Paso can be seen in a story entitled (in the *Plain Dealer*) "Two Men Narrowly Escape Death in a Sudden Flood." According to this account, on a street corner she overheard one man telling another about his experience with a friend when they got caught in a flash flood with their automobile. The power of that car was all that saved them. The article was patterned on the old "National Highway Twelve" story that had appeared in the *Plain Dealer,* but in the *Morning Times* it was a Studebaker Six because the Studebaker dealer was her advertiser in El Paso.[24]

Toward the end of 1916, her column in the El Paso paper became a regular part of the Sunday edition and appeared on occasion in the middle of the week as well. Since she had decided she would stay in El Paso even after the Guard left, she announced that she was sending for her mother, which meant moving to a house or an apartment because "Mother is one of those 'homey' women who could never be contented in a hotel."[25] And it did seem likely that if Minnie Hoerath could not have been happy at the Statler, she probably would not be any better pleased with the Paso del Norte. It was also likely that Minnie had announced she was coming rather than that Peggy had sent for her.

Peggy changed the title of her column several times, always, however, retaining her name as part of it. In early December 1916, under the heading "Peggy Philosophizes on El Paso Affairs," she offered assistance to people with their Christmas shopping, with making over dresses, and with decorating their houses. Although her "philosophizing" was given an impressive three columns in the paper, she was challenged to defend her effectiveness when a businessman suggested to her that people were not reading her column. To prove to him that she was earning her advertising fees, she asked all her "loyal friends" and readers to write and tell her what they thought of her column and promised to give a prize for the best letter.[26]

A week later she reported the results and thanked her readers for all the letters she had received, announcing that she would award the prize on January 21. Also, there was a note from one of her advertisers, S. P. Smith of the Leon Hotel, saying, "Since the story about my apartment and hotel appeared in your columns, Miss Peggy, I haven't had an empty room or apartment and at least fifty people whose names I can give have spoken to me about the story. It is the best advertisement I've ever had."[27]

Early in 1917, the *Morning Times* reported that the army planned to return National Guard units to their home states as soon as they could be replaced by regulars from Pershing's force which was reportedly on its way north out of Mexico. Peggy's column, now called "Peggy's Corner," had been concerned mostly with shopping news and descriptions of her attendance of the "Tea Dansants" at the Sheldon Hotel, with items such as an interview with a movie star, J. Warren Kerrigan, an account of a prize fight she had gone to, and the announcement that she planned to leave for the Mardi Gras in New Orleans sprinkled in.

But news that Pershing's return to American soil was imminent postponed her departure for New Orleans. She could not resist the invitation from a group of newspapermen, including Robert Rhode of the *New York Tribune;* Bill Griffin of the Hearst Service; and Nick McDonald of the Selig-Tribune Company, and rode with them to Columbus, New Mexico, where reliable rumor had it that Pershing and his troops were about to arrive.[28]

While they were waiting, she enjoyed the social life of the army base and loved all the attention she received. However, she declined any favored treatment. When she joined the other reporters for meals at the Clark Hotel,

Peggy would insist upon matching her dollar against the others to see who paid the bill, and when the hotel rooms were all taken and a refrigerator annex was all that was available, she refused to accept another's room and shivered and slept there while in Columbus.[29]

She was a much sought-after dinner companion not only by the other reporters, but also by the army officers. Though she gloried in the social life, "always she returned to the little telegraph car presided over by Irish Pat Murphy, the only Columbian who admitted he ran when Villa attacked the town,"[30] to send her stories to the *Morning Times* and to keep abreast of what was going on in the outside world.

By January 20, the dismantling of Pershing's base camp at Colonia Dublán began; and on January 27, American troops started the hundred-mile trek north to the border. With the soldiers came a pitiable band of political refugees — 197 Americans, 2,030 Mexicans, and 533 Chinese — who had been promised asylum by the U.S. State Department "to keep them from being slaughtered by Villistas."[31]

Reaching Las Palomas by February 4, the Expedition began crossing the border the next day. Peggy was outraged by what happened when the refugees tried to enter the U.S.:

> Starved though they were — many of them half naked and shivering in the crisp New Mexico morning air — their countrymen custom officials halted one little group after another, and demanded an export fee of three dollars each to enter the land of the free! . . . Military officials on the American side who had been detailed to take charge of the incoming refugee train, viewed the delay — first with curiosity, then with impatience — and it was none other than Captain Reed, General Pershing's intelligence officer, who stepped across the line and put a stop to the extortion.[32]

After the last of the refugees had reached American soil, "the commander of the first army which has ever returned bringing with it the unsolicited and willing population of the invaded state" led his troops across the border.[33]

Peggy's account of the return of the Punitive Expedition appeared with her byline on the front page of the *El Paso Morning Times* of February 6, 1917. Under the headline, "PERSHING'S TEN THOUSAND BACK FROM MEXICO DESERT SILENT, SWARTHY AND STRONG," with the subheading, "Hosts Which Chased Villa Over Sandy Wastes Return to Native Land Stoical, Unenthusiastic Fighting Machine; Their Orders Fulfilled," was a picture of her in uniform — hat with chin strap, long coat, and boots.

Columbus, N.M., Feb. 6 — There isn't a khaki-colored canvas tent in Mexico today. There isn't an American flag waving from a single pole. There isn't a long trail of alkali dust winding up from the road that leads into southern Chihuahua. No "gringo" taps echoed among the hills of Colonia Dublan last night or lingered over the still desert in the north. The punitive expedition is home. . . .

It wasn't the triumphal return of a victorious army or the dejected retreat of the defeated. It was a stoical, silent, unenthusiastic organization which marched through the border gate four miles below Columbus yesterday morning and saluted its commander. . . . They did not wave their hats or shout as they went by. Eleven months in Mexico had sent them back [an] efficient, unsentimental, hardened fighting machine.

The reception was somber and silent. A few people had decorated their cars with little American flags.

Two New Mexico National Guardsmen — sentries on duty at the gate — stood at attention as the general passed. His salute was curt. . . . Behind General Pershing rode Lieut. J. L. Collins, his aide, Capt. William G. Reed and Capt. Nicholas Campanole. . . . Their faces were seamed and white dust hung heavily on their faded uniforms.

Several miles down the road a group of children, who had been trucked out to meet the returning troops, lined the road, waiting. The officers on horseback came first and then as soon as

the dust from their horses' hoofs had settled a hundred tiny beams from the barrels of glistening rifles heralded the approach of the infantry. Out of the thin fog and ash-like dust they came — the boys who had walked — over hundreds of miles of dry country — over rocks[,] hills and almost impassable mountains — all the way there and now — all the way back.

Peggy found it a thrilling spectacle.

Their straight backs were even deprived of grace by the heavy equipment strapped around their shoulders, but no ugly uniforms or shabby shoes could take from them the lilting sound that arose from the road as they tramped along.

Above the marching troops, in a sight and sound new to military operations, "four aeroplanes dipped and circled."

There was never any doubt that Peggy Hull loved American troops,
victorious or vanquished. She was their champion, and she came through
for them now in her *Morning Times* article.

> Whatever the feeling in the hearts of true Americans today — what-
> ever the sentiment concerning the withdrawal of Pershing's forces
> from Villa's territory without the annihilation of the bandit or his
> band, the masses of the half-clothed, half-starved Mexican and
> Chinese refugees who called out friendly greetings to the return-
> ing army spoke eloquently of a mission that had not been in vain.
> They did not capture Villa, but they won the faith and friendship
> of two thousand of his countrymen.

---

> In Mexico today there are the ashes of a hundred or more camps
> made by American soldiers. And a silent road[,] gutted with ruts
> covered a foot deep with pulverized earth that eats into the flesh
> like acid[,] twists and turns [across] the desert and through the
> mountains to El Valle. It will tremble no more under the weight
> of heavy motor trucks. The punitive expedition is home and the
> Mexicans need no longer hear the bugle calls or listen to the strains
> of the "Star Spangled Banner."[34]

On page four of the *Morning Times* (page one of the Spanish language edition) there was a startling picture under the head, "Peggy Rides
at Head of Cavalcade of Distinguished United States Army Officers,"
which showed Peggy apparently leading Pershing and his troops out of
Mexico. The actual "event" had been recorded on movie film, probably
by Nick McDonald, movie cameraman for the Selig-Tribune Company,
whose parent company was famous for its creativity when it came to
news film.[35] Apparently no stills had been taken, for a composite had
been put together for the *Morning Times*. Although there are several
versions of this incident and how it came about, according to Peggy's
long-time friend, Irene Corbally Kuhn, the footage was the result of a
trick the men played on Pershing.

> When word came that the General was riding out at the head of
> the troops, . . . the newsreel men were tipped off that the best pix
> were to be had at a certain spot. Peggy was spirited to the rendez-
> vous on her horse, and kept out of sight. At precisely the right
> moment, as . . . General Pershing appeared on his charger, and
> just a moment before the newsreel camera started to grind, the

Peggy Hull and Pershing, Columbus, New Mexico, Feb. 1917, from *El Paso Morning Times,* Feb. 6, 1917. *(Photo provided by Southwest Micropublishing, Inc.)*

signal was given. Peggy trotted her horse into position, along side the General, the newsreel camera started whirring, the troops cheered, and the pictures appeared all over the U.S. and the world — "American girl correspondent leads troops out of Mexico with General Pershing."[36]

When the general had seen the picture, he had not been amused.

Afterward, Peggy claimed that her participation had been innocent. She had just ridden out to greet Pershing and welcome him home. However, Irene Kuhn's version must have come from Peggy herself, and certainly the picture's publication in the *Morning Times* seemed evidence of a much less naive involvement.

Of course, the Punitive Expedition had not succeeded in its assigned purpose — to break up Villa's band — but in the end it accomplished something that turned out to be much more important: It prepared American soldiers and equipment for U.S. entry into World War I.

In Mexico motorized equipment of all kinds was tested, and the army had the chance to smooth out the problems of transporting equipment and supplies by truck. Though Americans had built and flown the first viable airplane, the War Department was extremely short-sighted when it came to its military possibilities; by 1913 American military aviation was still in an embryonic stage. At the beginning of the Punitive Expedition the entire tactical U.S. Air Force consisted of thirteen antiquated planes, eight of which were sent into Mexico.[37] According to Haldeen Braddy, even though "the inadequately powered machines proved unsuited to punishing climatic conditions . . . [the] early-day airmen made aviation history through their reconnaissance and communication activities and by dropping supplies to stranded patrols."[38] Pershing himself wrote,

> The very primitive state of our aviation still gives me a feeling of humiliation. . . . These old planes were not in any sense properly equipped as compared with those being used by other nations even then.
>
> . . . Although at the date of our entry into the war more than a year had elapsed since the beginning of the Mexican Campaign, there were still only thirty-five trained fliers and about one thousand men in aviation, with only a few training planes, none of which were suitable for anything else.[39]

The Mexican Campaign also trained the men in basic and varied types of tactics, among them trench warfare.

Most commands were given some tactical training and the officers had the chance to learn something of camp life and to develop practical leadership in handling units up to the regiment. The training and experience the National Guard received during this service raised their relative efficiency considerably above that attained under ordinary circumstances. Thus the only training, except ordinary routine, any of our forces received during the years prior to 1917, was given to the troops then in Mexico and to those stationed along the border. . . . [In fact,] when the command left Mexico it was probably more highly trained than any similar force of our army had ever been before.[40]

The Punitive Expedition was the training ground not only for the army, but also for Peggy Hull. There she learned about the routine of camp life, the psychology of soldiering, the real military mentality; she developed the style and kind of war reporting that was to make her well known on and off over the next twenty-nine years, the reporting of the so-called "little stories" of war.

FROM the corn fields of a Kansas prairie farm to the Hotel Continental, Paris, is some jump, but Miss Henrietta Goodnough Hull, better known as "Peggy," made it in two "jumps," and landed right in the middle of a world beating story — landing in the middle of big stories being the best thing Miss Peggy does. . . .

[In El Paso, Texas, and Columbus, New Mexico], Peggy was the pet of the border army and she earned her spurs by right of conquest. . . .

[When Pershing marched out of Mexico] Peggy was the first across the line to meet him and the first to greet him. She jumped up and down in her little tan riding boots as the action, color, charm, billowed and piled around her. . . .

[She] was known from one end of the big camp to the other. Mere kids driving the gas-hog motor trucks out of Mexico saw her in her trim, olive drab riding suit, Stetson hat, red silk neck-chief and quirt and one could lip-read these unsung heroes of the punitive expedition saying "Peggy" as they rambled across the line in a halo of white dust. . . .

Peggy distinguished herself at Columbus, and it was perfectly natural that she should receive the coveted assignment to go to France over the heads of the male reporters. She packed her sheer linen party dresses away in a trunk, put on her old gray war bonnet, kissed her mother goodbye and started for Paris, admitting she was both scared to death and tickled to death.

The Cub Reporter,
*El Paso Morning Times*

## CHAPTER FIVE

# How Peggy Got to Paris

A week after her big story on the return of the Punitive Expedition from Mexico, Peggy left El Paso for New Orleans and Mardi Gras. Throughout the time she was there, despite the fact that she was sick most of the time, she sent stories back to the *Morning Times* from her headquarters at the New Orleans Press Club.

Her most successful advertising related to this trip was for the Galveston, Harrisburg & San Antonio Railway Company, a branch of the Southern Pacific; after her return to El Paso, she received a letter of thanks from W. C. McCormick, the company representative, in which he said,

> We have just completed returns from our sales to MARDI GRAS for this year and have compared the sales with those of a year ago and find that this year we sold three times as many tickets to New Orleans [on] account of this celebration as we sold a year ago. I believe that this . . . was due largely to the advertising done through your column.[1]

As gratifying as this was to her, she was getting restless again and decided to take a six-weeks' vacation trip to New York City. Her intention was to go to New Orleans and then proceed by steamer to New York, sending "letters" to the *Morning Times* describing the trip for her El Paso readers.

Before she could carry out these plans, the United States declared war on Germany. In such a crisis, a vacation seemed frivolous, and deciding to do her bit on the home front in El Paso, she settled back into column work. But her column now dealt increasingly with patriotic subjects like her participation in a "patriotic automobile parade." She also used it to castigate the young men of El Paso because all of those whom she had talked to expressed an intention to join the officers' reserve corps. Her lifelong frustration — being denied the right to become a soldier, of even the lowest rank — boiled to the surface.

"Everyone can't be an officer," she chided, "and it is the menial things a man can do with good grace and forbearance that proves his bigness as a man. If I were a man I wouldn't be ashamed to be a private."[2]

As her military passion grew, she began to think about another, different avenue to adventure. Evidence of it, as well as the conflict between the two sides of her personality, stood out sharply in her column of May 20, 1917, which included a picture of her making biscuits accompanied by comments on homey activities, and another picture of her in a trench coat, a piece of apparel which had only just appeared in local stores. "It is something like the soldiers wear in the trenches and I suppose that is why it was given the name of 'Trench coat.'" Pointing out that the style was hardly a month old, the store owner had said to Peggy, "You look almost like a soldier in that coat."[3] Naturally, this had pleased her tremendously.

Soon after, she announced that she was going away for awhile and that her mother, who was still with her, was going to look after her column while she was gone. Assuring her readers she was not going to get married, she said, "I'm sorry I can't tell you now just what I'm going to do but it is a great big secret and oh goodness, but you'll be surprised."[4]

The first one to be surprised was James Black, managing editor of the *Morning Times,* when she bearded him about it.

"Send you to France!"
[His] feet came down from the top of the desk with such a thud that his nose glasses fell off and clattered to the floor. There was a breathless moment . . . for [she] knew if those spectacles broke, [she] would have made a bad start.[5]

The War-to-End-All-Wars had been raging in Europe for more than two and a half years and the United States had finally officially entered the conflict. Troop ships were starting to carry American men across the Atlantic to fight and die on the European battlefields. Men who had gone from El Paso into Mexico with Pershing were now being readied for a new, more deadly military game; Peggy knew that, one way or another, she was going to go with them.

However, she said,

asking the managing editor of a Texas paper with about 25,000 circulation to send me to France as a war correspondent was as preposterous in his eyes and as presumptuous on my part as it would be for a munitions worker in England to have matrimonial designs on the Prince of Wales.

The glasses didn't break, but while the managing editor was gathering them up I began to realize the magnitude of what I had asked for. But, while his amazement frightened me, it gave me a bit of satisfaction, too; for it was the first time I had ever been able to jar his calm dignity. Then amusement gave way to resentment. He spread a paper before him as he answered me.

"How perfectly ridiculous!" There was scorn in his voice. "It would cost too much money, even if you could get a passport, which I am sure you couldn't. George Pattullo [*Saturday Evening Post* correspondent] has been in Washington for six weeks cooling his heels in the corridors of the state department, and he represents one of the biggest magazines in the world. I am surprised at you!"[6]

Peggy's heart was pounding, but she did not retreat. She had come to the interview prepared with an answer for every objection, and she was not above using the "big guns," her huge velvet-brown eyes, if reason failed; for she felt that this was what her whole life until then had been leading up to. When the discussion was over, Peggy left Black's office with the things she had gone there to get: a letter giving her a "roving commission" to do war reporting for the *Morning Times* and a guarantee the paper would pay most of her expenses.

Getting the *Morning Times* to sponsor her was not the only obstacle Peggy had to overcome. In Washington she found a great deal of confusion in the plans for the organizing, training, and quartering of the men called up for registration. Even in as public a place as a hotel lobby, people complained that public officials were wasting time with flag-waving and oratory. The difficulties she had in getting a passport, she found, compared somewhat with being charged with murder before a hostile judge. For one thing, whatever the reasons for the State Department's holding up Pattullo's passport, the official who had the power to make the final decision on whether to put "yes" or "no" on her application insisted that she "appeared too young" for such an assignment as going to France to join the American Expeditionary Force there.

She was, in fact, twenty-seven years old, no longer a prodigy, "the brilliant little special writer" she saw herself as; so, although most of her life she did look younger than her age, his objections were probably related to her sex. Many people felt that women had no business going to battle fronts unless they were nurses or Red Cross workers of some kind, and she was presuming to go as a war correspondent when no woman had ever been accredited for this type of work. The English had a phrase for it: "It isn't done." But Americans didn't do it, either.

United Press correspondent Webb Miller, who had been on the Border, too, was also in Washington picking up his credentials; he, along with some of the other correspondents, made bets that she would not get her passport cleared.

> Four o'clock was the hour set for the reading of the state department's passport judge. Webb wanted to go with me — so did the other newspaper men — I suspected to smile superiorly at me when the judge said no. I declined their offers and went alone. By the time I reached the main entrance my heart was beating so that it choked me and my hands were trembling so visibly that I was ashamed. What a lot of useless emotion I was going through over a passport — if I felt like this about the verdict how in the world would I feel if a submarine hit my ship.[7]

Happily, her fears were unfounded. At the State Department, a "handsome blonde man came and gave me all the papers."[8] Now all she had to do, when she got to New York, was get two visas, one from the French consul and one from the British consul, and she was on her way.

Of course, she was not accredited. The rules for accreditation of a war correspondent to the American Expeditionary Force were such that it was highly unlikely that the *El Paso Morning Times* could have provided for the accreditation of even a male correspondent, and the War Department had never accredited a woman correspondent though many, Mary Roberts Rinehart among them, had hoped to be.

For male journalists with the backing of large newspapers, the procedure was not inordinately difficult. Reporters had to apply to the secretary of war, furnishing "certificates" testifying to their character and physical fitness. They had to be in a position to take care of their personal expenses, including "motor cars requisite for the work," which they were permitted to hire from the army. They had to submit all their "correspondence" to an official censor before transmitting it and to swear to do and write nothing that could harm the army or war effort in any way. Since they were in the "position of a commissioned officer," they had to provide themselves with an "American officer's uniform, without insignia, and with a green brassard bearing the letter C in red." In addition, they had to deposit $1,000 with the War Department which was to be used to defray their expenses in the field and post a $10,000 bond. If correspondents failed to comply with the requirements or broke the rules in any way, their filing privileges were revoked, their credentials cancelled meaning the loss of accreditation, and they might even be court-martialed.[9]

Most newspapers with a circulation of only 25,000 could hardly afford such a financial undertaking; referring to the management's agreement to pay Peggy's expenses, the paper commented on the "heavy expense involved in having sent a staff correspondent to Europe"[10] to report to its readers in El Paso and the Southwest. The paper proudly claimed to be the only one west of the Mississippi to have its own correspondent "somewhere in France" and announced that her articles would appear exclusively in the *Morning Times*. Obviously, it hoped to increase its circulation substantially as a result of Peggy's reports. It also promised that Peggy's mother would temporarily take over her advertising spots in the paper.[11]

As soon as she had her passport, Peggy took the train to New York City to get the necessary visas. Her first impression of the Big Apple was not a happy one. She wrote to her readers back in El Paso:

> There is something deadly about this city — a sort of "too much" of everything. To live very long in this atmosphere would make me feel like a child who has over-indulged in chocolate creams.
>
> Perhaps I was dropped into this atmosphere too suddenly. It is a broad, vision-losing jump one takes — all the way from the sweet, genuine simplicity of an old southern home . . . to the artificial elegance of a New York Hotel lobby.
>
> . . . The people I have met here can't understand why I've chosen the southwest as the field for my career — they all immediately express sympathy with me because I'm not working on a New York newspaper. And then they get insulted when I say I would rather have the praise of one reader of the El Paso Morning Times than the fickle, fleeting acclaim of all New York. And I'd rather ride over the rock-strewn hills and sunbaked mesas of Texas than to motor merrily along over Fifth avenue.[12]

In her defensiveness she was not being quite honest with her readers. As ambitious as she was, she would have, if it had been offered to her, glommed on to "the fickle, fleeting acclaim of all New York" without a blink. Her El Paso readers loved her militancy in their behalf, however, and were reassured to know that they had a champion who would put those "snooty easterners" in their place.

The people she had met were not the only ones to express misgivings about her journalistic bona fides, and she discovered it was not going to be as easy to get the visas as it had been to get her passport. From the start, she was the victim of the usual bureaucratic runaround. The British consulate sent her to the French, and the French sent her back to the British. When she finally got in to see the British consul, a "thick set square-faced, heavily spectacled man," he scrutinized her "with open disapproval."

> What in the world did I want to go abroad for? Oh, newspaper work, what kind?
> "Feature stories about our expedition," I answered patiently. . . .
> "What do you call feature stories?"
> "Stories about our boys arriving in London — in France — in the training camps — stories about our base hospitals —"
> "Oh — have you a copy of your paper with you?"
> "No, . . . the only [copies] I brought from Texas I filed with the state department. In fact, my own government has had all the questions concerning my paper and my status as a correspondent answered satisfactorily — otherwise the passport would not have been issued."[13]

It was wasted breath. The consul said that did not mean anything to him.

> "What do you know about military affairs — what can you write about modern warfare — what has been your experience as a war correspondent?"
> "I've been on the Mexican border for the past eight months. I've made hikes with Major General Morton and his command and I wrote the story about Major General Pershing's return from Mexico." . . .
> "It is strange that you haven't a copy of your paper with you."

It was obvious he did not think it was "strange" at all.

> "Before I visa this passport, I will have to know what type of newspaper you are writing for and the kind of stories you write. You are entering a military area and I must be satisfied as to your real qualifications to be there — and your real business there." He said it as though he didn't like me — as though he didn't like any newspaper folks. . . .
> "Have you ever been abroad before?" . . .
> "No."
> "What," he exclaimed in a dumbfounded tone, "you've never been abroad before and now your paper is sending you over there as a correspondent?"
> "Yes."[14]

She was fast discovering it was "very inconvenient not to be a celebrated writer when one wants to go abroad during war time." Luckily, the State Department was willing to help her, and at her request, sent the copies of the *Morning Times* to the British consulate. The papers had been heavily marked, clipped, and underlined. It was obvious that "a great many of the opinions made in the paper had met with approval among officials at Washington."

Two days later she sat in the consul's office once more, but this time the atmosphere was much different. After he had looked the newspapers over thoroughly, he said, "Your paper is all right."

While he fumbled around for stamps and pen and ink he went on — "You know one can never tell in this country what a paper is — there are some rotten ones, you know — and they get along somehow."[15]

Peggy was booked to board the British liner, *Orduna,* on June 13, 1917, for the twelve-day voyage to England; in a journalistic letter to the folks back home in El Paso, she described her trepidation about it:

The night before sailing, the story of every ship that had been sunk during the war came vividly to my mind. The terror, the suffering, the awfulness of going down at night as described by [Floyd Gibbons] who survived the *Laconia* disaster, haunted me. I walked the floor in my room at the Biltmore hotel. . . . I thought of the sweet pea garden I hoped to have some day, of the cottage all furnished in wicker — of all those other natural and human things for which any normal young woman longs — . . .

My whole future was staked on that trip to England. I had given up all chance for a domestic life to hurry off on the trail of the American Expeditionary forces. Like an oldtime member of the sawdust ring when the circus moved, I had to go because it was the only life I had known; yet in the pink shadows of my luxurious room that night I regretted the adventurous side of my nature that had lured me off to battlefields and myriad scenes of misery when I might have been comfortably asleep under a Texas sky. . . . When morning came I was heavy-eyed and nervous.[16]

The next morning as the ship pulled away from the dock,

a certain fatalism caught at my heart and made me stand — gazing at the widening space between the wharf and the ship like a man, who facing a firing squad, looks beyond their rifles to the green hills. My chance to live. My chance to die. And whichever way fate turned the crank the throbbing of my heart could never change the verdict.[17]

It was reminiscent of her "Woman to Dare Death with Birdmen" style, and as usual, instead of its putting readers off, this melodramatic streak, an unbounded enthusiasm, and a child-like ingenuousness combined with worldly sophistication endeared her to them. It even inspired in others a desire to protect her from the harsher realities of life.

Shortly after the ship got under way, all her fears of being torpedoed were completely overshadowed by a more immediate peril.

> Something more vital, more overwhelming than . . . being torpedoed had over come me. . . . I did not care whether I lived to see you again or not — I didn't even remember the Morning Times or recall that I was going to join the American expedition. Everything in the world seemed infinitesimal in comparison to the awful nausea that claimed my whole being. I lost all trace of time but it must have been somewhere toward evening that a steward brought me a little card showing that I had been assigned to boat number three — in case of accident — and would I please be on deck for boat drill tomorrow morning? I don't remember what I said or did — but appearing for boat drill would have been harder than making peace with Germany. Besides, I doubted very much whether I would need a boat — if I didn't die before we were torpedoed, I would be so near dead I might as well finish the business.[18]

By the late afternoon of the third day, she managed to drag herself on deck where the salt air helped put an end to her seasickness. Once again her old sociable self, she started to mingle only to find that, except for an occasional phrase, such as "beastly boawh," "frightfully so," or "jolly well," she could hardly understand her traveling companions. They all seemed to be British!

The one person she could understand was an elderly man who decided that she needed a guardian and made it plain that he was going to be it. Usually flattered by male attention, she was dismayed when he began giving her instructions about when to get up in the morning, what exercise she should have, and generally trying to schedule every minute for her to the point that she felt that she was being left no freedom at all. Peggy could not let it go on. She had been running her own life for a long time and she intended to continue to; when he objected to her announcement that she wanted to spend some time writing about life on board the ship, all her "American spunk and independence asserted itself," and she told him in no uncertain terms that she made her own living and took orders from only her employers and the United States government. Fed up with "British paternalism," she decided that

American men were a lot more intelligent, for they knew "better than to tell a working woman how and when to do her work!"

Feeling outnumbered and overwhelmed by the British, she was delighted when she was setting up her typewriter in the lounge to hear a very American "Gee whiz!" The "Gee whiz" belonged to John Parkerson, a correspondent for the Associated Press. Naturally, they became friends. Later that day Parkerson introduced her to Gordon Dowding, a lieutenant in the Royal Flying Corps. Dowding had been injured and was returning from sick leave in the United States. She was attracted to him, at least partly, because he had lived in the United States before the war and "he almost talked American."

Since she had gotten over her seasickness, she had been growing increasingly fearful as the ship approached the U-boat "hunting grounds," and now fear haunted her constantly.

It was terrifying to sit there watching the pink clouds grow gray, thinking of all the sweet things life held and of the cold strangling death that probably awaited me just a few feet away.

. . . The last half hour between complete darkness and semi-night threw me into a panic. There was something so uncanny, so weird and death-like about it, a strange grayness that made me feel as though I was not alive and never had lived. Torpedo-itis had me in its grip. An acute attack it was, and through the terror of it, I could not sleep or eat. . . .

I was afraid to go to my cabin — I was afraid to leave the deck where the great boats swung from their davits, and even their presence gave me small comfort for if we were torpedoed, and in daylight, the chances were that our boats would be shelled. . . . The Germans had . . . demonstrated that they knew no law, no honor, no justice. In this, the final hour of their desperation, nothing would be too awful for them to do. . . .

Ashamed to acknowledge my fright, I hid among the funnels and ventilators at night. Making a pretense of unconcern by bidding everybody good night and ostensibly going to my stateroom, I [slipped] through a darkened side door and [passed] the long night hours walking the top deck. . . .

The wind whistled around the funnels, and the ship like a black spectre crashed through the water. . . . Playing in and around the rigging, the wind sounded like voices calling from a great distance, then it changed to a low moan, back again to a high far call only to die into a haunting, pleading plea from a drowning man.

What if it came [now], the torpedo? The question beat incessantly into my brain, it tortured me hour after hour, and kept me staring out across the sea, afraid to look, yet forced to. After all, death itself can't be so bad, it is the suspense, the waiting for it, the fear of it, that makes the last hours of life harder than dying.[19]

She was finally comforted by Dowding. Finding her on the boat deck scanning the water for torpedoes, "he didn't try to laugh me out of my fright, he didn't speak sarcastically about it, and most of all, he didn't try to 'command' me out of it." Instead, he took her by the arm and led her around over the ship, pointing out men in the crow's nest who were looking out for all of them and telling her that she should not be afraid with all those people guarding her.

With his assurance that if anything happened he would come for her, she was persuaded to go to her stateroom. In fact, she said,

My terror vanished like a fog under a summer sun. Here was I, the young woman who had so emphatically declared she could look after her own self, calmed and soothed when I had lost my resourcefulness by the fact that I was going to be "looked after." Oh, goodness, I can't keep from being a woman some of the time.[20]

It was not the first time and certainly not the last that Peggy was rescued by a handsome gentleman. An incurable romantic, she always looked for and usually found romance; it was hardly surprising that in submarine-infested waters, romance came through again.

After a good night's rest, she was informed by "good-news" Parkerson that during the night they had been running from a submarine; he had been awake all night. Dowding's cure for her fear was so successful that she did not even tremble when she heard about it. Further reassuring to her was the knowledge that the British liner had been joined by a convoy of U.S. destroyers for the last four days of the voyage. "Long, low, black, rakish-looking craft, they were — just as described in the old books about pirates — the modern touch being that smoke poured in great black clouds from their many funnels." The sight of the American flag was a comfort to her as, under orders from the American commander, the *Orduna* steamed a zig-zag course.

The usual intimacy of an ocean voyage and her inherent charm worked their magic. Soon everyone on board was calling her "Peggy," and she was enjoying the company of the other passengers who proved, on closer acquaintance, to be "so congenial that it might have been a private yacht." One passenger, whom she called "the entertainer, the beau brummel, the instigator of concerts, tete-a-tetes and the story teller of the crowd," delighted them all with his scandalous stories about royalty, stories that "you would never dare write to your family or friends."

When they neared the Irish Sea, they saw empty life boats and bales of cotton floating out to sea, grim evidence that German submarines had recently struck in the area. Even the realization that the danger was doubled near Ireland by mine fields did not spoil her elation at her first sight of the Irish shore: "Little farms, big farms, and back of them the mountains, all a mass of green, luxuriously growing in the warm sunlight. The fields were marked off with hedges and rock fences, studiously, carefully and accurately done."[21]

On June 25 the ship finally docked at Liverpool.

Since she had a date for lunch with Dowding, she was greatly annoyed when she was delayed for over an hour, first because the immigration officials had confused her with another passenger (Hill) and then because the officer in charge of clearing up the confusion wanted to talk to her about Pershing and Villa and the border difficulties when he discovered Peggy had been on the spot reporting on them.

After their lunch, she and Dowding took the train to London. During the trip she spent part of the time studying the rules of censorship in order to be prepared to write her stories for the *Morning Times* in "passable" form. "The censor is on the job here," she wrote, "and one must not even dream of writing anything that is not strictly according to the rules." She learned her lesson so well that her account of the voyage across the Atlantic brought the following letter from the British chief censor, Sir Douglas Brownrig.

CHIEF CENSOR ADMIRALTY,
June 27, 1917

Miss Peggy Hull,
Savoy Hotel, London:

Dear Madam:

I have passed your "goods" and sent it on its journey. May I add that, even after thirty-five months of this work, I have enjoyed your story?

I hope you will find, as time goes on, that Britishers are not so very different from Americans, in that we are both HUMAN, and we have our sense of humour all right, even though it is spelled with a "u," which you omit.

Yours very truly,
Do. Brownrig.

P.S. I wish you success on your mission and Godspeed.
D.B.[22]

Peggy used the letter to arrange an interview with the chief censor and also went to see the American ambassador, Walter Hines Page, who expressed surprise that she had been able to get to England. He had received a number of appeals from American correspondents in London, both men and women, seeking his help in getting to France, but the State Department would not give its approval. He could not understand how the *El Paso Morning Times* correspondent had managed to get permission to cross the Atlantic, let alone to go on to France.

Soon after she arrived in London, she was invited by one of her fellow passengers on the *Orduna* to come to tea and meet other American correspondents. This was followed by other invitations to social gatherings where she encountered the friction apparent between British and American officers. It was obvious to her that there was going to be "many a lively clash . . . not disastrous, you understand, but little word-wars that we've been trying to get off our chest ever since 1776."[23]

This tension had been exemplified by an incident that took place when General Pershing had been in London staying with his staff at the Savoy. Three or four American staff officers who went into the bar were having a friendly discussion when three English officers strolled in. One of them looked the Americans over critically and said sarcastically, "The war is over — They're here." It seemed to her to have been a strange welcome for their new allies. But she was confident that in spite of the fact that the British laughed at our army, our navy, our resources and our great wealth, our boastfulness, our bluffs, and our national pride, Americans would eventually prove that they could do something besides talk.

She soon encountered her old nemesis, the entrenched attitude epitomized by the three words "It isn't done," which the British seemed to cling to "with the unquestioning faith of a child," when she announced that she was going to France as a war correspondent. One of the men she was with looked at her with such disapproval that she asked him,

> "What's the matter?" . . . and all he could do was to stammer out, "Why, I say — it isn't done, you know!" A Red Cross nurse — that is different — it's done — but a woman war correspondent — heaven forbid! And just to think that a harmless, peace-loving person like myself has shattered one of the cherished traditions of the British.[24]

Her strong feeling of nationalism was further stirred at a luncheon which Charles Morris of the Associated Press gave for her at the venerable Cheshire Cheese. She got into an argument with an English accountant who had had too much to drink. As she described it, he made a few caustic remarks about America's entry into the war and enough criticism because we didn't do it a long time ago to stir up my love of country. . . . Being a true American I had to say something "big," so I ventured the information that if our great automobile factories turned their facilities over to the manufacture of airplanes, we could turn out three thousand each week. I'll admit I didn't and don't know a thing about it . . ., but I couldn't sit there and let him win the war himself. Well, he was furious. Three thousand planes a week! Impossible! Stupid of me to say such a thing! Just like an American! etc. etc. Wasn't he an expert accountant and didn't he know figures better than that? Anyway even if we could he didn't know that the British wanted to fly in Ford airplanes — they'd been "fed up" on Fords. Whereupon I suggested that the British would most likely be glad to fly in anything if they could get it — and my newspaper friends, realizing that the conversation was drifting into dangerous channels, led me away — victorious! I'd had the last word anyway.[25]

Even with this kind of mild unpleasantness, she was having a wonderful time partying and sightseeing while she waited for arrangements for her trip to France to be completed. Though she and Dowding had gone their separate ways, she did not want for companionship. Surrounded by military men, she dined with naval officers; danced to "Are You from Dixie?" and other popular American songs; explored Westminster Abbey, the Banqueting House and nearby spot where Charles I had been beheaded; and tried to cope with the different telephone system and traveling on the left side of the road.

In one of her columns for the *Morning Times,* she described various military uniforms; deciding that she liked the flying corps uniform best, she said she would have her picture taken in one and send it back to the paper so her readers could see what it looked like.

When it came time for her to leave London for Paris on July 3, she experienced something of the same feeling she had had just before she had left New York. Since she had come this far and nothing terrible had happened, not even an air raid, she told herself that it was foolish to be afraid, despite the comments made by some of the experienced travelers that the twelve-day voyage between New York and Liverpool was not half as dangerous as those few hours across the English Channel. Trying to put such thoughts out of her mind, she concluded she would just have to wait and see; she settled back in her train compartment to enjoy the

lovely English country-sides . . ., landscapes that looked as though an artist had planned them out — little scenes came to view as we swerved around a curve that revealed the work of a master's hand. Somehow the cows always stood just where they should — the hedges formed a certain angle, the trees grew in the right spot — there wasn't an artistic blunder or a technical error. Streams streamed just where they were the most effective — yellow poppies peeped up through the green grass along the right of way and spotted the wheat fields and meadows with their tiny, colorful bobbing heads.[26]

However, much as she adored it, the scene gave her pause:

How beautiful, how serene, how gentle and beckoning the land was. How sweet and how precious, life. My brain refused to comprehend the fact that only a hundred and fifty miles away men were in deadly battle — that heads were being shot away from bodies, that legs were being severed by heavy shells, that bayonets were tearing their way through abdomens; that only a hundred and fifty miles away there was no sunshine, no blue and green fields, no sleepy cows and yellow poppies.[27]

When the train arrived at Southampton, military police herded the passengers into a room to wait to be examined by government and war officials. Peggy could not believe she would have any problem since even the chief censor of the admiralty had not only passed her stories but had written her a complimentary note. So it was a shock to her when the military control officer in charge of her "case" took one look at her and said with obvious distaste, "Another journalist!" What she had not realized was that suspicious dislike was the typical attitude of the military toward newspapermen or women who wanted to report on the war.

When war had broken out in Europe, newspapers which tried to accredit correspondents to the British army in France had been met with the opposition of Lord Kitchener, British War Minister, who was supported in his antipress attitudes by most regular army officers. Even the London *Times* found itself dependent on reports from its regular correspondents in Paris, and their only source of information was the daily communiqués issued by the army, communiqués which were largely fiction. All correspondents understood and agreed that their reports must not help the enemy in any way, but the military believed that the correspondents' chief interest was in getting a story, whatever the consequences, and, therefore, reporters could not be trusted. Consequently, war news was subjected to strict censorship.[28]

Even though she had only a passport, not official accreditation from the War Department, Peggy's past association with Pershing turned out to be extremely useful to her. Going on the offensive, she said to the examining officer,

> "I'm desperately tired of being treated like a criminal. If any one has any kick against my presence over here it isn't the British army — it's General Pershing."
>
> "Oh, do you know the general and does he know you are coming?" He said it in such a sarcastic way that I lost my head completely, and for the first time on the trip told something that wasn't true. I said, "He should — I cabled him." His expression changed instantly and he passed me without another word.[29]

Irritated by the ordeal, she reported, "I leave it to some Texas cowboy to express my feelings about a few of the British consuls and military authorities."[30]

As she waited on board the small, crowded boat, she watched with apprehension as the sunlight faded. Yet the terror she had felt on the Atlantic crossing did not return, and she found to her surprise that she had exhausted, at least temporarily, her capacity for fear. After sitting for awhile on the upper deck and watching the searchlights moving among the clouds, she went below to her cabin.

Newspapermen in London had warned her that if she expected to catch the first train for Paris she must be off the boat as soon as it docked; so she was waiting at the gangplank the next morning at five o'clock. The French military and harbor officials passed her without comment, and she found a French-speaking Englishman to tell the cab driver to take her to the train station.

By seven o'clock the girl who had thought she wanted to be a soldier, who had had to settle for newspaper reporter, was in a compartment on a Paris-bound train. Her passion and training had now come together. She was, at last, Peggy Hull, war correspondent.

*It was July 4, 1917 . . . .*
I was in Paris [sitting in a side-walk café with two French-women. Suddenly] . . . A low murmur reached our ears . . . . it grew louder and louder . . . . and we heard the rhythm of marching feet, the military rhythm of marching feet . . . . the musical shuffle of the pre-cise . . . . left . . . . right . . . . left . . . . right . . . . the heart-ening sound of youthful marching feet . . . . the mur-mur grew into a roar! . . . Down the boulevard came the familiar khaki . . . . the broad sombreros of the American Army! . . . PARIS WENT MAD!

Peggy Hull,
"The Last Crusade, 1918, A.D.,"
*The Pointer*

# CHAPTER SIX

# A War Correspondent Without Accreditation

As Peggy had settled back into the taxi for what proved to be a jolting ride over rough stone paving, she had suddenly felt overwhelmed. Here she was, far from home, in a strange land where she did not even understand the language. It was what she had wanted; nevertheless, it was intimidating. But the villagers who watched her cab speed by on its way to the railroad station were smiling friendly welcoming smiles, and she was reassured by the sight of a blacksmith raising the Stars and Stripes alongside the tricolor in front of his shop.

The train, which followed the Seine River through Normandy, was slow and dilapidated, but she was fascinated by the countryside which, though "more magnificent in its beauty, more majestic with its pine-covered mountains and valleys filled with green grain and vegetables . . . [was] not so gentle, so complacent, so man-made beautiful as England."[1]

At the station in Paris, an obliging American helped her get a taxi to take her to the Continental Hotel. As soon as she had checked in, she went back out onto the street, found a sidewalk café, and started to take in the sights and sounds of Paris. She had barely gotten settled when the first wave of American troops marched into the city, and she could see firsthand the spiritually reviving effect the very sight of them had on the weary and dispirited French. Because it was the Fourth of July, their arrival on this day seemed especially momentous to the "true American."

A few days later she was granted an interview with Pershing, now commander of the American Expeditionary Force.

"A breath from home!" he said as Peggy was ushered into his office at his temporary headquarters on Rue Constantine.

He was standing in the center of the room, a room which was mirror-filled, heavily carpeted and hung with the masterpieces of dead painters, a room where once the brilliant men and women of all Paris had gathered. . . .

He appeared glad to see me, and I remembered the day at Columbus, New Mexico when he rode out of Mexico not so crisp, not so well groomed as now, covered with the alkali of many a mile from that long and dusty trail. . . .

At first I was a bit afraid that the great general might say this was no place for a girl correspondent and that I'd have to go home. If he had, it wouldn't have been the first time he had disciplined me.[2]

In fact, their meeting was going very well. He was all smiles.

"Why, Peggy! How in the world did you get over here — you don't mean to say you came all alone?" he asked.

"Yes — all alone — all the way from El Paso just so the people on the border could have news of you from one of their home folks," I explained. . . .

"I'm glad you are here," he said, . . . "and it was splendid of the Times to send you — I'm sure all the men will appreciate it. . . . You are a long ways from home — but you mustn't be scared — we'll all see that you get along all right."[3]

She was relieved by his obvious pleasure in seeing her. It meant that he had forgiven her for her part in the newsreel escapade.

Even overlooking journalistic pranks like that one, Pershing had never been especially fond of newspaper people. On occasion, during the Mexican campaign, he had gone so far as to try to control the news through Maj. John Hines, his official censor.[4] Events had conspired to change his mind somewhat, and he had come to see that it would be more helpful to him to try to use the press, instead of to restrict it. Nevertheless, there were still times when he was less than cooperative as when Westbrook Pegler had gone to GHQ at Chaumont to get an interview with him. On being admitted to Pershing's office, Pegler had said, "General Pershing, I'm Pegler of the United Press. Can you give me a statement on the general situation?" Pershing had stared at him and said, icily, "Pegler, get the hell out of my office."[5] Like Pegler, Peggy had incurred Pershing's displeasure. She was glad she was back in his good graces again; it made life a lot easier for her.

Her arrival in Paris had been noted in the Army *Chicago Tribune*, a small edition recently started with the idea of providing news and features for American soldiers in France.[6] Referring to her as staff correspondent of the *El Paso Morning Times,* the paper described her as "the latest addition to the ranks of American war correspondents in Paris . . . whose readers have learned to like and look for the chatty news letters . . . [and] whose experiences with the United States army in recent operations have qualified her as an interpreter of army life in garrison and in the field."[7]

In the beginning her reports were more those of the typical tourist than of a war correspondent because American soldiers had not yet become actively involved in the war. They were finishing their training at camps in safe regions of France, training for the new kind of war they would soon be fighting, trench and artillery warfare.

Peggy's inability to speak or understand French, a handicap she shared with most soldiers, led to both frustrating and amusing experiences, and she used them as the basis of her first communiqués from Paris. One described the first time she was paged by a bellboy in the Continental Hotel. She did not realize it was her name being called because to her very American ears "Mamselle Pezhgy" did not sound anything like it. And one morning as the hotel maid went to get her breakfast, the maid paused at the door, "looked over her shoulder," and said, "Tout de suite." Misunderstanding, Peggy thought the chamber maid had said she was "too sweet" and was extremely flattered. Her elation did not last long, for later when she and a captain friend went to see a mutual acquaintance and they asked an attendant to announce them, "he looked at the captain and said, 'tout de suite.' Then I knew something must be wrong," she wrote. "No one — not even a Frenchman[ — ]could call the captain 'too sweet!' "[8]

Because she found it next to impossible to tell taxi drivers where to take her, she often ended up walking. She suspected, however, that a lot of the drivers did know what she was asking but were pretending not to, simply because they were so much in demand. Venting her frustrations in several journalistic "letters" to her readers back home in Texas, she had her "revenge" in the humorous and sometimes unflattering portraits she drew of "offenders."

Enthroned on the front seat of a wobbly, lop-sided taxicab of a vintage of 1906 — with a flat tire, at least one broken window and a smashed mud guard, the lord-high-executioners of the feelings of the traveling public [hold] court. You can't plead with them — you can't beg them — you can't pay them four times as much as the regular rate and get them to take you any place they don't want to go. Before I started to see Paris with someone who could speak the language, I had placed the blame all on myself — I had

supposed they didn't understand me — now I know the meaning
of a lot of phrases. . . .

After walking eighteen blocks one evening I finally obtained a
taxi to take me to my hotel about a mile away — it was my first
ride and I shall never be afraid of submarines again. At first I
thought the driver was drunk, but other taxis careened by us in
the same swerving, violent speed. Men and women and children
hurried like ants to escape the threatening wheels.[9]

It seemed to her that hundreds of pedestrians must be killed every
day, but the desk clerk at the hotel assured her that there were many
days that not a single person was "run down." She simply could not
believe it. "Somehow I think the casualty list from the front — the con-
versations in which one speaks of ten thousand killed or one hundred
thousand dead — has made these people callous to the loss of a single
life."[10]

These human interest pieces were devoured by her fans in west Texas,
but the accredited (male) correspondents disdained such "little" stories.
They were waiting for the big ones. Peggy did her best to ignore their
condescending attitude. News was where you found it. She had come
to France to write stories for her readers back home and that was what
she was doing.

Several of the correspondents in Paris waiting for the American part
of the war to begin were her buddies, themselves fresh from the Pershing-
Villa campaign. Chief among them was Floyd Gibbons who had brought
his wife Isabella with him. The Gibbonses and Peggy picked up their
friendship again in Paris. Of all the correspondents she knew, Peggy
admired the thirty-one-year-old Gibbons most. To her he was exactly
what a war correspondent should be: strong, honest, direct, and ingenu-
ous, in fact, a lot like Peggy herself.

In early August she had her first experience with "billeting" when she
was among the "battalion of war correspondents from all parts of the
United States and Europe . . . of both sexes, all ages and sizes and . . .
varying dispositions," assigned to homes in the villages near the infantry training camp at Gondrecourt, 150 miles east of Paris. Of course,
she wrote the readers of the *Morning Times* all about it. Billeting, she
found, was

not half bad — unless someone tries to make it so. I have one of
the choicest little billets in the village. A front room on the main
street. It is a fine room with a great bed and a large mahogany
wardrobe and dozens of sepulchral urns, war lilies in glass domes
and odd old prints all over the walls. . . .

There are stables on the ground floor of all those houses and usually the only entrance is through a stall. There are no animals around my house, but the others are less fortunate — probably that accounts for the sour looks I get from my feminine friends when we start out on our tours every day. One New York newspaper woman lives over a general store which sells everything from beer to bedsteads — including babies — so she says because she hears them!

If I could make noises in a letter I would describe an average night and tell you how the colt got in the donkey's stall and how fiendish were the squeals and brays that resulted; how the owner descended, followed by his good wife in her night robe bearing a lamp; how the neighbors collected; how they talked it over and shouted at the colt and finally led it back to its own stall; how the poor ducks then woke up and began to quack; and then after [they were] quiet how the dog, mistaking the shouts for applause, redoubled his efforts and woke the ducks again and then — how clearly reveille sounded on the early morning air. It's a great life. The people amuse me and I like them.[11]

She was also amused by a surprise inspection that Pershing sprang on the nearby training camp.

We, the correspondents, had been forewarned. The poor soldiers hadn't. They'd been taking life not too strenuously — anyway most of them were recruits and didn't know the general like we do at home. He swooped down on them like an early morning Kansas twister. And when he left a lot of them felt like they'd been through one.[12]

In contrast to the amusing experiences were some more serious and frightening, one when she was sick and not able to make herself understood. She awoke in the middle of the night in terrible pain. Unable to rouse any of the service people of the hotel to get her a doctor, she finally dozed off until about seven o'clock when she awoke to find several maids and a waiter standing around her bed. Obviously, they had been trying to rouse her. Their physical presence did her no good, however; she was not able to make them realize that she needed medical attention. Finally, Isabella Gibbons, who came around to see her almost every morning, arrived and saw to it a doctor was summoned. He examined Peggy and said her appendix would have to be removed immediately. Feeling they needed a second opinion, Isabella called in another doctor. More conservative in his diagnosis, this doctor told them Peggy

Peggy Hull and a decorated French aviator (wearing the Croix de Guerre), 1917. *(Peggy Hull Deuell Collection, Kansas Collection, University of Kansas Libraries)*

probably would not need an operation, but he cautioned her to be more careful about what she ate, especially "war" bread.[13]

There were a lot of contradictions in life in wartime Paris. On the one hand, the beauty parlors where she had her hair done were operating as if it were the most normal of times. People always had a smile and a pleasant greeting, and she sometimes almost forgot there was a war on.

On the other hand, cafés closed at 9:30, and although the streets were better lighted than in London, the city was not so alive at night. There were no orchestras in the hotels after ten o'clock; only a few theaters were open. The transportation system closed down early, taxicabs refusing pickups after 9:30 and the subway and street car lines not running after eleven; so it was hard to get home if one did go out. The city fathers took it for granted that everyone worked hard all day and stayed home to rest at night. They should have known better. Even with all the difficulties, people were still going out and enjoying themselves, and as usual, wherever the lights were bright and people were having fun, Peggy was in the center of it.[14]

On a date to a roller skating rink, she was pleasantly surprised to find the calliope playing American music for the patrons to skate to and downright astonished that no one got drunk or caused any kind of trouble though there was a public bar on the premises.

At the same time, she was shocked when she first saw couples in a Bohemian café embracing and kissing between sips of wine. For someone who was no stranger to ROMANCE, who had a marriage and at least one major love affair behind her, this reaction might seem on first blush to have been overly "prim." The middle-American upbringing that she and her Texas readers had had, emphasized that it was not socially desirable to show affection in public, and Peggy herself was not publicly demonstrative. When she commented to dinner companions that she could not believe that the French behaved in such a brazen manner under normal conditions and that such amorous displays must be an effect of the war, she was surprised by their assurances that, on the contrary, it was just the way Parisians were. "If they love each other they consider it very silly and foolish not to tell the world about it — it is what they call sincerity." She resolved not to fall in love with a Frenchman, preferring "the good old American custom of holding one's heart secrets sacred." Though admitting to her readers that she was getting accustomed to this type of public display, she promised them she would not try to introduce such immodest behavior into the mores of El Paso when she came home.[15]

This Victorianism, typical of the time, was followed sometime later by her confession that the Place de la Concorde was her favorite spot in Paris, the one that she would always remember, because "an American aviator, who didn't mean it, proposed to [her] one moonlight night" there. She went on to say, "The fact that I saw him kissing a French girl an hour later should have taken the romance out of my only chance to marry — in France — but a young woman can't afford to be too proud in this steadily increasingly manless age." Anyone who knew Peggy would have been very surprised if this was indeed the only marriage proposal she had in France and even more surprised if the aviator had not meant it!

Infinitely more perturbing to her than public display of passion was what she found in the meat markets. Not only were there flies and dust on the food, but the markets lacked any kind of cooling systems. Not even Juárez, she said, could produce any worse-looking places than the ones in Paris; far from minding that two days a week were meatless, she was willing for all seven to be.[16]

Questionable food was not all that threatened to affect her appetite. One day when she was eating in a tiny café, two Canadian soldiers told about a bloody battle they had taken part in, describing how the heads of Germans had been blown right off their bodies. "I stopped eating," she said. "What an insignificant thing food, or work, or play, or anything is — when civilized men can deliberately mutilate each other — can throw the whole world into havoc and shower it with blood."[17]

Her first personal contact with the war came one night when she was reading in bed (a lifelong practice) in her hotel room. "A long shivering shriek arose from the street below. It was followed by the grating, coarse sound of many automobile horns and I could hear machines speeding down the Rue de Rivoli," she wrote. Concluding that there must be a fire nearby, she wondered why the sirens kept wailing and why she could hear the "whirring of aeroplanes." She soon found that it was something more serious than a fire when "there came a short, quick bang on my white door."

Before I could reach the door there came another sharp, impatient rap, and I opened it to find a little Frenchman waving his arms and talking very fast — I looked at him blankly. My stare seemed to excite him — he talked louder and faster and waved his arms furiously — then he looked at me quite disgusted — reached his hand around the door — snapped out the light — and walked away, leaving me standing in the pitch-dark room. . . .

Other Frenchmen hurried through the hall and as they passed my door I caught two words — "bosche" [sic] and "police." Then I knew — very suddenly — why the aeroplanes were humming over the hotel courtyard — why my light had been snapped out. I was going through my first air raid experience.

When I was a little girl thunder terrorized me. If mother wasn't with me, . . . I used to crawl under the bed or into a dark closet. Tonight the old fear came back, but tonight I was alone in a strange land of blackness. There were no mother's arms to flee to — no one to even say — at least so that I could understand it — a reassuring word. I felt my way back to my bed and climbed under the red satin quilt — I piled a great pillow on top of my head and waited. . . .

I thought of El Paso and the quiet summer nights back there — I thought of the wonderful park in Versailles which I had just visited — the wide forests so still and peaceful under the starlit sky. I thought of England and its placid countryside — its dreamy cows and flowered meadows — its lanes made for lovers — the most beautiful world our imaginations could conjure turned into hell — filled with unknown and unexpected horrors by the maddened kaiser-crazy Germans.[18]

Fortunately, none of the kaiser-crazy Germans' bombs hit her hotel that night.

Through her friendship with Floyd Gibbons, she soon got a chance to contribute pieces to the Army *Tribune.*

Her stories, under the general title "How Peggy Got to Paris," started with her departure from El Paso and concluded with her arrival in Paris and for the most part were the same as those published in the *El Paso Morning Times.* The announcement in the August 6 edition that the *Trib* would be carrying these stories described Peggy as "a typical young American woman" possessed of "grit and energy" and declared that her stories were "written in the frank and genial [manner] of the Rio Grande which will come like a breath of fresh air to the American soldiers in France." There is no doubt that the articles were well received by readers of the Army *Trib,* in fact, too well received, it turned out later.

In addition to this series, she wrote at least some of the Hank and Mike columns which purported to be exchanges of letters between Hank

("The Letter from Home") and Mike ("With the Americans in France"), discussing events, conditions, and concerns on the home front and the war front.

When "How Peggy Got to Paris" had run its course, she turned to a "reader help" column of a type she had done in Honolulu for the *Advertiser* and in El Paso for the *Morning Times*. This service was described in the Army *Trib* of August 22, under the heading "What Do You Need?"

I have just been told to be the godmother to all the American soldiers in France. I'm expecting you all to stand by me.

The soldiers down in Mexico last winter used to have me get all kinds of things for them in El Paso. I bought everything from French pastry to boots and overcoats — and it was lots of fun. So, if you need anything, all you have to do is to write the Army Edition, and we promise to find it for you, if it is in Paris.

We started our Christmas shopping in October, and you were only in Mexico then — now we're an awful long ways from home, and all the folks will be expecting something from Paris — so you'd better write the Army Edition right away and say how much you want to spend, and [we'll] make up a list and send it to you. . . .

One of the boys in the Expeditionary Force has written to the Army Edition for a "French-English conversation book" and I'm going shopping for it now. Please remember I am glad to get the most trifling things for you — even stamps for that matter. There is no charge for this service — it's just a little bit that the Army Edition of the *Chicago Tribune* wants to do for you. Sincerely,
PEGGY

To soldiers so far away from home this offer was a godsend, and Peggy, their fellow Yank, was a precious link to "home" for many of them. So homesick they could hardly stand it, some would even have been willing to be back at the Border coping with sand and cactus. The desert had not been so bad; it was a part of home. Their homesickness was, of course, exacerbated by the startling cultural differences between France and the United States. Few of them had traveled to a foreign country before. They had, obviously, not been exposed to the "culturally broadening" influence of television. Even the movies, such as they were, did little to contribute to an understanding of the real France, and books failed to convey the "foreign" atmosphere they found. Luckily, after a few weeks most doughboys began to get used to things, learn a little French, and even start to enjoy it all; in the beginning most were unhappy and disoriented. Especially for those who knew her because they had been on the Border with Pershing, Peggy was a reassuring presence, a bit of the familiar in a world suddenly full of unfamiliar things and people.

Early in September, Peggy had a real stroke of luck growing out of her contact with Mrs. Robert McCormick, whose husband was one of the owners of the *Chicago Tribune* and now a major stationed at the artillery camp at Le Valdahon. When her husband had been sent to France, Amie McCormick had followed to organize various kinds of war work. Peggy had volunteered to help, and one Saturday after they had spent most of the day making bandages for wounded soldiers, they were relaxing over tea at the Ritz when Mrs. McCormick suggested she and Peggy take an automobile trip through France so that she could see to extending her war work to the American camps outside Paris.[19]

Amie de Houle Irwin McCormick was no dowager. Only nine years older than Peggy, she had long been socially conscious and civic-minded. It was hardly surprising, then, that she would transfer that involvement from Chicago to Paris when her husband was assigned to Pershing's staff in France, especially since the McCormicks had not been married very long. In fact, Mrs. McCormick had been Mrs. McCormick only since March 1915. Before that she had been Mrs. Adams, well-known Chicago socialite and accomplished horsewoman, and the wife of Robert McCormick's second cousin. To the delight of the tabloid press, before the Adamses' divorce, Robert McCormick had even been "a member of their household."[20] Charming and lively as well as socially prominent, Amie McCormick appealed to Peggy as the perfect traveling companion; she was ecstatic at the prospect of the trip and enthusiastically agreed to help plan and make arrangements.

Assuming the responsibility of buying road maps and securing the necessary passes, thinking that this would be so simple and easy that they could be ready to start on Tuesday, she set out full of confidence on Monday. She got off to a fast start, encountering no problem at all in getting the maps. This surprised her, since one had to have a permit to buy almost everything else. Later she said, "I [was] glad I got the maps first. It only strengthened my belief that the trip was going to be one of the golden adventures of my life. A motor tour through France with Mrs. R. R. McCormick. . . . What a wonderful opportunity for a lonesome girl from the Texas Border!"[21]

Peggy's sense of excitement and triumph was short-lived, however. She ran into a major obstacle when, armed with their passports and other permits and credentials, she went to the prefecture of the police to get a permit to leave Paris. Expecting that if he did not speak English he would have an interpreter, she learned, after waiting three and a half hours in a dingy hallway, that it was up to her to provide whatever she needed to be able to communicate with the officials. She would have to return the next day with an interpreter.

Disappointed, she started back to her hotel. On the way she met Sidney Graves, a captain whom she knew from El Paso. He could speak French, and he agreed to help her. Language, however, was not the only obstacle in the way of the projected tour. She and Graves spent from Tuesday to Friday going from one building to another, one official to another, still no closer to getting the permit to leave Paris than when she had started on Monday. On their next to last meeting with him, after much unproductive discussion, the prefect finally read her the National Defense Law which, among other things, prohibited any pleasure trips by automobile. With Graves translating, she and the prefect conducted a frustrating exchange:

"But we aren't going for pleasure. Mrs. McCormick has a lot of money she wants to spend in establishing canteens for our American soldiers."

"Ah! Why [can't you] go on the train?"

"Because the train takes twenty-four hours to make the trip — there are no sleeping compartments and most of the time no dining cars."

She could tell by Graves's expression that the prefect was not impressed with her arguments. He was going to say "no" again. But now she was absolutely determined that she and Mrs. McCormick were going on the trip and they were going by automobile. As soon as Graves had said "au revoir" and expressed thanks to the prefect, thanks which Peggy felt he did not deserve, she asked Graves if he thought the prefect would refuse if a request came from an American general. He thought it was worth a try.

Thus they went to see a general who, when a colonel on the Border, had been Peggy's dancing partner at several garden parties. He agreed to write and dispatch a letter to the prefect. When they returned to the prefecture, "there was considerable difference in the atmosphere. We got the passes at 4 o'clock. At a quarter of five we rolled down the Rue de Rivoli toward the Charenton gate, out of which we were to really begin our six-hundred mile trip. We were on our way — four days late."

Within Paris gasoline rationing limited car owners to the purchase of one gallon at a time, so they had barely gotten outside the gate when they ran out of "essence." It took over an hour to find a place to buy more, but at least they were allowed three gallons this time and started on their way again.

At 8:30 it was quite dark and we were about fifty miles out of Paris, so Mrs. McCormick suggested that we stop for the night

97

at the next town [Mormant]. . . . As we drew up in front of a little hotel a great car dashed up and came to a skiddy standstill beside our machine. Two figures, grayish white in the half-light of the stars climbed out of the front seat, looked at how close they had come to crashing us and a voice said: "God but that was a close call." [The voice belonged to] Paul Rainey, . . . African hunter, adventurer, globe-trotter and now, official photographer for the American Red Cross. I had met him when I first came to Paris.

The two women spent a pleasant evening listening to Rainey's stories of hunting in the jungles of Africa. As interesting as she found his stories, Peggy mused that big game hunting had lost its glamour, becoming insignificant compared with "its rival — war."

The next day, the trip took on the more festive air of a tourist excursion.

We rode through the level lands and we climbed the mountains. We would come around a [curve] on a hill to find a valley miles wide, laid out like a vast piece of rare silk, its straight and curving fields making stripes of various hues. We found ancient villages tucked away between the mountains, villages that Caesar had battled for and which appeared to be desperately hanging on to their decaying outlines.

Their holiday spirit was dampened somewhat when they were about two hours away from Besançon, their destination. The car "threw a tire," and the chauffeur, far from being a shield and defender, did not know how to put on a spare. While they waited for someone to come along who did, they sat on the running board and listened to the sounds of a big mill wheel nearby and the thunder of guns to the north. Their closeness to the front was impressed upon them when

a German aeroplane flew brazenly across the soft summer night sky — we heard the siren shrieks of the little town we had just left and saw the little clouds of white which the anti-aircraft guns sent in the wake of the swift-moving Boche.

I don't know why I wasn't afraid unless it was because the greyish green evening with its mauve and pink clouds, the quiet slumbering fields, from which the workmen had gone home, stood out in such a tremendous contrast to the havoc that men were raising a few kilometers aw[ay that even] the Hun airman bent on the destruction of women and children and wounded looked less harmful from that secluded and peaceful spot.

Finally, a French soldier came along, changed the tire, and they drove on into Besançon, a town close to the artillery camp at Le Valdahon and the Swiss border, where Mrs. McCormick planned to establish a canteen.

Their return route to Paris took them to several villages where American soldiers were stationed. At one where they stayed overnight, Peggy characteristically stole some of the limelight from Amie McCormick by getting up early and going to breakfast by herself.

I had a little American flag pinned to my white fur, and as I walked into the breakfast room, seven American officers arose from their table simultaneously — one had noticed me and said, "By Jove there's an American girl." As I walked past them they all saluted — just as though I was a general. It made my heart feel good for I knew there was no foundation in the story that the French women were dangerous rivals.[22]

Though much less naive than she pretended to be in her columns, she used the report of experiences like this to reassure her women readers back in El Paso that the men in the American army regarded the women from home as the best in the world and were, therefore, presumably, being true to them.[23]

Some of the officers came to her table after they had finished their breakfasts, and she discovered that most of them had been in El Paso when she had been; they had a lot to reminisce about.

Her reports sometimes made it seem as if soldiers were continually either saluting her or cheering her. It may have been true. She loved all the attention so much that no doubt her own behavior often elicited these responses.

When she got back to Paris, Peggy was gratified to find that her stories in the Army *Trib* had attracted favorable attention in high places and that now the Press Office, which had not taken her seriously at first, had arranged for her to join a group of correspondents on a tour of army installations and parts of the French sector. She did not get to go because, on the eve of their departure, she became ill again.

Recovering rapidly, as she usually did, she was back in the *Tribune* office a few days later catching up on her shopping column duties when Major McCormick, keeping an eye on business, stopped in to see how things were going at the paper. Peggy's close contact with his wife had not hurt her stature in his eyes. Sympathetic because she had to miss the tour, he suggested that she might contribute some camp life stories with a woman's angle to the Army Edition. To this end, he told Joseph Pierson, the editor and business manager of the paper, to take her with him on the tour of the camps which Pierson was about to undertake to try to increase the paper's circulation. Pierson was quite willing to have her go along and thought that his credentials and pass would cover her, so they would not have to go through all the red tape of getting separate papers for her.[24]

But at Le Valdahon, the post adjutant denied her free movement around the camp because she lacked her own "proper credentials." However, he told her that Pershing was due to arrive on an inspection and said he would permit her to explain the situation to Pershing and to Brig. Gen. Peyton March,[25] the artillery camp commander, at tea in the mess hall. Since she was back in Pershing's good graces and General March, whom she also knew from El Paso, was reasonable and fair, she had hope that the generals would do something about her situation, relieving the post adjutant of responsibility in the matter.

At the "tea," she presented her case. She concluded by saying that, since she had missed the Press Office tour of the camps because she had been sick and was now in this credentials difficulty, she might as well go home. This emotional presentation had the hoped-for result: Pershing assured her that that would not be necessary, that something would be worked out for her. The upshot was that she was given temporary status as a YMCA worker. This enabled her to stay at the camp for awhile and to move around with some impunity while she was there which was even more than she had hoped for.[26]

Because she had not gone prepared to stay, she rode back to Paris with Pierson, gathered up her belongings and boarded the train to return to Besançon and Le Valdahon.

In Paris she had sometimes appeared in a uniform of the type she had worn on the Mexican border. It consisted of boots, skirt (which she called short but which was halfway between knee and ankle), American tunic, Sam Browne belt, and regulation campaign hat. Now she wore it to travel in because it was bulky and hard to pack. Thanks to this outfit, she found herself the center of attention, first from officers who saluted her, perhaps in confusion, then from civilians who could not seem to get enough of the "strange" sight she presented. Some of her fellow train passengers, she said, even counted her buttons.

> Those who couldn't come in[to the train compartment] and sit down and watch me walked ceaselessly up and down [the corridor] outside and looked in. I began to feel like a wild animal in a cage at a circus. They apparently expected me to do something — to dance or sing or cry, but the dignity of my costume forbade that. I just had to sit still and let them look.[27]

100

When lunch was served, she did not go to the dining car to eat because by then she was too self-conscious. The reaction of other passengers was only a prelude to what awaited her at the station where she made her first change of trains.

Here I was in the middle of a long platform crowded with civilians and soldiers — the only woman in khaki — probably the first one they had ever seen. They crowded around me; they pushed each other out of the way to get up closer; they inspected my boots, my uniform, my hat, my face and hair, my bags; they talked about me and laughed at me. They called their friends to see, and they all stayed around to watch what I was going to do.

Much as she would have liked to hide, she could not do anything but stay with her luggage and try to "tough it out."

Minutes that were hours of the tensest agony dragged by. Trains came in and unloaded more curious and staring folk. Finally a crisp, well uniformed Frenchman, with a chest full of decorations, elbowed his way through the crowd around me, stepped up in the most admirable manner, saluted and said in perfect English:

"Pardon me. I see you are an American, and if you do not know which train to take I will be glad to see that you get on the right one."

The sound of his voice, the easy flow of my own language, his thoughtfulness and respect flooded me with confidence and courage. I lost my self-consciousness — I lost my fear. I got over being angry because everyone ogled me, and when a poilu said, in half English and half French that my boots were "tres joli" I smiled at him.

A more serious problem presented itself when the train finally arrived at Besançon and she was standing in line to surrender her ticket to the ticket taker. She could not find the "safe conduit" pass one had to show before being permitted to leave the station.

It was late and I was tired and I had visions of waiting with a guard until an officer from the American camp nearby could come and rescue me. I turned in my ticket to the pretty girl, who looked at me in amazement. Two officers reached forward and said, "Safe conduit," and then glimpsed the uniform. Instantly their heels clicked together, their hands went to their caps and I — very scared — looked severe and unsmiling[ly] gave them back the salute that

Peggy Hull in heavy coat with fur collar and cuffs, at Besançon, near Le Valdahon, France, Oct. 1917. *(Peggy Hull Deuell Collection, Kansas Collection, University of Kansas Libraries)*

Major General Morton had taught me on the Mexican border.
It worked.

From the window of my room [in the hotel in Besançon] I can
see the group of children who followed me from the station. They
are still talking it over.

The military side of her nature having humiliated her once more, she
retreated into her ultrafeminine side again. "My uniform hangs [stiffly]
on its hangers and I've gone back to my first and only love — pink crepe
de chine."[28]

In the end she was permitted to stay at Le Valdahon for nearly six
weeks as the representative of the Army *Tribune* and the guest of General
March. During this time she was quartered with the female YMCA
workers.[29]

Her first morning in camp, she decided it was too cold and much
too early to get out of bed at reveille; she turned over and went back
to sleep. When she got up at eight o'clock, she found that breakfast was
over and the mess hall was locked. Clearly, she was not going to get
breakfast. Concluding that a little extra sleep was no substitute for biscuits, ham and eggs, and oatmeal, after that all she "had to hear . . .
was just one note of the bugle," and she was out of bed.[30]

At first she and the women YMCAs lived in the hospital because permanent quarters were not yet ready for them.

The weather had been perfect up to the date of my arrival. There
were no sick soldiers and we were told we could live there until
the doctor wanted the place. Then it rained and turned cold —
the next day . . . there were a lot of sick soldiers — not seriously,
but just sick enough to stay in out of the rain. We were asked to
move. I guess we were slow about packing because we didn't like
to go out in the rain either, and the message to vacate was deliv-
ered to us at the Y.M.C.A tent at the other end of the camp.[31]

They were told that they would be quartered in a barracks until the
YMCA building was ready.

It was at the supper table that we learned where we were going.
There was a midnight blackness outside. The wind blew against
the window panes and rain poured down their sides. We sighed.
Perhaps we didn't have to move until the next day?

We approached the hospital in a body — our wet raincoats playing drum-stick tunes off our boots. The major met us at the door.

"You ladies may stay here tonight if you want to — it is rather bad for you to have to move at this hour and in the rain too." The doctor had hardly finished speaking when we heard a man shriek. . . . Everyone of us was apprehensive.

"A man was injured today," volunteered the doctor, "and we have to operate on him tonight."

"We'll move," said nine women in one voice.

Normally, it would have been no great problem. She did not have that much: "one suitcase, a traveling bag, a legal case full of writing paper and carbons, a typewriter, a big coat and a mandolin." But that night it was a miserable operation. "We must have looked," she wrote, "like a caravan of lost souls swaying through the slippery paths, dotted at intervals by tiny beams of light that came from the barracks and administration buildings."

Wet and cold as they were by the time they had struggled through wind and rain with their belongings, they were pleased with their new quarters.

[They] are made of pine and the rooms are unusually large. The interiors are finished in a narrow brown wood called "ceiling" and it looks luxurious. Our beds are comfortable and just like the ones we had in the hospital. There's a stove in each room and after we had all arrived we rolled up our sleeves — set up beds, swept floors and built fires. There was mud on everything and we swept wet and cold — but cheerful.

The closeness, the mystical brotherhood, the almost festive togetherness that war creates has, of course, historically been reserved for men. It is a feeling from which they have shut out women and that they rekindle in peacetime in veterans' organizations and at conventions. Peggy could see no difference between this spirit of "brotherhood" in her group and that experienced by the "other soldiers."

There's a camaradiere [sic] about such a situation that makes one forget the discomforts and I'm glad to say that in our little group of women — and I was the only one who had ever lived a soldier's life before — there wasn't a whisper, a complaint, a dissenting word. Women who had never swept before or built fires or set up beds went after the work just like the regular campaigner does after the battle.

Well, we're moved and settled. The mud has been scrubbed off the floor — we've hung up the family portraits.

104

We wash in the basins and comb our hair by a thumb nail mirror. Reveille blows at five forty-five and there are no waiters or "petit dejeuners." If we miss breakfast . . . we don't eat until twelve o'clock.

I've lived in a tent. I'm living in a barracks — it leaks and the wind blows through. There is nothing I don't know about being a soldier in France except how it feels to live like a general.[32]

Once she had gotten well settled in, she began writing about the army activities she observed, like the training of the men to use trench mortars. She had to be escorted to the training ground which for safety's sake had been set up two miles away from the camp. To reach it, they had to follow a trail that led through a thick wood, and she had a hard time keeping up with the two American soldiers and the "tall, blonde and good looking" French lieutenant, who slipped and slid over the path made muddy by three weeks of rain. Not one to be inhibited by her lack of knowledge of technical military terms, she drew a word picture of what she observed for her stateside readers.

We eventually emerged on a broad plateau, punctuated at intervals with targets, long trench lines, knolls and flagpoles. Soldiers hustled back and forth across the tops of the trenches and through the narrow passage ways. Those in the trenches carried strange-looking objects in their arms.

In the center of a large hole which had been [carved] out of the side of the slender trench I saw a "hunk of stovepipe" — short, small at one end, and pointed skyward. It was mounted on a revolving basis. I wasn't very much impressed with it then.

Two men were adjusting a brass, curved instrument on its nose and from somewhere along the trench came a clear, far-carrying voice. "G — 1 — deflection 475 — elevation 74 3/4 — bomb — B, V, D, Fuse XV — fire six shots — commence firing."

A man who had a strange-looking object in his arms came forward. Another dropped a white bag down the throat of the ugly piece of iron — another punched it with a stick, and then the fellow with the oblong, gray object pushed the narrow end into the gun — a small, red-pointed brass fuse was fastened to the blunt end, and I saw the one man left in the hole lean down and put a small burning bit of wire into the lower end — and then run. An instant later there was a powerful concussion and the gray object started off toward the sky, the little tail wings that had aroused my curiosity whirling it upward and onward. . . .

Away toward the other end of the grass-grown range, blue and shimmering under the rainfall, fringed with burgundy-hued trees — topped with gold and orange, the whirling object sailed. Suddenly it turned nose downward, falling at a furious speed toward the target. There was a flash just as it reached the ground — a terrific explosion that . . . echoed through the hills like millions of flying splinters — dense black and white volumes of smoke swept upward from the ground, carrying with them wet clods of dirt[,] . . . a giant spray of smoke and mud — a great, broad, sweeping magnificent, awe-inspiring spectacle the kind of an effect the amusement parks are always striving for. Dull thuds from different points in the field told us the mud was falling — a few seconds more and the range was clear. Yet in a certain spot there was a hole that hadn't been there — a hole about six feet deep and eight feet wide.

From the concealed observation post in the side of a little hill I watched more firing. The mud spattered the roof of the shelter and even its thick timbers and big bags of sand didn't reassure me, for I knew if one of the "gray devils" unexpectedly changed its course and dropped anywhere near us — mother back in El Paso, Texas, would be lonesome all the rest of her life.[33]

Peggy Hull with officers at the airfield of the air wing attached to the artillery training camp, Le Valdahon, France, Nov. 1917. *(Peggy Hull Deuell Collection, Kansas Collection, University of Kansas Libraries)*

Obviously, Peggy was anything but lonely. In addition to tall, blond lieutenants, wanting to show her the excitement of artillery target practice, there were French aviators who were eager to take her on an aerial tour of the area. On her first flight, she was flown to the Swiss border, a beautiful trip but somewhat disappointing to her because it was so unexciting. Determined to give her the thrill which she had complained that the first flight had lacked, the French captain in charge of the squadron scheduled another a few days later so that she could observe artillery fire from the air. When she first saw the little single-engine plane he had picked for this trip, a much smaller one than the first, she began to wish that she had not made so much of the dullness of the first one. This plane, she thought,

> looked more like a mosquito than an airplane, and I had to be strapped in. I doubted the thing before we left the ground and the higher we went the less I liked it. We flew back and forth over the target range and the French pilot kept nudging me and pointing below. I kept wishing he would mind the controls for we would climb a little bit and then drop back almost unexpectedly. I lost all interest in the artillery fire and wondered how much higher he would decide to go before he took me home. . . . He made up his mind very suddenly to descend and instead of going down in nice long sweeping drops, he stood the plane on one wing and . . . began to spiral down — by the time I had caught my breath the earth was up here and the sky here. . . . I just toppled over against the fusilage [sic] and stayed unconscious until they carried me out of the machine.[34]

This was just one more example that there were two distinct and separate sides to Peggy's nature, constantly at war with each other: One side wanted to be treated like "one of the boys," while the other side retreated into "feminine" devices like fainting.

Nevertheless, time and again she proved that she was no *sunshine* soldier. On one occasion, having spent an exhausting afternoon in chilly drizzle, she was looking forward to eating and turning in early. But the sergeant announced that troops were "movin' at eight-thirty . . . so [she] changed [her] wet socks, . . . reached for [her] rubber boots" and rode with the "five thousand fully trained field artillerymen . . . [the] twenty-eight miles through a sweeping rain to the station where [the] trains were waiting" to take them to the battle front and where she and the YMCA workers, who accompanied them there, gave them snacks and said farewell to them.[35]

Peggy Hull in her favorite World War I uniform at Besançon, near Le Valdahon, France, Nov. 1917. *(In authors' possession, courtesy of Raymond A. Ruffino)*

Such things as these, not reports of battles or opinions of the progress of the war, were what Peggy Hull wrote about for the people back in Texas. What their loved ones — their husbands, brothers, and sons — were experiencing day in and day out were what her readers wanted to hear about and so were what made Peggy Hull herself important to them. It was her strength as a journalist; an unusual thing about her was that, though she was intensely ambitious, she was not very competitive. She did not climb her way to success over the bodies of other reporters. She was, instead, an opportunist who made her own opportunities. In France, denied the right to move with the freedom of the accredited men reporters, she took her "little" stories where she found them.

When Floyd Gibbons came to the camp from time to time, it was apparent to him that Peggy was having a wonderful time, dressed in her precious uniform, "holding court at the head of a table of . . . officers" on Saturday evenings at "Madame's," a popular Besançon restaurant located in a building which had once housed a convent.[36]

The crowning point of her stay at the camp came the day that General March presented her with a pair of spurs. He put them on her boots at a ceremony attended by the First Field Artillery Division. From the day she "won" them, they were among her most prized possessions.[37]

While Peggy had been glorying in her experiences and busily turning out her articles about camp life, a hundred miles north at Neufchateau, some of the men correspondents representing big newspapers had been lounging around their lodgings, bored and restless, squabbling among themselves. There was no real war news, at least none they were allowed to cover at that moment. The closest they, like Peggy, came to any action was their visits to the training camps, and since a lot had been done on the camps before, they did not find them worth writing about.

It was about this time that some editors stateside discovered Peggy's articles from the artillery camp first published in the Army *Tribune* and *El Paso Morning Times* and now being picked up by other newspapers. Before then the other correspondents had not taken her very seriously as a journalist. She was writing about the subjects they had rejected as unworthy; she was not seen by them as a professional threat. Now, suddenly, they were getting cables from their editors wondering why it was they could not seem to come up with anything for their papers when Peggy Hull was cranking out articles that were being published and that a lot of people were talking about. It seemed to the editors that the investment they had made in their correspondents was not paying off.

All at once the accredited correspondents began to take Peggy very seriously indeed, even more seriously than she had hoped. Smarting under editorial castigation, they now closed ranks and turned on the cause of their embarrassment, bombarding Maj. Frederick Palmer, the officer in charge of overseeing the journalists in France, with complaints. Palmer had to do something. What he did was write to General Pershing.

> If the privileges which she says have been given her have been authorized by the Commander-in-Chief and by the Commanding Officer at Le Valdahon, then she is receiving privileges which have never been given to any individual representing any daily paper with any European army during the present war; privileges indeed which are granted only to distinguished writers who use their material for lectures or for books or magazines, and do not enter into competition with the accredited news correspondents.
>
> The *Chicago Tribune,* Paris Edition, has not wanted for representation, if it would make use of its privileges. It has a regularly accredited correspondent, Mr. Floyd Gibbons. . . . The complaints against Mrs. Hull on the part of the accredited correspondents are unanimous. They add . . . that the work she is doing is undignified.
>
> . . . Mrs. Hull says that she was present at a luncheon given by Generals Pershing and March, when both Generals invited her personally to be their guest with the Army. The fact of her having received such an invitation has been widely advertised in her own paper.[38]

He concluded with the request that "some official authorization of Mrs. Hull's exact standing be given [to him] . . . in order to regulate the situation which has resulted from her assignment to the Artillery Camp."

This was a direct challenge to Pershing to give her some sort of official status or cut her loose. Peggy had counted on Pershing to keep his word that he would see to it she would "get along all right." But Pershing, with more important battles to fight than Peggy's, retreated under pressure; with that, "the army" forbade her to continue to use the pass she had been borrowing from Joseph Pierson. This meant she would be forced to return and be confined to Paris. When that happened, the roving reporter of the *El Paso Morning Times* could see no point in staying in France. Just as the real action was about to begin, her "colleagues" had succeeded in fatally handicapping her.

Whatever Palmer had said about the complaints being unanimous, Peggy, with good reason, believed that Gibbons, Ring Lardner, George Pattullo, and Webb Miller remained loyal to her. In fact, she said, Floyd Gibbons had brought her "all the funny stories that happened in the

American camps [that] he couldn't cable home — [she] wrote them and [her] stories were signed and on the front pages."[39]

About the time that the attacks on her had begun, an article entitled "From Kansas Cornfields to Paris, Via Denver, Hawaii, El Paso and Columbus, N. M., Being Something of the Life History of Miss 'Peggy Hull,' Times Staff Correspondent in France" appeared in the *El Paso Morning Times*. Its author, "The Cub Reporter," said Peggy had written to El Paso that "she had received no letters from home, and that her friends had forgotten her." In reply to this, the cub reporter wrote,

Bless your curly blonde* head and your little pug nose, Peggy, everyone loves you in El Paso and no one has forgotten you! The boys out at the base hospital miss you and your Thousand Island dressing and the dainties you brought them, along with a flood of cheer. The fighting men who watched you ride the best of the "kritter soldiers" to a standstill miss you. The hundreds of El Paso women and young girls miss you and pray that the Boche shells and torpedoes won't get you. . . . You are El Paso's kind of folks, Peggy Hull, and they love you from the tip top of that cute quill in your new Paris chapeau, to the tiny point of your petite boot. You're all the newspaper gang called you — you're a regular fellow, an unspoiled, down-stage American girl, who saw her opportunity, took it and is seeing history and writing it splendidly for the Morning Times.[40]

This reassurance came just when she needed it most. It did nothing, however, to alleviate the heartache she was suffering as a result of the jealousy and disloyalty of those she considered her own kind, and on November 10, she wrote a bitter farewell to her friends and rivals:

Dear Paris and France:
    I am going back to El Paso, Texas, Etats Unis. This bit of information which may not be particularly thrilling to the large and varied population of this country, will [nevertheless] be of some interest to at least three groups of persons who have been more than usually concerned about me the past two months — viz., all accredited and male visiting correspondents, the intelligence section of the U.S.A. and the press division. I like to make folks happy and that is why I'm writing this — I believe the above announcement will be satisfactory to the groups mentioned.

---

*Since she was a natural brunette, she was obviously either bleaching or dyeing her hair.

I have grown quite fond of Paris — it is such an unusual place — We haven't anything like it in Texas. I believe the Place de la Concorde is my favorite spot. It is rather hard to diagnose my exact feelings for it — a sort of proprietary half interest. . . .

There will be some advantage of trading the Rue de la Paix for San Antonio street, because I won't have to borrow money to pay my hotel bill at the end of every week. . . .

When I come to think about it — it really is a shame I have to go back now, for I've become an expert at dodging these ex-tank-driving taxicab drivers. . . . I really can't stay, however, as I've just read the story in the El Paso Morning Times in which the cub reporter announces "we love you, Peggy Hull; you're El Paso's kind of folks." After the reception I received from my fellow workers in France I feel that I prefer to be "El Paso's kind of folks," and to have even a cub reporter speak of me so sweetly is strange and holy music. But we've always felt that Texas was big enough for us all and I'll admit war corresponding is getting harder every day.[41]

She boasted of gains in circulation and advertising rates for the *El Paso Morning Times* as a result of her stories from the artillery camp, stories which had upset so many egocentric big-city newspapermen. She complained that her loyalty and years of experience had been ignored just when they should have mattered most, and she felt especially betrayed by the fact that "a general" (Pershing) had forgotten his promise to her.

Her final shot at the correspondents whom she held responsible for her having to leave France was:

When we've won the war and all you brilliant writers are out of jobs, come back to El Paso, Texas, and if you crowd my stuff off the front page there will still be two persons who'll look for it inside — mother and me. And I promise I won't fuss with the managing editor about it — or tell him you should be sent to Mexico or even ask him to put you in jail — I learned to be a good loser long before I came to France.

I cannot leave France without publicly announcing my gratitude and appreciation of the hospitality of Maj. Gen. Peyton C. March and his staff — of the Y.M.C.A. men and women workers when my colleagues were seeking my blonde scalp and of my admiration for the provost marshal general — who is a soldier first, but always a gentleman![42]

From this episode, she said later, she learned "not to get too big. The quieter you were about what you were doing, the longer you could keep at it. The minute you [got] too big, you [got] brickbats. [She realized she was not] clever enough to avoid some of the traps that might be set for [her]."[43]

Addressed to the officers and soldiers of the AEF, but apparently not published at the time, was a brief "s'long," what she called her "'good-night' to France," her swan song to the battle front.

For all the temporary bitterness she felt toward some of her colleagues, in this "s'long" her characteristic penchant for seeing the positive side of a situation prevailed, and she regarded the experience she had had during the summer and autumn of 1917 in the "glorious company of American soldiers and officers" well worth the miles she had traveled for it. The terrors of submarine and bombing she had "undergone gladly for that experience and . . . [she] would not [have parted] with it for twice the dangers."

She concluded, "No one can ever take this — the greatest adventure of my life — from me."[44]

*She beat the train* into the station by two jumps . . . for she leaped from the train steps and ran up the platform to greet her family and her friends. . . .

The crowd which had been waiting more or less impatiently within the station gates swarmed out over the tracks and Peggy was engulfed in a sea of human gladness. . . .

A sweet old lady . . . stepped up . . . and said:

"Peggy, . . . I thought of you often and prayed nights that you would get through the submarine zone safely. Your stories have been a comfort to me, and . . . I am glad you are safely home."

Peggy kissed the dear old lady through her mourning veil. . . .

Traffic to and from the evening trains was halted until Peggy and her party could get through the Union station lobby. . . . Everyone wanted to see the little girl who had braved the Kaiser's U-boats to get the news at the French front for the Times' readers.

The Cub Reporter,
*El Paso Morning Times*

## CHAPTER SEVEN

# The Heroine Returns to El Paso

On November 22, 1917, Peggy left Paris for the long and dangerous journey home.

Stopping for ten days in England, she saw the British with new eyes. The six weeks watching American troops being given final training to prepare them for combat had made her realize that her earlier assessment of how quickly the war would end because of United States involvement had been not only mistaken, but also unfair to the British. Now she could see that the English allies deserved more praise than criticism.

Her terror during the air raid in Paris had given her an appreciation for the courage of the civilians in London who lived under the constant threat of German Zeppelin and airplane bombing raids. She was impressed that no one seemed to complain about having to take shelter in the subways and sweat the air raids out, realizing that there were few English fliers at home to protect civilians because most of them had been sent to France to protect the soldiers.

After her experience with the pilots at the American artillery camp, she had great admiration for the exploits of the men in the Royal Flying Corps. The first to fly low enough to strafe trenches and marching infantry columns, they had even had pistol duels with German officers riding in their staff cars near the front. That they were more daring did not mean that they were less sentimental than the French pilots were about their "boats." They pasted their fiancées' pictures inside the fuselages and christened them with "such unwarlike names as Violet and Myrtle." One even named his plane "Peggy" after her.[1]

There were also women in the Flying Corps. They were not allowed to fly, but they were permitted to wear flying corps uniforms and act as chauffeurs and land transportation agents. A British officer told her that "the women had distinguished themselves for bravery during air raids, for cool-headedness in the dense traffic of London streets and for their tireless attention to duty."[2]

She was conscious, as she had been in Paris, of the effect of the war on transportation. In France and England, most people were prohibited the use of private cars, and only a limited number of taxis was permitted to operate in either London or Paris. Some people voluntarily complied with the governments' orders but, typical of any population, others had to be forced to. Furthermore, she had come to realize that effective transportation was vital to the winning of the war.[3]

On December 3 Peggy took the train to Liverpool from where she was to sail for home.

Although she felt she had been banished from the war zone by her reporter rivals, the "faithless" Pershing, and the army intelligence section, Peggy was returning to the United States with her trophies of war and three trunks full of Paris clothes, in a way, in triumph. She was especially proud of the trophies, gifts from various military men. Among them were a bamboo walking stick from a French aviator, a propeller "stick" from a British flying officer, an aluminum ring crowned with a Prussian button from a French poilu, a powder box made from a "75" shell,[4] and a little gold "dog tag" that Floyd Gibbons had given her to wear on a bracelet engraved with "Peggy. Correspondent du Guerre, A.E.F., France."[5]

At Liverpool she was subjected to a modified strip search, the lining of her uniform was ripped open, and her boots were "sniffed" by bloodhounds before she was permitted to board her ship. Though the police matron who searched her had spoken darkly of "documents" and "papers," Peggy never knew exactly what they had expected to find.[6]

German submarines still presented a grave threat to shipping, and though she was not as frightened as she had been on her way over, she was still nervous about the crossing as, indeed, were most other passengers and even the crew. Her worst fears seemed to be realized when one day, the ship well into open water, she was sitting alone in her cabin, lost in reminiscences. Suddenly the ship lurched, there was a loud noise, and an enormous jet of salt water shot across the sitting room of her cabin suite, carrying shards and slivers of glass in every direction. Although she heard no sounds of alarm or hurrying people, she was sure that the ship was being attacked, and a shell had hit the glass in her porthole.[7]

To her chagrin, she found her experiences had not made her any more courageous. Instead of rushing to save all the other women and children single-handedly, again she fainted. When she came to, she was being carried down a narrow corridor by an American naval officer. He put her down in a dry berth and assured her that the ship had not been torpedoed at all but that a "little gale — one hundred and ten miles an hour" had blown out the porthole. It was not the first time she had responded to danger this way, but it was about the last. After this experience she seems to have lost some of her capacity for automatic panic and reacted in a pluckier manner. Cynics might suggest that it was perhaps getting harder to find a handsome rescuer or that she was growing tired of the "game." Though basically she was the epitome of independence and self-reliance, it often seemed from her writings as if she saw herself as the heroine in a gothic novel. This romanticism appealed especially to her women readers.

It was a rough crossing, being the time of year for rough seas. She spent most of the voyage in her berth, so she missed the thrill of seeing the Statue of Liberty as the ship came into New York harbor. Her first indication that the ship was close to land was when the steward knocked on her door and said the "aliens officer" wanted to see her. Since she was now home, she could not see why she should have to go through "the same exasperating examination" that she had at foreign ports.[8]

It was nothing personal, of course. All returning citizens had (and have) to go through customs; and when she protested the high duties assessed on her clothing and souvenirs, the customs officer waved her away with, "The war, you know!" which she had found in the past six months to be "the indisputable and unanswerable excuse for everything unpleasant" that had happened to her. Now, it seemed, the war was responsible for a 50 percent tax on the value of every article purchased abroad. Had she known this in France, she said, she would not have come back in "anything but overalls." The final duty tally was $220; and when she showed the customs inspector that she had only about $2.20, he said, "Well, I'm sorry, miss, but your trunks will have to stay here until you get the money." She concluded that "the best way to land in one's own land is to do so with one's belongings wrapped up in a red bandana handkerchief. Not quite so impressive — but about $220 cheaper."

The thought of being deprived of her treasured war trophies as well as her Paris dresses spurred her into action. Taking "all the courage an ex-war correspondent could muster," she approached a perfect stranger, asked for and was given the loan of enough money to get her trunks "out of hock from the customs." Though she combined coquetry, chutzpah, and good-old-American-self-reliance, Peggy was not a calculating person. Rather, she possessed the tough naiveté of an intuitive survivor, a tough naiveté that served her well most of her life.

She had said in her farewell to the reporters in Paris that she was going to go straight home to El Paso; but unable to resist the temptation to be the center of attention, she delayed long enough to give interviews in both New York and Chicago and be photographed by the famous photographer, Elmer J. Underwood. It was "lots of fun for a country girl like me," she said.[9]

In Chicago the *Daily Tribune* report of her visit included a picture of her in a "feminine version of a Canadian soldier's khaki uniform, even to the Sam Brown[e] belt and cute little sombrero and chin strap." This uniform was a far cry from the uncomfortable, unbecoming one which had made her the center of unwelcome attention on a French train. And having gotten over her unfavorable first impression of New York City, she now told the *Tribune* reporter, "New York looked like heaven to me. . . . When I left France I had almost forgotten that there was anything else in the world but mud."[10] Then she announced that the series of stories she had contributed to the Army Edition under the title, "How Peggy Got to Paris," would be published in book form by George H. Doran and Company, but she was soon too busy writing new stories and searching for other adventure to settle down to the job of getting the material organized.

Although Peggy herself minded terribly, the people and the Chamber of Commerce of El Paso and especially the *El Paso Morning Times* reporters did not care that Peggy Hull had not been officially accredited as a war correspondent. When she finally stepped off the Golden State Limited, she found herself surrounded by admirers, the center of a gratifyingly tumultuous welcoming party. Bands played; local dignitaries made speeches; the "red carpet" was rolled out for the "only American woman war correspondent to reach the American first line trenches in France [an overstatement, at best] and to be the guest of the American Expeditionary forces overseas."[11]

She was finally what she had always dreamed of being: a bona fide, first-class celebrity.

"PEGGY IS HOME!" was the headline in the *Morning Times.*[12]

"That's Peggy," said the auto starter at the station.
"There goes Peggy," shrilled a Mexican newsboy selling the first edition of the paper as Peggy went down the street.
In the plaza, on the streets, in the hotel lobbies and wherever Peggy went the Sunday evening crowds recognized her.

The whole town seemed to be in love with her.

Responding to a comment that "Peggy grew fat Over There," "The Cub Reporter," who wrote the story of her homecoming, assured everyone that the five-foot, four-inch girl reporter was still a perfect thirty-six, but did concede that "French war bread, meatless, wheatless and eatless days in England, war rations at the front and fodder served from a goulash cannon has made Peggy plump, but not . . . a lump."

Around El Paso, Peggy wore a different correspondent's uniform from the one she had appeared in in Chicago. Describing it, the Reporter wrote:

> Her English serge field service uniform, made after the regulation British pattern by a British military tailor, with knee-length skirts, showed why the British and French officers insisted upon saluting her wherever she appeared.
>
> A jaunty little campaign hat which was bought on the Place de [l']Opera in Paris, with a chin strap snuggling under her chin, polished service boots, silver spurs, the Sam Browne belt which crossed from right shoulder to left side with a tan belt around the waist, clips for a sword, a green brassard with a cherry "C" for correspondent on the left arm, and a loosely cut military overcoat of regulation pattern completed Peggy's field service outfit.

But he pointed out that she had lost none of her "feminine charm in these apparently masculine war clothes. Her blonde beauty is enhanced by the rich tan of the uniform and the little French felt hat would be described by Mme. Mode of the Place de [l']Opera, as 'chic.'" Holding out a promise of even more exciting dress, the Reporter said that she had three trunks filled with Paris gowns and planned to wear them all as soon as she was rested from her long trip.[13]

In a box quote on page one of the December 24 issue of the *Morning Times,* Peggy expressed her gratitude to her local fans.

> I didn't have time to stop and tell you in the Union station last night how much I appreciated seeing you and how happy and complete it made my homecoming.
>
> You've no idea how I've looked forward to this re-union. . . .
>
> After I get my trunks unpacked and a couple of Paris frocks pressed, I will tell you all some of my experiences in the land of hot snails and cold war.

Several of her most prized souvenirs were put on display at the Popular department store: the walking stick made from a plane propeller, the aluminum ring set with the German button, a string of red beads made from nuts which she had bought in Paris from a crippled soldier, two military caps donated by their former owners, and a chunk of glass from the porthole that had been broken in the gale.[14]

Although she professed delight at being back to her more peaceful kind of reporting, Peggy was finding it difficult to make the transition. For the enlightenment and sobering reflection of her readers, she wrote a moving description of what Christmas eve might have been in El Paso if the "Huns" had mounted an artillery barrage along a line from Columbus, New Mexico, to Camp Cody,[15] and German airmen, guided up the Rio Grande to El Paso by the bright light of the moon, dropped bombs on the after-theater crowds and late Christmas shoppers, theoretically bringing death and destruction to Americans in the same way they had actually brought death and destruction to Europeans. In an especially affecting section, she painted a heart-rending picture of "the slim forms of children [lying] twisted and mutilated — some with stockings clasped in their tiny hands — beneath the roofs where they had lived in safety until — "[16]

It was a word picture that El Pasoans did not soon forget.

In another article, Peggy turned her attention to the liquor question. For decades Prohibition had been a red-hot issue in the U.S. Militant antiliquor groups, drawing support from a strong puritanical streak in the population, had become not only a "moral" but a political force to be reckoned with. In 1917 Congress passed the Lever Food and Fuel Control Act prohibiting "the use of foodstuffs for distillation and regulating beer and wine production" and proposed the Eighteenth Amendment for national prohibition. Since the latter would not take effect until three-fourths of the states had ratified it, in 1918 Congress passed the War Prohibition Act outlawing the manufacture and sale of beer and wine. These measures generally met with popular approval.[17] But now Peggy commented, "Everyone is wondering . . . what the war department is going to do about 'rum and the army.'" The question might have been settled in the U.S., she said, but not in Europe.

Defending the English who had been "severely criticized for serving a rum ration to [their] soldiers," Peggy quoted the arguments of a British officer with whom she had discussed the subject when she was in London. He insisted that rum was a "God-send . . . [to] the majority of the men in the British army [who] were unaccustomed to hardships in civilian life" and contended that "there was no hardship in peace times that could compare with the daily existence in Flanders' mud."

> To that mud . . . Germany owes the delay of its ultimate defeat, for it all but breaks the spirit of the men. It is a thousand times worse in the winter, for the soldiers must stand their watches in from two to four feet of liquid freezing mud. At 6 a.m. every human being's vitality is at the lowest ebb, whether he's in the trenches or not. . . . The man's cold and coffee won't warm him

alone. Coffee and a hot bath might, but there are no hot baths in the trenches — and no fires. So the only substitute we could find for home comforts, for hot fires and hot baths, was rum — and it does the work. It stirs the blood and takes out the kinks in our back bones.[18]

Immediately upon her return to El Paso, Peggy was sought after as a speaker. Her talks on war-related topics to diverse audiences revealed a talent for tailoring her presentations to the specific interest of each audience and mixing the humorous and personal with the serious and general. One of her first speeches was to the Woman's Club, where "many persons who never had seen her except in pictures, were surprised to see a young girl, exceedingly Frenchy and chic, wearing a Callot model of rich brown plush and topped with a close fitting hat made of gold cloth." Giving this talk the "woman's angle," she started by saying, "Ever since I can remember I've been told that war was a man's game — that the only part women played was the giving part. . . . However," she continued, "English women have done more than give their husbands, their brothers and their sons. They today are the moral and commercial backbone of Great Britain."[19]

Six weeks before the outbreak of war English people were flocking to tea parties and discussing the probability of a revolution in Ireland. The women — some of them, were clamoring for their rights. . . .
Then came the war that gave the English woman the freedom she craved. . . . Street cars, railways, motor buses, went under the management of women. Real estate offices, financial government positions, formerly controlled by men, went into the hands of capable women. The motive power of England was suddenly made up of women. Girls who had never worked before left their schools and governesses to cultivate their fathers' estates. Women who had never done anything but talk organized and equipped hospital units and the war office discovered there was a mobilized power at home that was proving a gigantic pushing force behind their army.

She pointed out that women realized with the terrible loss of men early in the war that "the positions they had taken over so hurriedly would be theirs permanently and they would have to build their lives accordingly." She had talked with successful businesswomen in London, with girls who drove the motor buses and girls on the tram cars and found for the most part, whatever their positions, they were planning the same sort of future.

The successful women told me they were contented. Business had a certain fascination — success held a certain satisfaction. First the war must be won and after that they would settle down into the existence that their bachelor friends had enjoyed before the war. They had their clubs, their hobbies, their vacations. They have become investors and shrewd financiers. Women who were assistant clerks four years ago are now on the road to independence. They are buying small country places on the installment plan. Some of them are adopting children and others are caring for those orphaned through the war. The bus and tram girls are doing the same. They are saving their money in the hope of having homes of their own — someday. . . .

In spite of the usual supposition that men, women and war will not mix well in the danger zone, the English women, to the glory of our sex, have proven that it is but a theory of other ages.

Though Peggy always disavowed the label, she often sounded like a feminist.

Contrasting the general spirit and atmosphere of England and France, she went on:

France is sadder than England. Probably because the people show their grief more easily. I saw no crying at the stations in London, where troop trains left. The English women sent their men away with a smile, and few of them wear mourning when they do not come back. The gardens and lawns are trimmed and cultivated with pre-war care, but in France many of them have died or gone to waste and the streets are filled with black-robed women [suddenly robbed of their homes and their] right to live in domestic happiness.[20]

At a luncheon in the Sheldon Hotel, she told the city's Advertising Club that the American troops were anxious to get into action to take some of the burden off the French who had done their part and whose armies had been "decimated by the onslaughts of the Germans," that the American soldiers did not like to be called "Sammies," the name which American correspondents had tried to tack on them, and that stories about friction between Americans and Canadians were not true, citing as evidence a scene she had witnessed in a Paris theater.

The comedian was making an effort to joke at the expense of the American soldiers. After one of these poor jokes a soldier rose in one of the boxes and cried: "Canadians, Americans, Australians:

Over the top!" and they went over the top and cleared the stage. When the gendarmes arrived they were promptly put out, and the manager was locked in his office.[21]

She delighted the Temple Mount Sinai Men's Club with a humorous story she had heard in England:

A man applied at one of the government offices for a position, and an official asked him: "You want a job? Well, what can you do?"

"Nothing," replied the applicant.

"Well, why didn't you apply sooner? All those high salaried jobs are gone."[22]

She spoke several times at Fort Bliss. Describing one of her first appearances at the camp, the *Times* reported:

More than 500 soldiers of a truck train at Fort Bliss stood at attention last evening when Miss Peggy Hull, Times staff correspondent who recently returned from the western front in France, appeared before them. The greeting extended Miss Hull was one of the most spontaneous and enthusiastic she has received since returning from the French battle front.

Miss Hull spoke to the soldiers for several minutes, reciting incidents of the war, relating humorous tales and stories of army life at the front, and describing the work of the Americans now in France with General Pershing.[23]

She told another group at Fort Bliss that she had had a "terrible time" in France before she had gotten the uniform she was wearing. Civilians had to have the permission of French officials to go anywhere, and when she appeared wearing one of her "regular Parisian outfits," a French officer denied her request for "a pass through the war zone because [she] wasn't military." She had gone "right out and got[ten] this uniform." After that, she assured them, she had had no problem.[24]

In yet another talk at Fort Bliss, she commented on the fact that the average Frenchman was enough shorter than the average American that the trenches the French dug were not deep enough for Americans to be safe in. Also, soldiers in the first lines had to be as quiet as humanly possible, never speaking above a whisper, for the enemy was close enough to hear even normal levels of noise. And she concluded that it was up to the British and Americans to win the war because "France has fought until she has nothing left to fight with."[25]

Peggy Hull in uniform wearing the spurs presented to her by Gen. Peyton C. March in 1917. *(Courtesy of Alice Goodnough Reissig)*

Speaking to members of the local Red Cross, she cautioned them about believing all the atrocity stories that were circulating.

> Stories and rumors in Paris crop up over night like mushrooms, and are thicker than they ever were here in the Villa days. Any officer or private in Paris for a few days' leave can tell such hideous details of the front that — well, there were days I never cared to eat and to sleep, because my dreams were filled with horrors. Right after the first raid on American trenches, the story drifted through our ranks that the men taken prisoners had been horribly mutilated. A few of them, it was told, were hung up and used as dummies for bayonet practice. Such reports as these . . . are not believed by the fighting men of the allies. They know better than to believe everything they hear.[26]

At least partly due to her connection with the YMCA canteen at Le Valdahon, her talk sponsored by the local unit drew a large and appreciative audience. Especially pleasing was her comment that the work of their organization at the battle front rivaled that of the Red Cross in giving first aid, serving hot drinks, and dispensing other comforts to the wounded and exhausted soldiers. To ringing applause she said, "Members of the Y.M.C.A. beat troops to the battle front . . . and were ready for service when the soldiers arrived. It would not surprise me at all if Y.M.C.A. men get to Berlin in front of the soldiers."[27]

Referring to one of the dangers to the "health" of soldiers overseas, she warned those about to be shipped out that "the French woman of the street was probably the most entertaining companion that could be found, an artist in this capacity." However, she continued, the YMCA was working to protect American servicemen from the dangers of involvement with such women.[28]

Proving she was no prude, she told them of a humorous experience.

> It is the custom of the French that when you admire anything they have, they want to give it to you. I admired [a swagger stick belonging to a French aviator] and he said, "It is yours." I might say that I thought I had gotten myself in trouble a little later. I remembered that I had admired his scarlet trousers.

A prohibition petition had been circulated at the meeting, and playing to the antiliquor element in the crowd, she assured them the YMCA was doing its bit to discourage alcohol consumption among soldiers in France, even setting up a "hut" to serve coffee and chocolate near a French wine shop close to American headquarters.[29]

Her most successful performance was before a high school assembly in January 1918. Having read her reports in the *El Paso Morning Times* which described her experiences beginning with her departure from El Paso in June 1917, and having heard talk about her activities as a correspondent, the students were wild to see and hear the "Plucky Yankee Girl Reporter" in person. With her flair for the dramatic, she did not let them down.

> Booted and strapped[,] khaki-clad, wearing her military hat, held securely by a chin strap, and carrying a bamboo walking stick, [she] walked out on the stage [to be] greeted with loud cheers.[30]

The students listened spellbound while she told them about her experiences.

She had spoken to so many groups that by the end of February there were few people in El Paso who had not heard her tell firsthand about her adventures. So when someone in one of her audiences had protested because she did not talk longer, she took public cognizance of the possible effect of this wide public exposure.

> I know I'm a woman, and I suppose I should live up to the reputation of my sex, but I've told the story of my trip to France and back, I have gone over in detail the horrors of ocean travel, the food shortage, the quarrels with the military control officers, so often that I can't imagine any one wanting to hear it . . . again. I am writing a book about my trip, and every one I ever knew has to have me tell the story all over again — until I almost wish I'd never gone to France.[31]

Actually, she was reveling in the attention she was getting, and she was further gratified to hear from Webb Miller that she had not been forgotten in Europe, that not everyone had been glad to see her leave. It was obvious that he expected that she would soon return to France.[32]

As much as Peggy wanted to go back ("it had been so long, it seemed to me, since I had been a military person"),[33] she knew it was not immediately possible. Having returned in debt, she had to concentrate on work that would bring in money. When she had first returned to El Paso, she had been the "guest" of the Sheldon Hotel for a few weeks. At the end of that time, she moved back to the Paso del Norte which she loved and where the management agreed to let her fix a room into a sort of studio in which to do her writing; and she knuckled down to her advertising work and column.[34] In spite of her romantic nature, she could be practical-minded when it was necessary, and she had a real capacity for self-discipline when she needed it. Once again her column concentrated on the businesses of El Paso which were her major sources of income.

The column still mirrored the remarkable split in her nature and was often a study in contradiction. For instance, while one section in her February 3, 1918, column dealt seriously with very real world problems, the advertising parts were startlingly frivolous. Referring to the lessons the American housekeeper could learn from the average French housewife, she pointed out the French could "take the most discouraging ingredients and make a palatable dish out of them." She continued:

> When we sit down and think of the appalling waste in years gone by — waste that we didn't dream of then — didn't consider because the necessity for conservation hadn't been driven home to us. Now — when we face the possibility that our boys at the front may have to go hungry if we don't watch our larders — it's different!
>
> We Americans have been spoiled. Competition has given us luxuries that are unheard of over there — now — and everyday the war will demand more and more sacrifices from us. Let's don't cry like babies if every public utility isn't up to the standard we crave.

In sharp contrast to this was a reference to jewelry made from military insignias. She had noticed quite a number of girls and women wearing crossed guns or sabers, or a staff pin "just as they came off the officer's tunic." English women, she wrote, had them made up in gold and diamonds.

> And the French women — goodness, a French woman wouldn't wear a plain bronze pin for anything in the world. . . . A French woman simply will not wear anything that isn't the last word in beauty and smartness — no matter whether there's a war or not.[35]

This was a nonsubtle approach to getting her American women readers to rush to "The Jewel Shop" in El Paso with their U.S. staff pins to have them duplicated in gold and silver and decorated with diamonds so as not to be "outdone" by the European women. She seemed able to make the most breathtaking switches from savant to huckster, not really so surprising when one considers that to her personally, economics being what they were, the advertising was often the more "serious" part of her writing.

In addition to her regular advertising, she did movie reviews. One film that affected her greatly was "The German Curse in Russia," the work of fellow Kansan, war photographer Donald Thompson.[36]

I discovered that seeing the picture once wasn't enough. I sat through the second showing — there were so many scenes I did not grasp the first time. . . . The scenes of the revolution are those which actually took place, and [Thompson] was fortunate enough to be in Petrograd at the time to get them. Maria Botchkareva, the woman who has struggled so hard to save Russia from anarchy, is seen at the head of the Battalion of Death. In fact, Thompson has given the world an authentic animated photographic history of Russia since the beginning of German intrigue. No one in El Paso should miss it.[37]

Most of her reviews, however, were of entertainment films with stars like Norma Talmadge and Wallace Reid.

Since her mother and stepfather were now living in nearby Deming, New Mexico, Peggy frequently spent weekends with them. On one of these visits, she was entertained at Camp Cody. There she renewed her acquaintance with Eugene Millikan, now a captain, whom she had known when she was a cub reporter in Denver and he was secretary to Colorado Gov. George Carlson; with DeLos Walker, now a lieutenant, who had also been a reporter in Denver; and with several officers including Col. W. H. Raymond, whom she had met in Columbus when General Pershing returned with his troops from Mexico. She attended the officers' dance at the armory, reporting, "I haven't had such a good time since I danced on the veranda of the officers' mess in the artillery camp in France."[38]

After spending four days in and around the camp, she felt qualified to pass judgment on those who were unhappy with conditions there. She made it plain that she had little sympathy with the complainers. "If the men are kicking about conditions in Camp Cody, what, I wonder[,] will they do when they get to France?"[39]

As for herself, getting back to France occupied her thoughts more and more. Not only had Webb Miller encouraged her to return, but she also had a letter from Gen. Peyton C. March, now chief of staff in Washington. March had obviously been chagrined about what had happened to her in France, for in his letter (dated March 18, 1918) he wrote:

I have often thought of you as you left the front and have always admired your pluck in beating the men correspondents in getting news and you will always have my best wishes wherever you go.[40]

By spring, having saved up enough money to get her started and having recovered from a case of mumps, Peggy felt ready to go back to

France. It was not her nature to "treasure" hurts, and so her bitterness over the attitude of most male correspondents toward her had faded. This time, however, she was determined to be a fully accredited war correspondent when she saw Paris again.

Peggy's intention to return to Europe was announced in the *Morning Times* by the "Cub Reporter" on April 7, 1918. He was not too surprised when she said, her first day back on the job after recovering from the mumps, "I'm going back." He did not have to ask, "Where?" because she had told him that the editor of the army edition of the *Chicago Tribune* had offered her work before she had left Paris. He continued:

> Maybe you think you'll miss her, but I had to sit next to that empty chair and look at her dust-covered desk for many long weeks. I remember how we used to gather around the telegraph editor when she was going over and coming back if there was news of a torpedoed ship. When Paris was bombed we were all scared to death. Now, we've got to go all through the same thing again.

Peggy let everyone know that she was more than willing to take the risks, to go back and take the Army *Trib* job so that she would be able to send back reports to the American people of her visits to naval bases, army camps, and finally to write an eye-witness account of the fall of Berlin.[41] She could expect no financial support from the *Morning Times* for this second trip to Europe. It had been an interesting venture for the paper to have her sending back her "chatty little stories" about life in Paris during wartime and about life at American army training camps in France. Now, with the Americans going into the fighting in large numbers, there was a need for more coverage than could be supplied by a young woman who probably would not be allowed to get anywhere near the fighting. So the management of the paper negotiated with the *New York Times* and the *Chicago Tribune* for additional war news service.[42]

Although she had to have been smarting at losing out to a largely impersonal and "foreign" news service, she went all out to prepare a special section, "Farewell El Paso," which was included with the paper before she left. This section contained pictures of her at various shops around town, making preparations for her departure, accompanied by her usual advertising of those shops, some of which made references to her experiences in France.[43]

Because she expected to be gone for a year, she made several trips to visit her mother and stepfather at Deming.

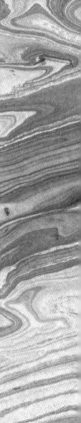

*Vladivostok is,* with one exception, the worst port in the world. Port Said is the only place which surpasses it in vileness and wickedness. Thousands of criminals were turned loose during the revolution. They flocked to the nearest port and the city became the center of their operations. . . . "Kopeck Hill," the center of immorality, flourished without restraint. Murders occurred every night.

It was into this port of degradation and chaos that our soldiers were landed for their first Far Eastern duty.

Peggy Hull,
"U.S. Honor Impaired Due to Lax Discipline of Troops in Siberia"

# CHAPTER EIGHT

# Accreditation at Last — to Siberia

Peggy arrived in Washington in the summer of 1918 with one goal in mind — to get permission to return to France, this time as a fully accredited correspondent. She knew it would mean a battle with the bureaucracy, and she was prepared for it. But in the capital city, she found that everyone was talking about an expedition that was being readied to go to Siberia. She immediately gave up all thought of returning to France, for it seemed to her that Siberia represented a lucky break: Journalistically, it was a new area which probably would not be filled with reporters who would resent her competition. Also, she was still under the spell of the movie, "The German Curse in Russia." Finally, it was a place she had not been before.

Telegraphing and writing to every editor she "had ever known and to a lot [she] hadn't," she began the search for someone to send her as a representative of his paper and underwrite her expenses. Then she went to the office of General March, confident that he would be helpful because of their past friendly association. To get to him, she had to go through his aide and son-in-law, Maj. Joseph Swing.

"I want to go to Siberia!" she said to Swing. "What are the chances?"[1]

He told her to wait while he consulted the general. When he returned, he said that General March would talk to her about it.

The meeting got off to a bad start. As she entered the room, she tripped on a rug and was catapulted into March's arms. Mortified, she regained her balance and stood speechless. March, sympathetic to her embarrassment, tried to put her at ease.[2] Complimenting her on her work in France, he said,

Your stories are the sort that give the people at home a real idea of what the American soldier is like and what he likes and dislikes.

I'd like to see you go with the Siberian expedition. These men are likely to be lost sight of in view of the big things that are happening in France. If you can get an editor to send you, I'll accredit you![3]

She left March's office determined nothing would stop her. However, when, after several weeks, her search for a sponsoring editor had yielded no positive responses, she very nearly decided that it just was not meant to be. Yet it simply was not a part of her nature to give up something she wanted as desperately as she wanted to be an accredited war correspondent; in a final effort, she wrote to S. T. Hughes, editor-in-chief of the Newspaper Enterprise Association, the Scripps-McRae (later Scripps-Howard) syndicate whose primary outlet was the *Cleveland* (Ohio) *Press*. On the basis of what he had learned about her experiences along the Mexican border and knew of her work record on the Cleveland newspapers, he finally agreed to give her the assignment.

That hurdle overcome, she set out for the Office of Military Intelligence, which was responsible for issuing the passes and credentials that all accredited correspondents had to have. Once again, she was faced with the prevailing attitude toward women when Capt. Carl Ruth, "an old newspaper man," told her that she might as well save her time and not bother to even present an application for there was "a very clear order to the effect that no woman shall be accredited." He knew this was the case, he said, because there had been hundreds of applications from women, and they had all been turned down.

But Peggy had not come this far to be put off with an answer that sounded like the Englishman's "It just isn't done." Arguing with Ruth, she told him that she had General March's blessing, a claim which Ruth clearly did not believe. In exasperation, she said, "If General March tells you to accredit me[,] I guess you will[,] won't you?"

He gave her a smile which showed that he thought it was highly unlikely and replied, "Oh, of course . . . but you'll have to get the order."

Vowing that she would have it in an hour, she left his office, and "exactly one hour later [she] returned with [a] memorandum signed by General March: 'If your only reason for refusing Miss Peggy Hull credentials is because she is a woman, issue them at once and facilitate her procedure to Vladivostok.'"[4] Even a diehard like Ruth could not disregard a direct order from the army chief of staff.

So Peggy was at last ready to start her ten-thousand-mile journey to Siberia, proudly carrying the first war correspondent's pass ever given to a woman by the War Department.[5] A very impressive document, it was eight by eleven inches, printed on heavy vellum paper, and it said:

The Bearer, Miss Peggy Hull, whose photograph and signature are hereto attached, is hereby accredited to the Commanding

General, American Expeditionary Forces, Siberia, United States Army, as news correspondent of the Newspaper Enterprise Association with permission to accompany said troops, subject to the Regulations governing Correspondents with Troops in the Field and the orders of the commander of said troops.

This pass entitles the correspondent to passage on military railways and, when accommodations are available, on Army transports, with the privileges of a commissioned officer, including purchase of subsistence, forage and indispensable supplies when they can be spared.[6]

It included the printed name of Newton D. Baker, secretary of war, and the signature of M. Churchill, director of Military Intelligence. Dated September 24, 1918, it showed she was assigned to the headquarters of the American Army in Siberia under the command of Maj. Gen. William Graves. In addition to all the practical advantages of accreditation such as the right to transportation, housing, and forage, accredited correspondents were "entitled" to military salutes; the guards at headquarters were supposed to present arms when correspondents appeared there. "Being human I liked that better than anything else in my military experience," she admitted. "I suppose nearly all of us have a little Napoleon complex in our natures."[7]

On her way to San Francisco where she was to embark for Vladivostok, she stopped in Kansas to visit her brother, intending also to see her father and the rest of the family who had been living with him at Dorrance since they had moved back from Arkansas. She found that her father had, in the meantime, moved his family to Salina, fifty-five miles east of Dorrance, so she had to leave without seeing them.

Sailing from San Francisco on October 15, she traveled to Yokohama on a Japanese freighter, arriving on November 6, and sailed from there for Vladivostok.[8]

The nature of the expedition to which she had been accredited was not clear even at the time. With the Bolshevik movement in Russia and the Treaty of Brest-Litovsk in March 1918, by which the Soviet government made a separate treaty with Germany, the western Allies found themselves in a dilemma. First, with the eastern front gone, the Germans were able to remove the troops which had been fighting there and launch a mass offensive in France on March 12, 1918. Second, the Czechoslovak Legion, made up of two groups who had been fighting alongside the Russians — the Czechs and Slovaks who had been living in Russia and those who had been in the Austro-Hungarian forces and taken prisoner by the Russians — wanted to continue the war against the Central Powers. Since obviously they could not pass through German

## Correspondent's Pass.

OCT 14 1918

**WAR DEPARTMENT,**

Washington, September 24, 1918.

The Bearer, Miss Peggy(Henrietta G.) Hull, whose photograph and signature are hereto attached, is hereby accredited to the Commanding General, American Expeditionary Forces, Siberia, United States Army, as news correspondent of the Newspaper Enterprise Association with permission to accompany said troops, subject to the Regulations governing Correspondents with Troops in the Field and the orders of the commander of said troops.

This pass entitles the correspondent to passage on military railways and, when accommodations are available, on Army transports, with the privileges of a commissioned officer, including purchase of subsistence, forage and indispensable supplies when they can be spared.

NEWTON D. BAKER,
Secretary of War.

Official:

M. Churchill

The Adjutant General.
Director of Military Intelligence

Peggy Hull
Signature of the correspondent.

Headquarters American Army Siberia
November 15, 1918.

Wm Graves
Major-General Commanding.

Peggy Hull's Correspondent's Pass, 1918, first one issued to a woman by the War Department. *(Photocopy, Peggy Hull Deuell Collection, Kansas Collection, University of Kansas Libraries)*

Upon receiving permission to leave the Army the correspondent will surrender this pass to the Censor, who will cancel and file it.

and Austrian lines to reach the western front, they sought permission to cross Siberia by means of the Trans-Siberian railway to Vladivostok where they could be transported by sea the long way back to the western front.

To this end they placed themselves under the overall command of the French, who had promised to provide the necessary ships, and began negotiating with the Soviet government for safe passage across Siberia. The Bolsheviks agreed but made the stipulation that the Czechs must first turn over all arms except those necessary for self-defense. Almost immediately, there was trouble, for some Czechs smuggled unauthorized arms aboard the trains, which, of course, upset the Bolsheviks.

On the other side of the coin, local Communist groups sometimes delayed or impeded the trains, difficulties which the Czechs suspected were the result of orders from higher up. Not unexpectedly, fighting broke out between the Czechs and the Bolsheviks; by the latter part of May 1918, it had developed into a small war, being waged all across Siberia. By late summer, the Czechs controlled the Trans-Siberian railway from the Volga to Vladivostok, helped create friendly governments in the cities they captured, and cooperated with the White Russian military forces.

Both Britain and Japan felt they had justification for intervention in the "Russian situation." The British concluded that the Bolshevik leaders were nothing more than German agents working for the kaiser and did not represent the Russian people. Therefore, they decided to intervene to help the White Russians and restore the eastern front against the Germans. The Japanese favored intervention to further their economic interests. These factors resulted in Britain's and Japan's landing troops at Vladivostok in April 1918. There was very little press coverage of the Siberian situation due to censorship and a preoccupation with the western front where the Germans had launched the massive offensive.

Meanwhile, President Woodrow Wilson had been considering sending an economic commission to Siberia as a gesture of support for non-Bolsheviks. With news of the Czech situation, he decided outright military intervention in their behalf would be "appropriate." Wilson's idea was to send a modest force, small enough that the Russians would not regard it as an invasion, to protect Vladivostok and a portion of the Trans-Siberian railway so that the Czechs could consolidate in the interior. Since the intervening troops would establish only defensive positions, they could claim to be neutral while actually maintaining a pipeline to the anti-Bolshevik armies. They could also serve as a curb on the Japanese who, General March was convinced, had plans for expansion in the area.

The decision to send an American force was made on July 6, 1918, and Maj. Gen. William Graves was selected as commander. His force, made up of contingents from the Philippines and the United States, consisted of 296 officers and 9,056 men.[9] His orders from Wilson, which were vague and contradictory, called for him "to steady any efforts at self-government or self-defense in which the Russians themselves may be willing to accept assistance"[10] (the meaning of which still puzzles historians), while at the same time remaining neutral in the internal struggle in Russia. In view of the political situation, this put Graves in the position of being open to criticism from all sides.

When he arrived on September 1, 1918, Graves found that "Vladivostok was a microcosm of Siberia: the old order had broken down and nothing stable had arisen to take its place."[11] He commented, "The fact that we were not troubled by custom inspectors and quarantine officials was my first initiation into a country without a Government."[12]

The British newspapers were permitted to publish only reports favorable to the intervention, which meant "hysterical and anti-Bolshevik reporting." Although American newspaper reports were more restrained, they, too, justified intervention on the grounds that "the true voice of Russia had sought the help of the Allies."[13] In fact, though the Associated Press bureau in Tokyo got a more accurate picture of the situation from Japanese sources,

> newspapers preferred to print the unfailingly optimistic views of a string of sources such as "well-informed areas in London," "army officers in Washington," "the Russian Embassy in the United States," and the Russian Committee in Paris — all White Russian exiles, all emotionally involved, and all highly subjective.[14]

When the armistice was signed between Germany and the Allies on November 11, 1918, the troops who had been sent to Russia now found themselves fighting what in reality was a new war: "the Allies, with troops from sixteen countries, against the Bolsheviks."

Finally, any objective reporting was next to impossible after the Red-peril scare became the dominant theme of the Allied press. The Bolsheviks had now replaced the hated Germans as the enemies of all that was decent.

Peggy arrived at Vladivostok on November 14, 1918, eager to start writing reports on the American troops involved in this tangled situation. From the first, she was struck with the sharp contrasts she found there. The harbor, surrounded by the steep hills on which the city was built, presented an exotic sight to her as her ship entered the bay. The city itself was glorious with its wonderful old Roman architecture.[15] Her ship had hardly docked before she discovered that underneath this beautiful exterior "filth reek[ed] amid wealth." As she and the American officer who had come to help her passed through the customs house, he advised her to hold her breath. She tried to, "but one accidental whiff sent [her] reeling toward the door. A dirty wharf and a collection of human beings not half so well kept or clean as the average village dog back home — that was [her] welcome to Siberia."[16]

Winter, which began in Vladivostok around the end of October, was not a time of picture postcard views of deep, white snow. In fact, it usually snowed very little, and there was almost no wind; most foreigners did not realize just how cold the place really was, a hazard to the troops and foreign correspondents stationed there. It was now November, not the best time to be introduced to the area.

On top of the inhospitable climate, Vladivostok was one of the worst ports in the world, a place of "vileness and wickedness" where thousands of criminals who had been turned loose by the revolution had gone to set up their operations. With inadequate police, murders occurred every night, and the American soldiers took advantage of easy access to vodka ("sold . . . in little tin cans; similar to . . . old fashioned coal oil cans") and cognac to "forget their old troubles and create new ones."[17]

From the wharf Peggy was taken to meet General Graves at his staff headquarters, a Russian home on the main avenue. There, from a window, she had a good view of the street below where in less than fifteen minutes, she said, she counted a total of thirteen nationalities.[18] It was strange to her to see such a conglomeration of different ethnic groups; later she tended to contrast the "half-breeds, Mongolians, Manchurians, Chinese and Koreans" unfavorably with the Russians she met.[19] The Orientals here were very different from those she had known during her two years in Hawaii.

Unimpressed with her official accreditation from the War Department, General Graves was not pleased when she arrived in Vladivostok, regarding her presence as just another problem associated with his mission in Siberia. His attitude was very different from what she was used to from military officers. The ultimate discourtesy, to her, was that he would not let her use his bathtub, one of the very few in the city. Fortunately, she found the navy in the person of Adm. Thomas S. Rodgers to be more cooperative than the army; he permitted her to use the bathtub on board his ship.[20]

Conscious of her new status as a fully accredited correspondent, Peggy felt that she had to be careful not to upset the men by taking advantage of being a member of the "frailer sex." On the other hand, her reporter's instinct and her air of self-assurance based on previous military experiences sometimes led her into difficulty. For example, she did not improve her standing with Graves when she asked him about the absence of military police in the area. On the defensive, he replied curtly that he had "ideals about the American soldier" and did not "like to think it . . . necessary to put a military policeman over a man to make him do his duty as a protector of life and liberty!"

Although she felt the general was sincere and considered his attitude "a sweet thought," she pointed out that it was not long after their conversation that his " 'protectors of life and liberty' had wrecked a building, been mixed up in several shooting scrapes and had become so reckless that he [Graves] found it necessary to sidetrack his ideals for a while." In her opinion, it was as a result of just such attitudes that "the Russian people had been thoroughly disillusioned about the Americans."[21]

She had "fallen in love with" the educated Russians she had met and had found them delightful companions; she was hurt and embarrassed to feel that the Russian people who had once looked with love on the United States and on Americans as the greatest people on earth now felt only bitterness because of the conduct of the American soldiers. "What would we think," she asked,

> if the Russians had sent an army of 8000 [sic] to our shores to help us, and instead of moving to the places where they were needed they calmly settled down in San Francisco, occupied the best buildings in town and the best barracks while our own soldiers slept in box cars? How would we feel if their automobiles and trucks raced through the main street regardless of human life? If their soldiers insulted our women — and our cafes were filled with drunken foreigners who made life miserable for everyone?
>
> Yet this is exactly what happened in Vladivostok. And after my experience with the army on the Mexican border and in France I feel that I am qualified to judge fairly.[22]

Some Russians were quite open about their dislike of Americans. At one of the places she had lived, Peggy "had put an American flag on the gate outside [the] door. The woman who owned the house, in high rage, tore it down."[23] Heartsick, Peggy remembered the day in the French taxi when through the window she had seen a village blacksmith proudly putting up the Stars and Stripes beside the tricolor.

However, she realized that the role of peacemaker was a hard one, especially in such a confused situation:

Our program, as far as I can learn, is to sit tight until it is determined which is the proper party to support in the regeneration of Russia. . . .

General Graves and the other allied commands wish to give their entire support to the proper party but how to determine which is the right one is a question which is putting more than one wrinkle in their foreheads. . . .

Siberia is on the threshold of its blackest period. Twice a victim, first to monarchy and then to anarchy — its people this winter will die by thousands. They are freezing to death now and the coldest weather is still to come.

Farther inland, where the disorganization of the railroads has made it impossible to carry supplies, they are starving to death, while roving bands of Bolsheviki and bandits terrorize the unprotected communities.

Murder, pillage, starvation, and bitter cold — what a desperate outlook.[24]

[Even worse] the Czechs whom we were supposed to have relieved at the front starved to death and froze to death because their supplies did not reach them [because] we were dickering with the Japanese for control of the railroads.[25]

During the winter of 1918-1919, the friction between American and Japanese troops in and around Vladivostok led to individual brawls as well as "inadvertent clashes between patrols," indications of "disharmony among the intervening forces. The coming of spring brought more serious friction."[26]

While American troops were barracked in buildings formerly used to house officers of the czar, the less fortunate war workers, members of the relief commissions, Red Cross and YMCA workers had to take whatever they could find as shelters. In one case, nine American nurses were sleeping in a room which Peggy regarded as barely large enough to accommodate one comfortably. She observed that in this bitter-cold climate, the Russian idea of comfort bore "no relation to the American conception of the word, and there is no sanitation."[27]

From a comfort standpoint, she was in Russia at the worst time of the year. The December mean temperature in Vladivostok being fourteen degrees (F), and January's five degrees (F), it was difficult and expensive to heat the houses. The solution as far as home owners were concerned, she said, was to seal up windows with putty, paste, and paper "so tightly that a breath of cold air [could not] get in" while "a whiff of warm air [could not get] out," and the houses remained sealed up this way until the spring rains came. The heat for each room was supplied individually by a stove made of bricks, sometimes faced with tile, that reached almost to the ceiling. With this type of heating, the room would be cold in the morning until a fire was built to warm it up. By evening the rooms were too warm. Added to this was a total lack of ventilation so rooms captured and imprisoned the daily buildup of dead air odors. As a result, it was a real shock to enter a Russian house after having been out-of-doors.

To illustrate the Russians' suspicion of the English and Americans "because of their penchant for fresh air," she wrote a highly exaggerated tale of an experience she had had with it. She had, she said, known she was going to be in Vladivostok for at least a month, and she felt she simply could not live in a room that was so hot and filled with such putrid smells. Immediately after she was settled in her first rented room, she broke the seals, dug out the putty, and opened the window to let in some fresh air. The next morning, the magnitude of her crime was dramatically brought home to her.

A Chinese servant came in with a cup of coffee and upon seeing the window ajar ran chattering excitedly out of the room. A few seconds later the Russian proprietor, his wife and all the servants flocked in. They pointed to the window, shivered and gargled strange words at me. I could tell from the vehement way in which they talked and flung their arms that they were angry and I wasn't quite sure for a moment whether I was going to be yanked out of bed and thrown in the icy street or not.

By this time the loud voices had attracted the attention of the other roomers and they crowded in. A Russian officer who spoke a little English explained, "The Proprietor thinks you are quite mad because you have opened the window. He says you must pay him one hundred roubles at once because you have ruined the room by letting all the heat out and he will not be able to rent it again this winter."

One hundred roubles meant $12 in American money! I was annoyed at that but I was in a rather embarrassing position. I didn't exactly enjoy having so many foreigners standing around my bed discussing my peculiarities while I was powerless to do more than peep above my blankets.[28]

She was forced to move that day; as she left, the proprietor, who grudgingly accepted her offer of fifty roubles instead of the hundred he had asked, was busily sealing the window again. More in sorrow than in anger, Peggy realized that she had made a contribution to the general anti-American feeling and that her room would probably never be rented to an American again.

When she arrived at her next "home," she discovered that word of her "vandalism" had reached her new landlord and he was taking no chances with her. "Along with the tightly sealed windows there were two great thick wooden shutters and just before sundown they were slammed together and barred and [she] was left a prisoner with the accumulated smells of many Russian predecessors."[29]

As amusing as this account was, the lack of sanitation in Vladivostok was no joke. The stench was pervasive, "sickening and depressing." The Orientals particularly suffered from "catarrh, lung or throat trouble." Cafés were filthy.

"The food [is] served by dirty waiters and it is prepared, no doubt, by dirtier cooks," she wrote.

> Americans have the feeling that they have been dumped on a garbage heap. . . .
> "Think of it!" exclaimed a white-haired American colonel, early in May, "it is springtime in the states and the country is full of sweet smells and — "
> A gust of wind swept up from the dusty street. He reached for his handkerchief to cover his nose and mouth. One cannot breathe the dust of Siberia with impunity.
> The morale of the Americans, Canadians, English, Italians, French, and Czecho-Slovaks [has begun] to wane during the spring.
> . . . Everybody [feels] the same as the American soldier who rushed out of his barracks the first warm morning, threw his hat in the air and shouted:
> "Heigh-ho! spring has come! Bring out your gas masks!"[30]

Another shocking aspect of life in Vladivostok was the widespread cruelty to animals. Peggy was particularly upset at the number of blind horses she saw and the rather routine beatings of both dogs and horses which she observed. It was just one more instance of the barbarism which existed side by side with civilization.

Disregard for the pain and suffering of animals, she felt, was symptomatic of a pervasive indifference to all suffering. The story of the "death train" epitomized for her this terrible indifference. In December 1918, American railway workers imported to try to do something about the deteriorating condition of the railroads[31] reported that a "death train" which had originated in Samara, had arrived at Nikolsk with 775 of the original 2,100 "passengers," chiefly political prisoners, dead, most from typhus, typhoid, dysentery, scurvy, and pneumonia. Others, it was said, had been shot as they tried to get food and water at the stations.

Red Cross workers had come from the town out to the train and done what they could to give the sick and dying medical help, but in the conditions and bitter cold, it had been a losing battle. As soon as the worst cases had been removed, the train had suddenly fired up and chugged away, to be swallowed up by the rolling prairies and the endless wheat fields. No one knew what happened to the 800 people still on board.[32]

Whether or not the story was exactly true as reported, these reports of terrible things were not isolated, and time has shown that many of them were true, for conditions at the time were chaotic and with all the warring factions there was little regard for life. Though Admiral Kolchak, whom the Allies supported, was a relatively honorable official, the soldiers of other anti-Bolshevik leaders, like generals Semenov and Kalmykov,

> under the protection of Japanese troops, were roaming the country like wild animals, killing and robbing the people. . . . If questions were asked about these brutal murders, the reply was that the people murdered were Bolsheviks and this explanation, apparently, satisfied the world. Conditions were . . . horrible in Eastern Siberia, and . . . life was the cheapest thing there.[33]

It was General Graves's judgment that the most horrible murders were not, as world opinion wanted it, committed by the Bolsheviks; rather, quite to the contrary, the anti-Bolsheviks, the Whites, killed "one hundred people in Eastern Siberia, to every one killed by the Bolsheviks." Graves felt that the Japanese could have put a stop to the murdering but did not because they hoped that if things got bad enough, "the United States would become disgusted with conditions, withdraw her troops and request Japan to go in and clean up the situation."[34]

Once again, the history of Russia was the story of her suffering people.

During most of the time she was in Siberia, Peggy was apparently confined to Vladivostok. She wrote to General March to complain that her activities as a war correspondent were somewhat circumscribed, she believed, because of her sex. In a letter to Graves, chiefly devoted to comments on the government's policy in Siberia, March came through for her again. His reprimand to Graves shows him to have been the exception to the rule, his attitude ahead of his time. He wrote:

> Of course you understand that sex counts for nothing in this modern game and Miss Hull is like any other newspaper correspondent in regard to being permitted to see whatever you let any one

else see. No favors to be shown her, but on the other hand, no repressions either.[35]

This letter was apparently responsible for the fact that she was occasionally permitted to go outside of the city, and after all the terrible things she had seen there, it was a relief to Peggy when she could get out of Vladivostok and visit the American garrisons along the route of the Trans-Siberian railway between there and Blagoveshchensk. She found the quarters occupied by Americans in Blagoveshchensk to be quite comfortable. Formerly used by the czar for his officers and soldiers sent to the area to guard exiles and political prisoners, the buildings had walls fourteen inches thick, double windows, a stove that reached almost to the ceiling in every room; some quarters even had bathtubs which by now to her were the epitome of civilization and luxury.

Even here Peggy met an officer she had known on the Mexican border. He was Maj. Fitzhugh Allderdice who had the responsibility, with his two companies of soldiers, of protecting the line of communication to the north of Evgenevka. She found these men "more contented than those stationed in Vladivostok" and concluded that it was probably because they had an occasional chance at "real combat" since sometimes a few Bolsheviks in the area got brave enough to start something.[36] Allderdice said there had been numerous Chinese and Manchurian bandits in the area when the troops had arrived, and the peasants had been going to market in armed groups to protect themselves. He had sent out a few patrols, they had taken care of the problem, and now the bandits steered clear of the military posts.

With the typical American prejudices of the time, Peggy analyzed the possibilities for good to come out of the intervention:

> If the allies eventually decide to garrison Russia and Siberia and establish a stable government, then the dreams of a few Americans will come true, and in the realization, the people of Siberia will learn more of progress and thrift by the example constantly before them than they could possibly get in any other way.
>
> They may not be pleased when they see Americans tilling the land, but as the years go by and their conditions improve along with the development of their country there is bound to come an intelligent and educated race.[37]

At the same time she realized that the social atmosphere of the foreign settlement in Vladivostok, the settlement made up of the future

Peggy Hull with unidentified soldier, probably in Siberia. *(In authors' possession, courtesy of Raymond A. Ruffino)*

purveyors of the sterling example, was the same as that in most small towns in America, rife with petty jealousies and titillating gossip. She detested it, especially since at various times of her life, she had been its victim. Avoiding the company of those who made up this group, she spent most of her leisure time swapping tall stories with soldiers and sailors, and this, no doubt, gave the tea-party regulars even more to talk about.[38]

In the middle of January she went to Japan on a sort of rest and recreation leave. There she was struck by the difference between the American and Czech soldiers, themselves on leave. The Americans were rowdy, drunken, and apparently unconcerned about the rights of others while the Czechs were models of responsible behavior. The story she wrote about the situation was uncomplimentary to American servicemen.

Peggy's stories which attempted to deal with the military and political situation were marked by the same inaccuracies and distortions as the reports of the male correspondents. Because of strict censorship, official news sources rarely gave correspondents any reliable information about what was going on. As a result, they spent most of their time

149

trying to substantiate what usually turned out to be wild rumor. In a tongue-in-cheek account illustrating this problem, Peggy wrote:

> Siberia is the newspaper man's heaven. He never has any difficulty in finding news. His only trouble is deciding which news to select. . . . It all depends on what one wants. . . . Siberia is as full of rumors as an appleskin before being peeled is full of apple.
>
> Sometimes, late at night, my doorbell rings. Drawing my dainty canton flannel pajamas around my body and winding three thicknesses of blankets around my shoulders, I peer out my front window to see who is freezing on my doorstep; usually I see W. C. Whiffen, Associated Press representative, "Dad" of the newspaper bunch and dean of far-Eastern [sic] correspondents.
>
> "On your way," he shouts, as he spots my breath steaming out the window; "on your way. The government has been overthrown for the ninety-sixth time, and the new government has put in a plumber's assistant as Foreign Minister!"
>
> "Great stuff," I murmur, tossing on eleven layers of garments. . . . "Great stuff, not to say hot dope! The people of America will be passionately interested in that!" And I am just ready to slide down the banisters and join Dad Whiffen in his hunt for hot dope, when the patter of feet rings loud and clear on the pavement. Looking out of the window again, I behold Dad Whiffen once more, steaming back up the street. . . .
>
> "What ho!" I shout from the window, "have you got all the dope on the Plumber's Foreign Assistant Minister?"
>
> "Nyet!" howls Dad Whiffen. . . . "That story blew up. Now I'm on the trail of a good one. Kutchyourtungoff, the celebrated Cossack leader, is reported to have bitten Lenin in the ankle and given him a compound case of hydrophobia and lock-jaw. Hurry up! Hot Dope! Let's get to it!"
>
> So I fly down and get to it. Getting to it means that I slip, slide, skate and fall over 200 versts [one verst being approximately two-thirds of a mile] in Vladivostok and vicinity in an attempt to verify the tip. I scurry to American headquarters where I get the stereotyped, ever ready, multigraphed answer, "I don't know."[39]

It was her opinion that they should put a sign bearing "I don't know" on the front door of the headquarters. It would save everyone a lot of trouble.

"From the A.E.F.," she continued:

> I dash to Czecho-slovak headquarters and with the aid of one French phrase, two German nouns, a Russian verb and a Chinese

article, I find that the Czechs are fraternity brothers of the . . . officers I have just left. Undespairing, although I have followed the same trail many times before, I manage to reach the box car one league away in which rides the . . . accommodating Russian general to whom I always flee, because he knows everything before it happens and has a pleasant habit of making it appear almost ten times more important than it really is and absolutely truthful.

"Ah," says the . . . Russian in English, "it only too true is[,] my kind friend[.] Kutchyourtungoff to his country gives everything in this brave and act noble." . . .

Returning across that one league with three falls, a bruised knee, a sore head and a sprained wrist to my credit, I approach Japanese headquarters. . . . As usual, the guard looks at my teeth and in my ears. . . . I am searched for concealed weapons, bombs, hand-grenades and armored cruisers. Having convinced themselves of my innocent motive . . . I am convoyed through a line of 39 aides, 26 adjutants, 14 chiefs of staff and other appurtenances employed by the ostentation-loving Nipponese army.

Apologetically I announce my mission and the colonel, who speaks English, frowns slightly, rubs his hands together. . . .

"It would displease very much my country to know that this crime was committed, for it would, no doubt, have a tendency to unify the Russian people, which, you know, is not congenial to us or in line with our ambitions."

. . . [Next] I turn my face toward the gray-clad figure which stands in front of a big door five miles to the west. . . .

One can do a lot of thinking in a five-mile hike, and as I neared the suburbs of the city, I remembered . . . that I had over-looked the one place where they were in direct communication with western Russia. . . . I speeded up the lagging legs and breathlessly came to a halt under the British flag. "Jolly ripping news, isn't it, bah Jove!" exclaims the tall blonde major with sea blue eyes, "Rawther!"

"But," I [say] impatiently, "have you any confirmation of its authenticity?"

"Eh, wot wot wot?" irritably [says] the blonde major, "if your bally over worked railway engineers would arouse themselves from their winter's sleep we might jolly well have an opportunity of chewing Lenin's ankles ourselves, topping idea wot wot!"

Dauntlessness is a requisite which all Siberian reporters must possess. Already Dad Whiffen may have stumbled upon the hidden source of confirmation. . . . I must hasten away while there is still unvisited a point of information.

151

"Mais oui, mademoiselle," began the dapper horizon-blue clothed [French] officer, "I think it is maybe how you say it true. Mais ca serait if M'sieu Lenin have bite dat chien Semenov. La Belle France how she have suffered, mais we suffer worse in Siberia. It is many months we are here, still nossing can we do."[40]

She heard no more because she was so exhausted from her exertions she dozed off sitting up. During her nap she dreamed that she had also made it around to the offices of "the Chinese, the Poles, the Serbians, the Germans, the Roumanians, the Ukrainians, the Pomeranians."
"But hardly," she went on,

had my . . . eyelids flopped for wink number two when the irresistible and irrepressible Whiffen flashed through the door . . . and I came instantly back to consciousness of my duty.
"Has it been confirmed?" I asked eagerly, ". . . about Lenin?"
. . . Whiffen had a perfect Russian convulsion and after it passed said in an awed voice, "Are you still working on that story? Why it's so old that the Baptist annual wouldn't print it. Since I gave you that tip I've been working on the report that the Czechs had all joined the Bolsheviks, that Kalmykoff had gone crazy and wiped out the American contingent at Khabarvosk, that Japan had declared war on the Allies, that Czar Nicholas had turned up alive and well in Petrograd with a new son and had reestablished the monarchy. But this late one is the best of all; let's beat the other fellows to it and go meet 'em and get the first interview."
. . . I slipped inconspicuously through a back door and . . . beat . . . an unmilitary and un-war correspondent-like retreat for the U.S.S. *Brooklyn*. . . . I staggered up the gangplank and begged the officer of the deck for news from the front. He covered a wide yawn with a fur mitten and looked at me suspiciously.
"Front," he says, "what front?"
"The Bolshevik front," says I.
"Oh, hell!" says he, and walks away.[41]

At the conclusion of this fanciful account of the difficulties encountered by all correspondents in getting reliable news in Siberia, she said she returned to the American headquarters where she and the sentry there "closed the day's events" by singing an anonymous musical lament popular with the soldiers and set to the tune of "My Country 'Tis of Thee." It was called "Dos Vedanya to Siberia."

Siberia 'tis of thee
Sad land of treachery,

Of thee I sing.
I hate your rocks and chills
Your woods and Bolshevik thrills.
My heart with shame does fill
For you and me.

I came to fight for thee
In Freedom's sympathy.
I stayed to *sing*.
Land where my nation's pride
Died with mine side by side,
Land where we only hide
The Bolsheviks to chide.

Some day we'll have to fight
For Freedom's holy right
Then we'll go home.
We'll leave this land of lust,
Of hate, of filth, of foreign dust,
With hearts in deep disgust
We'll sail for home.[42]

It was even more frustrating when she did get a decent story. The newspapers back home were usually not interested in it or her attempts to evaluate the military situation; so most of her reports from Siberia were of the same type she had written about her experiences on the Mexican border and in France.

Difficulty in getting their stories from Siberia published plagued most of the reporters. An expedition that was at best a sidelight to the great war in Europe and at worst an exercise in confusion and frustration even to those directly involved had to compete for newspaper space with stories of the armistice in November 1918, followed by the intense interest in the peace negotiations, the struggle over American membership in the League of Nations, the steel strike and coal strikes of 1919, and other postwar domestic problems.

Although she had been wild to go, hoping that her reports would ensure that the soldiers taking part would not be forgotten as well as to secure her place in the annals of journalism, Peggy did not like Siberia, and for the first time she had seen a less than heroic side of American soldiers. That this was due, for the most part, to the fact that our forces found themselves in an untenable and disheartening position did not entirely mitigate her disappointment in them. Her time in Siberia was an anticlimax to her experiences both along the Mexican border and in France. On the two earlier occasions she had, at least for a time, had a privileged position with contacts which made it relatively easy for her to write stories which were readily accepted and published. Now she, along with most other correspondents in the area, found herself frustrated, disillusioned, and largely unpublished, or her stories were cut up and shortened enough to rob them of information and charm.

When she had first arrived, Peggy had reported that the American soldiers in Siberia were not suffering from anything worse than boredom, that they had never been better clothed, better housed or better fed. She even went so far as to assert that "this is just like a vacation in a winter resort."[43]

Several months later, what she had seen and experienced had so changed her attitude she felt that, far from a holiday atmosphere, there was not even the most basic "pleasure anywhere in life in Vladivostok. Not even in walking along the main thoroughfares, no matter how bright and sunny the day." She was referring to the soldiers' old nemesis, homesickness, exacerbated because they were "marooned in filthy Siberia."[44] In fact, she felt a great deal like the three soldiers she had overheard in a café:

> "You can pan this country all you want to," said one, "but, believe me bo, if the climate was warmer and the people here spoke English and weren't so blamed dirty, I'd just as soon live here as San Francisco."
>
> "Me, too," said the second.
>
> The third swallowed a pirozhnaia [a little filled pastry] at a gulp.
>
> "You guys are both right," said he. "Siberia would be a swell dump if it was a regular country; and the Russians would be swell folks if they were Americans.
>
> "And if they was a lot of swell restaurants on the moon, and the old Murray Hill gang lived there, and the place was crowded with swell dames, and I could get three days a week off and spend them in New York, and somebody'd pay me $200 a week for living there, I'd just as soon live on the moon as not. Just as soon as not."[45]

Peggy's later comment, "Those years will never be forgotten," was at least partly a wry one. It was with great relief that in June 1919, she went to Shanghai to await transportation home when the United States began preparing to withdraw American troops from Siberia. The Canadians pulled out that month; the Poles, Serbs, Italians, and Czechs all left by September; one British battalion left in September, the other in November. The first shipload of Americans did not leave until January

17, 1920, the last, March 31. The Japanese remained until October 1922 and left then only as a result of U.S. pressure.

In this apparently futile exercise, 27 American soldiers had been killed, 52 wounded, 8 had died of wounds, 135 had died of disease and other causes. Fifty had deserted.

At the end it was General Graves's observation that:

> the Japanese, without cessation, and in the most obnoxious way, interfered in Russian affairs from the day I entered Siberia until the day I left.
>
> . . . The Siberian people were sure that the presence of foreign soldiers made it possible for the Cossacks to murder, beat, and rob men, women and children. They are sure to come to this conclusion, because the stubborn facts justify it. These facts have been, and may continue to be hidden from the American people, but they are not hidden from the Russian people.
>
> . . . I doubt if any unbiased person would ever hold that the United States did not interfere in the internal affairs of Russia. By this interference, the United States helped to bolster up, by its military forces, a monarchistically inclined and unpopular Government, of which the great mass of the people did not approve. The United States gained, by this act, the resentment of more than ninety per cent of the people of Siberia.
>
> . . . I was in command of the . . . troops . . . and, I must admit, I do not know what the United States was trying to accomplish.[46]

Given the situation, it is little wonder that little attention was paid to Peggy Hull's significance as the first woman to be accredited as a war correspondent.

*Somehow* nearly all the friends I had in those days of Blood and Sand, and Eucalyptus Horsemen, [are] famous. But then — they were men and that does make a difference.

Peggy Hull,
*China Press*

## CHAPTER NINE

# Capt. John Taylor Kinley and the Shanghai Years

Peggy's decision to return to the United States from Siberia by way of Shanghai turned out to be a fateful one, for she got a temporary job on the *Shanghai Gazette*,[1] an English-language newspaper.

Shanghai was the most sophisticated of Chinese cities; the International Settlement, the 8.3-square-mile bastion of European trade and culture,[2] protected the English and Americans living there from the harsh realities of Chinese life. In fact, the Settlement offered a privileged, even luxurious kind of life to Occidentals, based on very favorable exchange rates and cheap Chinese labor.

It was also the busiest of ports, its docks full of ocean liners and river steamers; like most ports, it abounded in all the pleasures money can buy, its old world and "border" streets lined with brothels, opium dens, and dance halls. Sailors particularly were the prey of the fleshpots and were the frequent objects of muggings or worse and the victims of disease.[3]

From night spots such as the Eldorado and the Boxers' Café Buffet and Palais Crystal Garden, the blare of jazz bands filled the evening air, and painted Chinese and chalk-faced Japanese ladies of the night swayed to their rhythms while they waited for customers.[4]

Life within the International Settlement was filled with parties, polo, and other pleasant pastimes, and for residents of the Settlement, even those, like Peggy, who had to work, too, it was still a happy round of dinners, tea dances, and horse races. Westerners dined on boned capon and pâté de foie gras while to the north and west in the "real" China, people were starving or drowning, depending on the kind of weather the region was having that year.[5]

On sight she fell under the spell of the "Paris of the East."[6] Nevertheless, as infatuated as she was with the city and as much as she enjoyed the life of the International Settlement, she was not blind to the real China and its suffering. This was at least partly due to the fact that she was assigned to cover the student riots of 1919 which started in Shanghai and developed into a nationwide strike against the government of Peking.

The riots had been touched off by the news that the Shantung Peninsula, which Japan had taken from German control during the World War with the announced intention of returning it to China, would not be returned after all but would be kept under Japanese control. This was a betrayal of Wilsonian principles on which the Chinese had pinned great hopes, and it left the door open to the spread of anti-American propaganda by both the Peking government and the Japanese in an attempt to place all the blame for the Shantung decision on the United States.

As Peggy saw it, this ploy was not working because the Chinese students saw through it and got support from the merchants and other groups in their attempt to bring down the government with a boycott of Japanese goods. She was sympathetic to the students' appeal to the United States to send "progressive young men, capable of managing factories, of opening new industries, of teaching the Chinese laborers new trades." In fact, Peggy believed it was "the young American's great opportunity," especially since the Chinese had "a deep and lasting devotion to Americans."[7] She even seemed to feel that it might, at some later time, be the land of opportunity for her, too.

Not everything about Shanghai was totally ideal, however, for during her stay, she was sick from the hot weather. Therefore, when she returned to the United States, she did not go at once to Kansas to visit her family because her mother had written her that it was "frightfully hot" there, too. Writing to her father and half sister, Alice, in Salina, she said that as much as she would like to visit them, particularly since she had missed them on her way to Siberia, she would wait until the weather in Kansas was cooler.

She was preparing to go to New York to see about having her book published and to look for other writing assignments. Apologizing for her apparent neglect of him, she wrote:

> I . . . have always meant to keep in touch with father, but my path to fame and fortune has been just as hard and rocky as everyone's and when my work is finished I am no good for writing letters.[8]

Once again, her book deal fell through; but she did get several articles published, including four for *Leslie's Illustrated Weekly*. Showing her versatility as a writer, two of them were based on her recent experience in the Far East — "United China Demands Her Rights," which was concerned with the student riots, and "The Land of Roaring Rumor," which dealt with the difficulties of being a war correspondent in Siberia. The other two articles, done on special assignment, were "Steelworkers' Wives Want No Strikes," which was critical of the attempt of steelworkers to unionize, and "In Search of Pep or Pulchritude," which suggested that the Turkish baths could offer the means of losing or gaining weight. This article probably grew out of her constant efforts to control her own weight.

When she finally returned to Kansas in April 1920, she visited relatives in Bennington, her father and his family in Salina, and her favorite aunt, Myrtle Wright, in Oketo, where she was the talk of the town. Peggy, extremely conscious of her effect on young people, felt that they, especially, needed romance and romantic heroes; she did her best to provide them when the occasion arose. One such opportunity presented itself in the person of fifteen-year-old Eulalia Weber. Eulalia, a school friend of Peggy's cousin, was invited to meet her illustrious relative.

To Eulalia, Peggy, with her peroxide blond hair curled around her face and big, expressive brown eyes, was a glorious figure. Indeed, it was hard for her to decide whether she was more enthralled with the hair, eyes, and long black, very low-cut, velvet dinner dress Peggy was wearing or with the stories Peggy recounted of her adventures as a war correspondent in wonderful France and remote, mysterious Siberia. At a time that most of the newspaper work done by the women she knew involved the society page, Eulalia, who had already decided to be some kind of writer, determined that someday she would be a *newspaper* writer like this glamourous war correspondent.[9]

Peggy could not get Shanghai out of her soul, so after she left Oketo, she headed for the West Coast and back to China where, for the next several months, she worked on the *Shanghai Gazette* again.[10] After a short time she got restless. In the fall of 1918 she had been bound for Paris when she had gotten sidetracked to Siberia, and now she felt a longing to go back to France. She had contacts there. One was Floyd Gibbons, editor-in-chief of what had been, during the war, the army edition of the *Chicago Tribune,* afterward continued as the Paris edition, an English-language edition now being put out for the American tourists who were swarming to Europe.

As she had expected, her long friendship with Gibbons was helpful to her; she became, temporarily, a part of the newspaper crowd in Paris.

One of this crowd was Irene Corbally, a young newspaperwoman who in 1921 was hired as fashion editor of the Paris edition.[11] Peggy and Irene soon became friends. It was not, however, a case of like calling to like, for they came from very different backgrounds: Peggy, from a farm in Kansas, did not graduate from high school while Irene, from New York City, had attended college. In addition, the recently divorced Peggy was ten years older than Irene and much more experienced; to Irene, sophisticated. Though not a "flapper," Peggy was a woman of the twenties, that strange, half-liberating decade for women of silk-stockinged legs exposed to admiring glances, one-piece bathing suits outlining the curve of the breasts, diaphanous negligees, Mary Garden perfume, cold cream, face powder, makeup — "vamp" advertisement side by side with "housewife and mother" pitches. With her flair for clothes, her peroxided hair, and independent spirit, Peggy was a flamboyant woman, and Irene admired that flamboyance as well as Peggy's relaxed sense of humor, use of slang, and tendency to tease.

They were living at the same cheap hotel on the Rue St. Antoine in late 1921 when Peggy decided to go back to Shanghai and the *Shanghai Gazette*. In her usual outgoing way, she invited her newspaper friends in for a farewell party in her room. About a dozen people crowded into the room to give her a proper send off the evening before she left for Marseilles to catch the boat for Shanghai. Champagne flowed freely. They toasted her "again and again and again";[12] Irene, who had just had a serious disagreement with her current boyfriend, began feeling more and more sorry to see Peggy go, not only because it meant losing a valued friend, but also because she was jealous and resented losing her to an adventure that she "wanted for herself, too."[13]

After Irene had unwisely accepted a glass of cognac on top of the champagne she had drunk, someone suggested that she should go to China with Peggy. When her boyfriend, instead of objecting, joined in and started giving her advice on how to get the most out of a trip to the Orient, the disconcerted Irene left Peggy's room, rushed to the newspaper office, announced her resignation, and then returned to her room at the hotel to start getting ready.

The next day she saw Peggy off for Marseilles, got her affairs in order, and bought a train ticket to Marseilles for herself. When she got there, she found there was no berth left on the *Inaba Maru*, the Japanese freighter on which Peggy had booked passage. By happy accident, by the time the ship sailed, as a result of a cancellation, a berth became available in Peggy's cabin.

Throughout the six weeks' voyage, Peggy and Irene were the only Americans in the small group of "whites," which included a "tweedy" Englishwoman who was their cabin mate. The woman expressed "shock" at Irene's and Peggy's practice of completely undressing before putting on their nightgowns. Much to *their* amusement, this woman was able, by "a complicated laborious process of unhitching and unhooking, unlacing and unbuttoning herself under that cambric coverall," to get into her night clothes without ever really uncovering herself.[14]

Their other cabin mates were not so amusing, at least to Irene. Since Peggy had traveled on freighters before, she was somewhat resigned to the presence of cockroaches, but the beasties sent Irene right up the wall, and she could not rest until the stewardess made an effort to get rid of them.

Peggy had had enough experience with the Japanese that she was not surprised at the curiosity of the radio officer about two American women traveling alone. As she explained it to Irene, "All Orientals believe that women traveling alone to the Orient are going there . . . either . . . to become a *fille de joie* . . . Or, . . . to engage in espionage."[15]

At Port Said, Irene had an experience that in the long run had more of an effect on Peggy than on her. Just after they docked, an Egyptian fortune-teller who was especially interested in Irene and her fate came on board. With Peggy standing by, Irene finally agreed to let him tell her fortune. He predicted that she would soon marry and give birth to a daughter, but then the happy times would give way to a period of great unhappiness. At the time Irene was bothered by the seer's prophecy, but the skeptical (although as she said later, searching) Peggy had laughed it off. "Whew! [she had said]. A nice cheerful bird! Forget it!"[16]

Irene had forgotten it. But after Irene had married, had a baby girl, and her husband had died suddenly, it had been Peggy who had remembered and whose skepticism had been shaken.

Proceeding by way of Cairo, Aden, and Ceylon, by January 15, 1922, the *Inaba Maru* dropped anchor at Singapore. Peggy was surprised and pleased to see a familiar sight as she looked around at the other ships in the harbor. "It's the old China Mailer, the *Nile*," she said excitedly. "I knew the skipper up in Vladivostok. Kingsley, his name was. I'm going over."[17]

When she boarded the *Nile* and asked for Kingsley, the cabin boy took her to the captain's cabin. But as she entered, "instead of the short, dark-haired, black-mustached Kingsley there was a tall, handsome blond," whom Peggy recognized as the chief officer with Kingsley at Vladivostok, an Englishman whose name was John Kinley.[18]

Peggy was amused by the coincidence in names and intrigued that Kinley not only remembered her, but showed her a snapshot he had of her taken two years before. Since he was tall and handsome, had blue eyes and blond hair, Kinley was all the things physically that Peggy found most attractive in a man. On the Border, crossing the Atlantic, in France and Siberia, it was the tall blonds with sea blue eyes whom she could not resist and into whose arms she invariably fell for comfort and protection.

John T. Kinley, second husband of Peggy Hull and captain of the China mailer, *Nile*, later a harbor pilot at Shanghai. *(Peggy Hull Deuell Collection, Kansas Collection, University of Kansas Libraries)*

164

It was little wonder that, Kinley's seeming to requite the feeling, she fell in love with him the next morning during their breakfast date. When Peggy returned and told her about what had happened and how she felt about John Kinley, Irene could see that in all probability she and Peggy were not, after all, going to be living together in Shanghai, that it looked likely that if things worked out for Peggy, Peggy would not even be around to look after her. This was a blow since she had come to depend on Peggy for not only moral support but also sewing and mending, things at which Peggy was accomplished but which Irene was not at all good at. Although Irene was disappointed, she tried not to show it and declined Peggy's suggestion that they both leave their ship at Hong Kong and wait for Kinley to pick them up there on his return from Java and take them on to Shanghai on the *Nile*.

John Taylor Kinley, who had been born on the Isle of Man, came from a long line of sea captains. He was the youngest captain in the Pacific area and was something of a hero, having rescued 150 Chinese from their sinking ship in a typhoon. For this bravery he had been decorated by the Chinese government. Swearing that he had been carrying the torch for her from the time he had met her two years before in Vladivostok, Kinley was taking no chance of losing sight of Peggy again and sent her frequent radio messages during his week's voyage between Singapore and Hong Kong. Irene could understand why Peggy could not resist him.[19]

Although Peggy again urged her to get off at Hong Kong with her, Irene realized that because of the romance, she would be at best in an awkward position and at worst in the way, a situation she did not want to be put in. Her only course seemed to be to stay on the *Inaba Maru* and to go on alone. As it turned out, she was not quite alone, having the company of Peggy's eleven pieces of luggage, which were left when the sailing time of the *Inaba Maru* was suddenly changed to a day earlier than scheduled due to the threat of a shipping strike. When they parted, Peggy and Irene expected to see each other in a few days in Shanghai. But the *Inaba Maru* was the last ship to leave Hong Kong for six weeks. The strike shut down the harbor which meant that Peggy and John Kinley were "stuck" there until it was settled. In those weeks Kinley was so attentive and romantic, Peggy was swept away, and on February 22, 1922, they were married in St. Andrews [Episcopal] Cathedral.[20]

After the wedding, they had a rousing celebration on the *Nile*. The next morning when she woke, Peggy was surprised to find John sitting in a chair across the room. She sat up in bed and said, "What's the matter? Why don't you come and get in bed?"

Kinley answered heatedly, "Well, you wouldn't let me. Every time I'd try to take off my shoes, you'd say, 'Nobody's going to put their shoes under *my* bed!'"[21]

When the shipping strike was finally over, the Kinleys sailed for San Francisco, stopping at Honolulu on the way. The report of Peggy's marriage in a Honolulu newspaper contrasted her attire ("some sort of a fetching pink creation") with that of the time when she had been there on her way to Siberia in 1918 in her khaki uniform. While they were in California, Peggy visited her mother and stepfather who now lived in Alhambra.[22]

It was not long before Peggy's marriage to John Kinley ran into trouble.

Living on the ship was no big problem. Peggy was used to constant traveling. It even gave her the chance, in Honolulu in 1923, to renew her friendship with Irene Corbally, now Kuhn, since Irene and her husband were living and working there.[23] She kept herself busy, offering a shopping service to *Nile* passengers, giving them advice as to things to be found in the stores in the ports where the *Nile* put in.[24] She took pleasure in sending such gifts as red mandarin suits to her little nieces in Kansas.[25]

Accustomed to being independent and, at the same time, the center of attention, she found it very difficult to cope with a husband whose job it was to charm the women passengers and glad-hand and drink with the men. Some who knew John Kinley had been doubtful about the chance for success of the marriage from the start;[26] for her part, Peggy was career-oriented enough to bring her own set of problems to their union.

After living for awhile in San Francisco, in January 1924, she returned to China with her husband when he was given a new job — bar pilot at Shanghai. Optimistically, Peggy announced that she would not be back to the States for another ten years,[27] obviously counting on the more settled, less social nature of John's new work to help make their marriage happier.

Life in Shanghai was comfortable, even luxurious for most foreigners. An annual income of $3,000 to $5,000 made it possible for an American to live there on a scale available only to those with incomes of $10,000 to $15,000 (which at the time was quite a lot of money) in metropolitan areas in the United States.[28]

A major change had taken place since she had previously been in Shanghai, a part of the aftermath of the Russian revolution. When Admiral Kolchak had been killed in 1920, thousands of White Russians who had fled to Vladivostok to escape the Bolsheviks had had to flee again when the city fell to the Reds. Some had gotten passage on ships out of Vladivostok, but others had had to cross Siberia to Manchuria to find seagoing transportation. Wherever they had started from, they had sailed south to Shanghai, and this flood of refugees settled there, taxing the economy and changing the social climate.

Since most of these Russians arrived without friends, money, skills, or training, even the ability to speak Chinese or English, they were reduced to competing for jobs that required no skill or training or language fluency — jobs as janitors, gardeners, chauffeurs, bodyguards for wealthy Chinese. This brought them into conflict with the native Chinese in the same economic situation. The Chinese called it "breaking their rice bowls" (taking their jobs).[29] The fact that the Russian refugees were on an economic and therefore social level with the native Chinese changed forever the way the Chinese regarded whites. They were no longer impressed and/or intimidated. Furthermore, coming at a time when the country was starting a period of great social upheaval, this Caucasian "loss of face" ultimately helped pave the way for a "new order." In the short term,

hundreds of young girls entered the night life of the city as entertainers. . . . Many of them were lush, snow-white creatures, with hair the color of pale honey and eyes like violets in spring. . . . They were intoxicating. . . . The day of the once famous "American" courtesans was gone.

Overnight, Shanghai [had become] a cabaret town. A city of expensive night clubs where the most beautiful of émigrés appeared as entertainers, it [had become] also a city of tawdry, sordid dance halls . . . with Russian hostesses [and] risqué floor show[s].[30]

Thriving in this gaudy, seething atmosphere, Peggy threw herself into the social life of the International Settlement. One of the most popular hostesses in the city, she wrote for several English-language newspapers and was a war correspondent of sorts when factions led by General Chi of Kiangsu Province and General Lu, struggling for control in China, brought the conflict right to Shanghai. Describing the "press gangs" (military companies whose job it was to force civilian men to join the army or navy) who worked the Chinese sections of the city so diligently, she reported that many Chinese who had jobs in the Settlement feared to return to their homes lest they be dragged into a struggle which they did not even understand. In the belief that it would protect them from the unsettled political situation, many took to flying the British flag.[31]

Peggy also worked on a series of feature stories about life in China, illustrated by John. Already in a socially secure position thanks to her husband's position, Peggy had personal standing in the international community since newspaper writers at the time "numbered among their friends the British subjects of his Majesty the King who constituted the Scotland Yard of the International Concession, as well as His Majesty's top servant, the Consul General."[32] The foreign newspaper writers found themselves even more tied to each other than they had been in Paris because of the widening gulf between the white inhabitants of the foreign Settlement and the native Chinese.

In this group were Edna Lee (Booker) Potter, a reporter married to an American diplomat, and Irene Kuhn, who had moved back with her family to Shanghai from Honolulu. Floyd Gibbons, now divorced, was a temporary part of the circle whenever he was in the area on an assignment.

Peggy's stories of life in Shanghai demonstrated that she had not lost her touch as an acute and objective observer of life around her. She did not have to worry about housekeeping with the easy availability of Chinese servants eager, because of stiff competition for jobs, to please their "masters."

At the same time, these "servants" were no longer above taking advantage of the generous natures of the people they served if those people, like Peggy, had generous natures; she reported with some amusement on how she was "taken" by one of her servants who invited her to go on a shopping trip to buy gifts for the servant's "number two girl" who was soon to be married, and a little later on another for her number three girl. On both occasions Peggy found herself very cleverly maneuvered into paying for all her servant's purchases.[33] Peggy, who as she grew older was becoming more prodigal, was hardly typical of Settlement employers.

On shopping trips with her servants, as they drove "through crooked, narrow streets, scraping past infants and adults," Peggy was horrified at the lack of caution of the native Chinese as they walked or rode in rickshaws or pushed wheelbarrows. Going indifferently on their way, they ignored the honking horns of dangerous automobiles and the angry shouts of drivers. She observed that they seemed to have an unshakable belief in the god of good luck, and when one darted across the road in front of a speeding car and was barely missed by it, he smiled with self-satisfaction, believing that "the evil spirit which [had] been shadowing him for some time [had] been crushed by the speeding machine."[34]

Peggy was intrigued by obvious Western influences on Chinese culture. Shen Hung, who had been a student and actor in the United States, adapted Western plays for Chinese audiences, his first choice being "Lady Windermere's Fan," for he believed that "the wit of Oscar Wilde is the sort that Chinese can understand and appreciate." She reported that Shen also planned to present Ibsen's "A Doll's House" and, most remarkable, in one of the really radical changes brought about by Western influence, that women were appearing on the stage, even before motion picture cameras and in Western dress.[35]

That Shanghai had become the "Hollywood of the Orient" was no accident. It was the direct result of the fact that C. C. Bau, the organizer of the first Chinese motion picture company, had gone to Los Angeles when the industry was starting there and learned the business after which he returned to China and set up his own company. Most of his actors were also his office staff, and when not acting in pictures, they worked in the business departments of the company.

As evidence that Chinese movies had a long way to go to rival those made in the United States, Peggy described a marriage proposal as presented in a Chinese movie:

Aside from the fact that the hero looks very much as though he was treating the heroine for rheumatism in her right hand and wondering how she felt about it, one could hardly call this a passionate love.[36]

Although some of her observations on the "strange" habits and customs of the Chinese in Shanghai were humorous, her writing reveals a sympathy and fondness for them in spite of the fact that she was somewhat influenced by the prevailing attitude of the Settlement that the native Chinese existed primarily to serve the foreigners living in Shanghai. She was also acutely aware of momentous social undercurrents, and she warned English readers that there was a real danger of their losing out to Russian communism if they did not mend their ways. Critical of the type of European who was "nobody" at home and so preferred to live and work in the Far East where he was automatically considered "somebody," she quoted Aldous Huxley's *Diary of an Eastern Journey.*

He may be ill-bred, stupid, uneducated, no matter. His skin is white. Superiority . . . is a matter of epidermis. No wonder if he loves the East.

Though it was obviously much too late for such admonitions, Peggy loved the East so much herself, she could not face giving up quite yet. When she saw the Soviets treating the Chinese with courtesy, acknowledging their equality, she insisted that, if nationals of other white countries would wake up and also treat the Chinese with courtesy and equality, there was still a chance the Western position in China could be preserved. "China is worth the struggle, but the Russians are going to get it, if you don't watch out!" she wrote. Europeans, of course, were not suddenly going to start treating the Chinese with Courtesy and Equality, and her only reasonable suggestion for England, if England did not want to lose influence in the area, was to "meet the situation with the same weapons used by her enemies . . . propaganda."[37]

As hard as she was on Europeans and Americans living in Shanghai, Peggy leveled her sharpest attacks against the American tourists who, after spending a few days during which the women shopped and the men sat in the bars drinking, returned to the United States as experts on the situation in China. An example of these "ugly Americans," although the term was not yet in vogue, appeared in an article she wrote for a Shanghai newspaper in which she described the insensitivity and ignorance of two tourist couples, the Bentons and the Smiths, who stop off at Shanghai for two days and then return home

> and Benton, as a member of the commercial club, is tendered a luncheon and asked to make a speech on conditions in China. Now Benton's memory of China is rather hazy. He can recall a number of large buildings on one side of the river bank, and he never thought to ask what they were. And after he left the ship there were two cheerful days in the hotel bar while his wife shopped. However, that would never do to tell at a business men's luncheon. So he decides to pick up a few items in the newspapers and use his imagination.[38]

Utilizing these two sources, he comes up with the following expert opinion to share with his fellow club members:

> My impression of China and the Chinese can be summed up in a very few words. I don't see any future for them. They are about three thousand years behind us and any country that's lagging that far doesn't stand a chance to catch up. They don't seem to understand running a government — too much graft everyone says — and you know that a government to be successful today must have strictly honest men in power. They have lots of trouble with bandits — lots more than we do — why if we shot as many hold-ups as they do out there, I think it wouldn't be long until we could clean them out, but it don't seem to make no difference to the Chinese. That's the whole trouble with 'em. You can't get under their skin. No, as a round the world traveller, I'd say frankly there isn't much hope for China.[39]

While Mr. Benton is edifying his business cronies, Mrs. Smith is entertaining the Thursday Sewing Circle:

> After she [has] displayed the Spanish shawl, the Chinese coat, the cross stitch luncheon sets and her mah-jongg they all [settle] down

170

to munch ginger while Mrs. Smith [gives] a talk on China. "The majority of Chinese live under the most distressful conditions. . . . I can't understand how Americans and foreigners living in Shanghai can close their eyes and their hearts to the misery around them. Hundreds of poor Chinese women spend all their lives in dirty little boats — even their children are born there — and the boats are not any larger than some our boys use for fishing in the summer.

"It was quite cold when I was there and I saw hundreds walking the streets without shoes, and both men and women doing the most terrible kind of work — the kind we have trucks and derricks for — carrying coal and running big wheelbarrows. I really think our trunks were brought to the hotel that way.

"I have worried a great deal over conditions out there, and coming home on the boat I thought out a plan. We could appoint a committee of our most influential women to see the different Chinese governments and get an appropriation of land and money from them. Then we could build a lot of these little modern bungalows they have so many of in the big industrial centers. We might raise enough money here for the bath tubs. Just think how wonderful it would be to take those wretched people out of those filthy boats and give them a decent place to live in."[40]

There is a general murmur of assent for the proposed remedy from the gathering and then someone asks about the foreigners in Shanghai and how they live.

"Mansions, my dears!" exclaims Mrs. Smith, "why nearly every house I saw was as big as the President's home in Washington!"

Although it was an exaggeration to claim that foreigners in Shanghai all lived in mansions, it was true that most of them lived pretty well. Peggy discovered, however, that many young men who had come to Shanghai with high hopes of adventure and dreams of wealth soon became disillusioned. While it had all been so exciting and their salaries had seemed so enormous in the beginning, after a while they found their work just as hard and dull as it had been in London, New York, or Vancouver and the pay, though good, not enough to support luxury and self-indulgence. It was easy for them to get into serious financial trouble with the easy credit (the chit system) extended to foreigners by most Chinese merchants.[41]

Peggy's tendency to see herself as younger than she was, was reflected in a column she wrote for the *Shanghai Times* under the heading "Shanghai Sub-Deb's Letters," with the byline "Norma," probably after Norma Talmadge who was one of her favorite actresses. Using the journalistic device of addressing these "letters" To The Editor, Peggy presented their author as a flighty sixteen-year-old girl from a wealthy family whose other members, especially two sisters, she belittled. Underneath the frivolous comments in these fictitious letters, however, was some pointed social commentary.[42]

Though Peggy found Shanghai life interesting and at times exciting, she did not feel the writing she had done there had added anything to her prestige as a newspaperwoman. Most of her friends from the Border or her Paris days had done better occupationally than she. Indeed, it seemed to her that "nearly all the friends [she] had in those days of Blood and Sand, and Eucalyptus Horsemen, [were] famous. But then," she had concluded, "they were men and that does make a difference."[43]

Furthermore, despite her optimism, after having given her marriage another try, she could see it was still not working out. It was the second time she had "married in haste."

Neither Peggy nor John was the type to "repent at leisure"; once they had decided to part, Peggy was eager to get away from the area. In addition, she was homesick; so she made plans to return to the United States in the company of Mr. and Mrs. Roy W. Howard for an "extended visit." Howard, managing director of the Scripps-Howard Newspapers and the Newspaper Enterprise Association which had sent her to Siberia, proposed that she do some feature stories for the syndicate; and she planned to visit with relatives and with Maj. Gen. and Mrs. Charles G. Morton with whom she had kept up a friendship since their El Paso days, and who had spent time with her and John in Shanghai.[44]

Now, to her horror, she found that it was much more difficult to return to her native land than it had been to leave it.

## CHAPTER TEN

# Peggy Hull Kinley, Alien

When Peggy and John Kinley separated in the fall of 1925 and Peggy decided to return to the United States to become a permanent resident once again, she discovered that she had become a woman without her country. The American consul in Shanghai explained that she had lost her citizenship by her marriage to an Englishman and could only be admitted to the United States as a visitor.[1] Even to do that, "she would have to get letters from three prominent businessmen guaranteeing that she was [returning] to the States only on a visit, would not accept employment of any kind, and that she would stay only six months."[2]

In October she left Shanghai and went to Canada, where she completed the sale of her series of articles on "China and Her People" to the *Montreal Daily Star,* which had carried her work from time to time, beginning with her reports from Siberia. Then she went to see the American consul there to try to straighten out her citizenship problem. To her dismay, he told her the same thing the consul in Shanghai had: She was no longer an American citizen, that as a British subject she could visit the U.S. for a period of a few months at a time, but if she wanted to stay longer, she would have to enter as an immigrant under the British quota which was already filled to 1930.[3]

The problem was the sexually discriminatory expatriation act of March 2, 1907. It legislated that an American woman who married an alien lost her American citizenship. A man, of course, retained his citizenship no matter whom he married or when, unless he took deliberate action to forfeit it. It was true that the 1922 Cable Act (a landmark piece of legislation in that for the first time a government recognized a woman's citizenship as separate from that of her husband) had negated

Peggy Hull with her father, Edwy Goodnough, and her half sisters, Alice and Eleanor Goodnough. *(Courtesy of Alice Goodnough Reissig)*

part of the 1907 law, but in doing so it had created a situation, which, no longer exclusionary, was now selectively discriminatory, for it stated:

> All American women marrying on or after September 22, 1922, shall retain their citizenship, but all American women having married previous to that date shall be classed as subjects or citizens of their husbands' countries and shall be subject to the laws regulating the immigrants from such countries.[4]

and so singled out those who had married before that date. This meant that Peggy, having married Kinley in February 1922, had lost her right to American citizenship and would have to enter the U.S. as a British immigrant, while someone like actress Constance Talmadge, who had married an Englishman only a few months later, retained hers when she was divorced.

So Peggy was faced with the prospect of having either to go back and forth between Canada and the U.S. for the next four or five years or settling permanently in Canada; she feared — at least publicly — that if she stayed in Canada and tried to earn a living there, she would probably starve to death.[5] While that was undoubtedly overstating the result, the inescapable fact was that Peggy was an unabashed AMERICAN and could not imagine being anything else.

Returning to the States (and after a visit with her family in Kansas), she turned to the most potent weapon she knew to fight her battle for her citizenship — the press. In late February 1926, she sent her story to the major newspapers in New York City; it was picked up by the *Boston Evening Transcript,* the *Detroit Free Press,* the *Lincoln* (Neb.) *Journal,* and other newspapers around the country. Under the heading, "Born in Kansas But Must Leave United States by May 1," she called upon "all sane-thinking, logical Americans to put themselves in [her] position," and asked:

> Is it possible to contemplate anything more ridiculous, more obviously untrue, than the assumption that I am no longer an Ameri-

176

can? . . . Is it possible that by the simple use of legal phraseology my natural heritage of generations can be taken from me?[6]

Soon the National Woman's Party, through its publication, *Equal Rights,* took up the cause to have the discriminatory part of the Cable Act repealed. As a result of these pressures, at the end of March 1926, Congress was considering several immigration bills and holding hearings on married women's citizenship; Emma Wold, legislative secretary of the Woman's Party, reported on the bills and hearings in various publications.[7] There was reason to believe that the wrong would soon be put right. However, characteristically, Congress was slow to act.

In addition to carrying on her personal struggle to regain her citizenship, Peggy was doing freelance writing and publicity work. In April she proposed an idea for an article series to Robert E. Sherwood, editor of *Life,* a very popular magazine of humor and satire (no relation to the later picture news magazine). It involved a contest which required readers to pick out historical errors in a series of letters purportedly written by a sixteen-year-old flapper named Joan Kinley traveling abroad and describing, erroneously, what she saw. Some of the boners were to be very obvious, such as "the Eiffel Tower was built during the World War as a defense against air raids,"[8] while others would be more difficult; and a prize of $2,500, the cost of a European tour, would be given to the winner. Sherwood agreed to give it a try, advancing her $1,500 and sending her to Europe, promising that if the volume of entries proved it to be a success, she could try a similar stunt in the United States with a tour of American cities offered as a prize. The contest afforded Peggy a European trip and a rest from her citizenship problems. Her "letters" appeared in *Life* weekly from May 6 to June 24.

After she returned to the States, she resumed her battle with the government, but by October 22, 1926, all she had succeeded in getting was an extension of her temporary admission, granted by the commissioner of the Immigration Service in a letter which authorized her to stay until July 1, 1927. Furthermore, it "requested" that she keep the Immigration Service posted on her movements and ended with "Hoping you have enjoyed your visit to our country, I am," and it was signed by the commissioner.[9]

This last particularly enraged her.

But in the breathing spell provided by this extension, she had to concentrate all her energies on eking out a living, and that was becoming increasingly difficult for her. She still found advertising and publicity work, but with added financial responsibility in regard to her mother, who was now permanently separated from Will Hoerath, Peggy turned to short story writing, hoping that it would prove to be an added source of income. Unhappily, there seemed to be little market now in this country for the type of writing she did best, and her stories were rejected.

Come what might, she was determined not to leave the United States. As the deadline for her departure approached, she threw herself once more into the battle with the Immigration Service. Her first shot in this renewed campaign was a letter to the *Chicago Tribune,* published on June 26, 1927, in the column "Voice of the People," under the title, "No Longer an American." Reminding the paper of her association with the Army Edition during the war, she summarized the history of her alien status and the danger of her being deported, concluding that if this happened,

> it means that I must give up the little foothold I have gained after long absence from the United States, go to a foreign country and try to earn my living while waiting for a quota number. It means that mother who is dependent upon me must shift for herself. While I face poverty and loneliness in another land, hundreds of immigrants will be admitted each month — men and women who know nothing of our traditions, our customs and little of our language. The American government will spend thousands of dollars attempting to teach these people to become good American citizens, while a made to order American is exiled.

Recognizing that she was not pleading her case only, she continued:

> There are hundreds of American women facing this same ruling. Those who have the means can carry their fight to the courts, but for us to whom lawyers' fees are prohibitive, there is nothing we can do but submit.

Of course, Peggy had never been the submitting type, and this time she was just as unsubmitting as ever. When she received a letter informing her that the secretary of labor had denied her application for another extension of her temporary admission to the U.S. and that it would, therefore, be necessary for her "to leave this country on or before Aug. 15, 1927," she told a reporter for the *New York World* that she would not obey the order.

> If I leave this country, they will have to carry me out. . . . I was brought up in the heart of the United States, with the idea that I was living in the greatest country in the world. My people have always been fighters for legislation to secure greater freedom and tolerance and abolish discrimination. Just because I was married

to an Englishman six months before September 22, 1922, I am an alien in my native land, while Constance Talmadge, for example, who married an Englishman after that date, may retain all her rights as an American citizen. Is this Cable Act a law which fosters patriotism?

Can it possibly have any constructive effect upon the country?[10]

In the final analysis, Peggy was not deported. Officials of the Labor Department claimed that the letter she had received which insisted that she must leave on or before August 15 had been a mistake. As Assistant Secretary W. W. Husband observed, no American woman had been deported for this reason, and Peggy was in no danger of being. Further, he said she would automatically be given an extension of her visitor's permit.[11]

Even though Husband wanted to refer to it as simply a "form notice" which had no real meaning, the letter which she had received had said, quite specifically, that she must leave the country on or before August 15. It said nothing about the mere formality of asking for an extension if she chose not to leave.

Maybe Peggy exaggerated the danger of her being deported, as Husband contended. On the other hand, perhaps she counted on her persistence and her use of the press to publicize her case to the point that the embarrassed government would hesitate to enforce the immigration law as it applied to her. As Emma Wold pointed out in a letter to the editor of the *New York World,* August 8, 1927, several district courts had ruled that American-born alien women, who had succeeded in remaining in the U.S. more than a year by the piecemeal extension of their visitors' permits six months at a time, had fulfilled the residence requirement for naturalization. On this basis, she felt Peggy Hull Kinley was in no real danger of being deported. But Peggy believed she had done battle with the bureaucracy and, if she had not won the war, had at least fought them to a standoff.

Whatever the case, now, since she seemed finally free of the threat of deportation, she was ready to turn her attention to some new writing projects, like the American Travel Contest for *Life.* To her chagrin she found that Sherwood had decided to write the letters himself under the name Kay Vernon.[12] She felt she was due an additional fee for her idea if not the execution of it, and the turn the affair had taken surprised and disappointed her.

However, this was not a totally unlucky time for her. Her friend, Irene Kuhn, was now in New York working for the *Daily News;* even more important, Harvey Deuell, whom she had fallen in love with in Denver in 1915, had been moved to his home territory and made city editor of the *Daily News*.[13]

In 1927 they met again.

It was not a minute too soon, for her writing career was not going well. Harvey tried to help her by sending some of her stories to an editor friend of his for criticism and marketing suggestions, but the reply from his friend was not hopeful. He said that one story was in quite good shape, but another needed substantial editing, and it was obvious that in spite of her attempts to make up for her lack of formal education by working on composition on her own, Peggy had problems, especially with punctuation.

She did not see her literary shortcomings as the real source of her difficulty, and cast about for outside causes to blame for her failures. She thought, for instance, that the right pen name might hold the key to success for her, so she tried a variety: Joan Kinley, Eleanor Goodnough, and even Peggy Hull. But her stories were rejected by the magazines she sent them to whatever name she used. She even explored the possibility that some of her stories might be used as plots for motion pictures. These, too, were returned by the agent she had sent them to with the agent's assurance that they were fine, but.

In her frustration, she turned on Robert Sherwood, and in February 1929, sued him and *Life* for $5,000, charging them with the theft of her American travel idea. She found, however, that their verbal contract was not sufficient to protect her interests. Furthermore, Sherwood was no longer the editor. He had been fired for taking a political position in the magazine which had angered the owners. The lawyers for *Life* held that, for one thing, her letters had not been satisfactory, and for another, the magazine had already paid her for the general idea; therefore, she no longer had any claim to it. Peggy maintained that she would not have sold her idea for as little as $1,500.[14] She did not win the suit. This failure, coming at the time she was writing under the name "Kinley," was becoming increasingly attracted to occultism, and was in the frame of mind to believe that there was a-great-deal-in-a-name, made it easy for her to take seriously the warning of a numerologist that she would not have any success as a writer until she dropped the name Kinley forever.[15]

In July her mother died.[16] It was a terrible blow to her. Though the sixty-three-year-old Minnie had not been in good health, her death was unexpected. Peggy had often contributed to her mother's support; of course, she had never made a permanent home for her, and Minnie, separated from Will Hoerath several times, never quite forgave her daughter for this failure. More than once, when Peggy had seemed to be settled in a more or less permanent position, Minnie had felt that Peggy had definitely implied that she would make arrangements for them to live together; whether Peggy had ever really held out this hope or not, it had not worked out. There was always their conflict over the kind of personal life Peggy should lead.[17] Her mother had such definite ideas as to what nice girls did or did not do, and she never hesitated to tell her daughter just how far short of the ideal she considered that Peggy was falling. Not being a masochist, Peggy could not see living her life under constant reproach.

Beyond that, Peggy had always been on the move, had not stayed in one place long enough to make a truly permanent home for anyone, even if she had been inclined to. Even so, she could not help feeling regret at her mother's funeral, for she knew that her mother had not had a very happy or satisfying life, and she felt a little guilty that she had not done more for her.

She also felt awkward about being the sole beneficiary of their mother's small insurance policy. When she broached the subject of Minnie's failure to include Edward as a beneficiary, though he may have felt sensitive about it, her generous-hearted brother told her to think no more about it — to keep the legacy with his blessing.[18] She was grateful to him not only for letting her off the hook psychologically, but also for making it easier for her financially.

She was not one to dwell on regrets in any case. When the funeral was over, it was over, and she returned to New York to pick up her life. She had been living at the Hotel Bretton Hall in The City; now, starting to long for a more normal existence, perhaps even with the idea of proving to Harvey that she was ready to live in a more settled manner, Peggy moved into a cottage on Long Island that had "ruffled curtains on the sun porch and geraniums blooming in the windows" and vegetable and flower gardens. She also acquired two cats, a black one, Lord Kitchener, and a gray, General Grant.[19]

On July 3, 1930, a bill introduced by Rep. John Cable which essayed to correct some of the difficulties of his 1922 immigration bill was passed by Congress and signed into law by President Herbert Hoover. The significant part of the law as far as Peggy's situation was concerned provided that

> the native-born woman who lost her citizenship by marriage to an alien prior to September 22, 1922, may be repatriated by a simple affirmative act in a court of competent jurisdiction; that is, she may go before a naturalization examiner, prove that she has lost her citizenship by marrying an alien, that she is eligible to become a citizen under our naturalization laws, then go into court and take the oath of allegiance. . . . After her naturalization such

181

woman shall have the same citizenship status as if her marriage
. . . had taken place [after September 22, 1922].[20]

Willing to go through this simple "naturalization" procedure to become
a "native-born" citizen again, Peggy wrote to her father for documenta-
tion of her American birth. In October he sent her a notarized statement testifying that she was his daughter and had been born in Kansas,
that her mother had been born in Ohio, and that he, her father, had
been born at Oneida, Wisconsin, and was a descendant of the Drurys
of Massachusetts;[21] Peggy again became in law what she had always
been in fact — a full-fledged American.

In May 1931, due to her reputation as a war correspondent, she was
able to invade another male-dominated field when she took part in the
radio broadcast of a mock air attack on Manhattan Island. She was asked
to describe one of the first German air raids over London in the early
days of World War I and later to serve as one of the eight NBC announ-
cers (the other seven were men) describing the practice air raids on New
York. Among the CBS contingent was Eddie Rickenbacker; Gen.
Douglas MacArthur gave a short introductory speech from Washington.[22]

She found this to be exciting stuff and hoped it might be a stepping
stone to a career in broadcasting. Floyd had managed to get *Literary
Digest* to sponsor a regular radio program called "The Headline Hunter,"
in which he gave his opinions on issues of the day and told of his
experiences as a reporter. Never mind that to a lot of people he was,
as *Time* magazine described him, "garrulous, hysterical, and frequently
absurd."[23] He was a popular hero with a rapid-fire delivery. Sometimes
hitting 245 words a minute, he was advertised as the fastest talker in
broadcasting.

Douglas Gilbert described a typical Gibbons performance in the *New
York Evening Telegram* which was quoted in *Literary Digest*:

> Gibbons breezes in [to the studio at the NBC building], his huge
> bulk a mountain of overcoat, his soft hat pegged at its customary
> cocksure angle. The linen oval patch shielding his left eye-socket
> glistens whiter against a ruddy face. . . . He sucks deeply on a
> cigaret, chest muscles tautening his vest, and exhales. The gray
> cloud blurs a framed sign . . . "No Smoking."
>
> He leans toward the "mike," his torso outspanning the back of
> his chair by six inches on either side. He shoots a quick glance
> over his shoulder at a studio visitor. The full lips of a rugged "ring-
> side" face curl into a friendly smile, foiling the glint of his one
> blue eye.

Floyd Gibbons, about 1930. In June 1918, Gibbons lost his left eye, suffered a concussion, and sustained a flesh wound to his arm at Belleau Wood in the Battle of Chateau Thierry. *(Culver Pictures)*

. . . His hamlike hand moves beyond his reading script for the glorified cigar-box that is the table "mike." Draws it forward, a foot and a half from his face. He looks up toward "Thorgy" [the announcer]. Like a rector intoning a service, Thorgersen's ecclesiastical basso booms the introduction, and then — "Floyd Gibbons." . . .

"Hello, everybody! Prepare for the hottest news of this hottest national issue — Prohibition! I just breezed up from the *Literary Digest* [public opinion poll] counting-rooms, and, boy, it's almost too hot for me to handle. Get a load o' these latest returns from the capital of our national Sahara, Birmingham."[24]

183

It was the kind of performance Peggy would have loved to have been involved in. Of course, she did not begrudge it to Floyd. She and Floyd had always seen journalism and the practice of it in the same way. They were buddies. And she certainly never saw him as absurd. No, she could not begrudge Floyd, but she would have liked to have a program of her own, and she was disappointed when it failed to develop for her. Her disappointment was mitigated somewhat because now there was Harvey.

Peggy had once said to her sister Alice, regarding the men in her life, "They didn't cross my path; I crossed theirs."[25] She was beginning to think her and Harvey's paths might run together now.

Harvey had never married, at least partly because as an only child he still had the responsibility of his mother, and as Peggy had long ago learned, it was a responsibility they both took very seriously. Then, of course, it was also partly that he had been completely career oriented.

From 1927 to 1931 they spent more and more time together, establishing a bond. In all the years since his father's death, Harvey had rarely had a vacation away from his mother or even an evening by himself. Now, as they sat talking until the early hours about the places she had been, the things she had seen, Peggy became his Scheherazade; Harvey, who had spent his life being practical and responsible, yearned to be transported to a more romantic clime. What Peggy did not really understand was that he expected to take the "old clime" along with him.

That was not apparent then. What did seem apparent to both of them was that they had never really gotten over each other, that they had been searching for each other all the years since they had first met. Harvey was coming not only to love her, but to depend on her, for she alone could shore up his flagging self-confidence. No one with whom he worked had ever suspected that Harvey Deuell lacked self-confidence. Those who had tangled with him might even have hooted at the suggestion. Nevertheless, Harvey feared he would never reach the top — managing editor — because he knew *Daily News* owner and publisher, J. M. Patterson, did not like him. Peggy started to work to help Harvey change his behavior toward Patterson, hoping that that would improve his chances for promotion.[26] Enthralled by Peggy, dependent on her, Harvey decided he must be married to her. Peggy was more than willing, but there was a stumbling block: She was still married to John Kinley.

She felt that a quick American divorce would quite adequately free her. Harvey, obsessive about doing things the "proper" way, wanted her to go back to China to get her divorce.[27]

Harvey's mother was still not happy about the prospect of Peggy as a daughter-in-law. She had hoped he would never marry; failing that, her attitude seemed to be that if Harvey felt he absolutely had to get married, the very least he could have done was choose a more "presentable" and socially prominent woman. Peggy was only too well aware of Mrs. Deuell's objections to her and, realizing that she was starting out at a disadvantage, uncomplainingly did as Harvey asked and sailed for Shanghai to divorce her second husband.

*Jan. 29* — In company with other Americans I stood on the roof of the tallest building in the international settlement for three hours watching the planes drop their bombs. With the others I saw the resultant flames destroy hundreds of tenement homes in Chapei, where dwell close to 1,000,000 Chinese laborers. The tenements crumbled like pie crusts and the ruins burst into flames as the terrified Chinese fled into the narrow streets, running in packs like bewildered animals. Thousands huddled in the debris. It was a frightful scene of human misery.

Peggy Hull,
*Chicago Tribune*

# CHAPTER ELEVEN

# "The Battle for Shanghai" by Peggy Hull

Peggy had intended, as soon as she had started the divorce proceedings, to go north to Tsingtao, Tientsin, and Peiping with the stated purpose of gathering material about Chinese women for a series of articles. "The women of the United States are keenly interested in the Oriental woman [*sic*] and have been particularly sympathetic with them in their attitude toward the occupation of Manchuria," she said in an interview in the *China Press*. "American women want to know more about the Chinese woman, about her daily life, about her home, about her thoughts and her ideals." So she had decided, she continued, "to let the men handle all the war correspondence. She [was] interested in peacetime stories."[1]

This was not the first time she had resolved to retire from war reporting. As before, the resolve hardly lasted long enough for her to state it. This time, she had barely gotten unpacked before Japanese forces attacked Shanghai, beginning the latest in a series of conflicts between China and Japan, which had started with the Mukden Incident in Manchuria in September 1931, when the Japanese had begun their campaign of national aggression which eventually led to World War II in Asia. Now, in January 1932, they opened up a second front at Shanghai hoping to divert international attention away from Manchuria. One of their first actions was to bomb Chiang Kai-shek's headquarters at Lunghua, only fifteen miles from the International Settlement.[2] Since the *New York Daily News* was caught with no reporter on the scene, Harvey cabled Peggy: "Go to work; you're our correspondent."[3]

So Peggy went to work. For the first seventy-two hours, she did not sleep; for the next thirty days, she usually slept sitting up in a chair. Often on the brink of exhaustion, she lived on the exhilaration of excitement. Regularly scooping other correspondents because she had found someone with a private shortwave radio, she was usually able to get her stories across the ocean in about twenty minutes, much ahead of most other reporters who had to take turns using the cable. With all the waiting, it sometimes took some of them up to four hours to transmit a story.[4]

As important as having a private wire line was having access to the roof of a tall building, for from such an observation post reporters could see what was happening miles away on the ground and in the air. Peggy and her friend from her Kinley days, Edna Lee (Booker) Potter, discovered and shared a lookout post atop a flour mill. "It was hazardous, but from its vantage point they could watch the progress of the battle through field glasses."[5]

As soon as he could, Harvey sent a reporter to relieve her, but even after "help" arrived, Peggy continued to work feverishly, still writing and sending stories for the Chicago Tribune-New York Daily News Syndicate[6] which appeared in those newspapers as well as others. She had always wanted to be where the action was. Now she was in the thick of it, and instead of reading a script prepared by someone else as she had done for the radio broadcast of the mock attack on Manhattan Island, she was describing a real bombing she had seen only minutes before from the roof of the flour mill or the Cathay Hotel.

On Friday, January 29, she and several other Americans watched the first major assault — the bombing, by Japanese planes, of the working-class Chapei district of Shanghai, a district in which about a million Chinese lived. She wrote:

> The tenements crumbled like pie crusts and the ruins burst into flames as the terrified Chinese fled into the narrow streets, running in packs like bewildered animals. Thousands huddled in the debris. It was a frightful scene of human misery.[7]

The thousands who survived converged on the International Settlement, seeking sanctuary. At first the borders of the Settlement were kept closed, but finally officials relented and opened them, admitting a flood of desperate refugees which swept into the peaceful streets of the Settlement. From then on those streets were their home. Conditions were terrible, but the streets were safe, for the moment anyway, because the Japanese, for obvious reasons, hesitated to attack the International Settlement.

A week later Peggy watched a much closer assault, this one against the North (railroad) Station.

[It] began almost as soon as it was light enough for their ground troops to see. While their naval cannon hammered at the ruin, their bombers rose from their aircraft carriers in the river, and dropped their 100-pound projectiles.

At the same time, other planes took the air, and began the incendiary attack on Pootung. . . .

The reverberations of the bombs shook the windows of the Cathay Hotel.[8]

The correspondents from neutral nations, like Peggy, were in a fortunate position in that they were courted by both sides and permitted to move back and forth between the opposing military forces. As a part of this courting, she was invited to have dinner aboard the *Idzumo,* the flagship of the Japanese fleet, as the guest of Adm. Kichisaburo Nomura. During the evening she was greatly annoyed by Nomura's contention that American men could not fight, a condition that he blamed on American women.

He pretended to admire the vitality of American women, but said American independence weakened American men. He said he felt that the Japanese women were superior to American women because psychologically they gave their vitality to men.[9]

Peggy Hull and Admiral Kichisaburo Nomura aboard his flagship *Idzumo* during the 1932 Shanghai war. Nomura was subsequently Japanese ambassador to the United States at the time of Pearl Harbor. *(Peggy Hull Deuell Collection, Kansas Collection, University of Kansas Libraries)*

However, Nomura presented her with a picture of himself inscribed "To Miss Peggy Hull" and signed "Yours sincerely, K. Nomura, Vice-admiral I.J.N." More important, he gave her a safe-conduct pass,

a piece of unbleached muslin, a square not much larger than [her] hand. In one corner . . . was a red symbol. It was . . . an Oriental design stamped on the cloth. Running down the right side were big black characters. [As he handed it to her, he said,] "If you are ever in danger with the Japanese troops, show this. You are the only foreigner to whom we are giving this type of identification."[10]

A few days later she arranged an interview with the other side in the person of Gen. Tsai Ting-kai, commander of the Chinese Nineteenth Route Army, who had become something of a hero to a lot of Americans because of his "gallant defense of Shanghai."[11]

To get to his headquarters, Peggy hired a car and a driver, Sasha, who was one of the Russians who had fled the Soviets in the early 1920s and had eventually ended up in Shanghai. She had employed him several times before. Since he was a "neutral," too, he was permitted to drive through both Chinese and Japanese lines. Neutral status was a necessity when the battle lines changed as often as they did in the seesaw of war.[12] Of course, fighting did not stop when neutrals got in the way, and from afar a bullet or artillery shell could not tell friend from foe, neutral from partisan. Reporters took their chances if they went into the war zone.

On this day Peggy and Sasha had driven right into the middle of the current war zone. Unaware that at the moment the Chinese were in retreat, they were suddenly caught in heavy cross fire. Abandoning their automobile, they raced for the cover of a mound-shaped Chinese tomb standing in the middle of a field.

As they crouched in the half-light inside the damp, smelly mound listening to the whistling artillery shells, exploding mortars, and crack of rifle fire around them, their one hope was that, as they had dashed toward the tomb, they had not been spotted by the Japanese soldiers they had seen silhouetted against the near horizon. It was, Peggy realized, most likely a vain hope.

Suddenly, the tomb was filled with a terrible sound, a sort of rasping panting, the sound of an animal poised for the kill. The sound was coming from Sasha. Even in the dimness she could see his body trembling almost uncontrollably, his face, a mask of murderous hatred, hatred focused on her for having gotten him into such a situation.

He had been so faithful, available whenever she needed him, driving her to the Japanese and Chinese lines. Until then he had seemed to be totally unafraid. But everyone who knew Sasha knew that terrible things had happened to him in the past, that before he had left Russia, he had been a soldier, that he had been wounded and left for dead on a Russian battlefield, that he had lain for a long time on the cold, silent earth of that battlefield, cold, silent bodies around him, then finally dragged himself many, many miles before he had been rescued by other refugees and brought to China.

It was, perhaps, not so surprising that the terror of the present had triggered the memory of all that past horror, horror so great it was whipping him into a savage frenzy. What an ironic twist it would be, Peggy thought, in the middle of a battlefield with bombers circling overhead, the battle raging so close, to be killed by her own companion and helper.

Instinctively, moving as silently as she could, she reached out and pushed the wooden door of the tomb. It moved enough to admit a shaft of sunlight that fell on Sasha's face and broke the spell, refocusing his attention. In an instant, he scurried like a huge crab on hands and knees to the doorway and through it. Outside he stood up, looked about him, seemingly in a daze, and then burst running out into the field.

Peggy watched fascinated as he ran crazily, not away from, but *toward* the oncoming Japanese soldiers. Suddenly he stumbled, "flung both arms around his body, hugging tightly, and fell face downward in the brown, winter earth."[13] She had hardly been conscious of the shots that killed him.

To that moment, she had thought they had a chance, but it was obvious it had been hopeless all along. Sasha was dead; she as good as, for his death had not disturbed the advancing line of troops. Sasha had been nothing more than a flushed quail to them. They had seen him break cover. They knew that where there had been one, there might be others. On they came, walking carefully toward her hiding place, guns at the ready, hunters stalking game. "As far as [she] could see, the fields were covered with them. Groups of short, stocky, khaki-clad, dark-skinned men bore down, their rifles smoking at exact intervals."[14]

She suddenly realized she did have a chance, a very slim one, supposing, of course, that the Japanese did not direct an artillery barrage at the tomb or riddle it with rifle fire from a distance. She grabbed her purse and clawed through it. "Somewhere in one of the pockets was [a] piece of unbleached muslin, a small square not much larger than [her] hand,"[15] the "safe conduct" Admiral Nomura had given her.

It was not there. Frantically, she dumped the contents of the purse onto the floor and scratched through them. It was not there; she "hadn't put the pass in [her] pocketbook! [She] had left it in [her] desk at the Cathay Hotel!"[16] Her one chance and she had botched it.

On the brink of despair, she leafed through her passport. There it was, folded neatly! She took it out with shaking hands and, believing that when they shot her, the soldiers would aim for her heart, she fastened the little cloth with hairpins over her left breast. But she knew that if, in their first glimpse of her, the Japanese mistook her for a Chinese soldier, she would be dead before they saw it.

Luckily her coat and beret were tan, the Chinese uniform gray, so she was all right there. She felt that if they could instantly see she was a woman that would be another advantage. She fluffed up her hair as much as she could with no comb. Then she crawled out of the tomb and on trembling legs stood up to face her killers. Strangely, she "felt a curious, quieting comradeship with them. They, too, might be about to die; they, too, might be walking in the last moments of their lives."

193

Describing the scene later, she wrote:

> Almost calmly I stepped forward, my arms . . . raised above my head, and I saw both surprise and bewilderment growing in their faces. A young officer, who was a few steps in advance of them, called a broken command. They stopped instantly.
>
> Not more than twenty paces separated us. As the lieutenant moved toward me, his revolver in his hand, I walked out to meet him. I made no effort to speak but with my right hand, I pointed to the muslin identification tag on my coat.
>
> . . . His eyes rested on it. . . . Slowly . . . he bowed toward me, respectfully and obediently. . . .
>
> "You are lost?" he asked. . . .
>
> I replied slowly, trying to control my voice, "I did not mean to come here. I did not know there was fighting."
>
> . . . He spoke kindly. "You are safe. Three of my men will take you to headquarters. General Shirakawa will send you to your hotel."
>
> . . . This was more than I had hoped for or expected. . . . [To] be taken to headquarters and provided with a motor car and escort only equaled my astonishment at the thought of meeting General Shirakawa again. We had last met in Siberia.
>
> When I entered his office two hours later, shaken and unable to conceal the ragged edges of my fright, he thoughtfully recalled our last meeting at an Allied tea party in Vladivostok in 1919. He smiled at me, his brown eyes twinkling in friendliness and relief. "You know," he said softly, "if you do not give up your war corresponding, you are surely going to end your life on a battlefield."[17]

Even though her eventual meeting with General Tsai was something of an anticlimax after what she had been through on her first attempt to interview him, she was favorably impressed with the tall, thin young commander. Later, at a tea party he gave for the war correspondents, the Japanese contributed the "excitement of two attacks from the air."[18] Several years later Tsai gave her a picture of himself, which he assured her was the only one ever given to an American woman. Having learned that she had been the first woman accredited as a war correspondent, he inscribed the picture to "Mister" Peggy Hull, paying her the highest compliment it was possible to pay a woman in Chinese custom of the time.[19]

As "Staff Correspondent of the [Daily] News," Peggy was at her best describing the effect of the war on the people — on the foreigners whose homes were in the International Settlement and, in devastating contrast, on the Chinese people themselves.

## TERROR REIGN PERILS ALIENS IN SHANGHAI

Feb. 1 — Despite the truce and the temporary lull in the fighting, American and British residents of Shanghai were prepared for a reign of terror, approaching the Boxer uprising of 1900.

The Cathay Hotel, one of the most impressive in the Orient, where scores of foreigners reside, was in a state of siege, its shutters up, its massive steel gates closed, following an attack by snipers yesterday. . . .

Japanese are building entrenchments everywhere, and reinforcements for the Chinese Nineteenth Route Army are approaching. Further fighting is almost certain to bring the foreign area under constant artillery fire.

Although sniping in the foreign settlement has been checked, the streets are unsafe for members of any nationality. Yesterday's guerrilla warfare carried bloodshed into a part of Shanghai which corresponds to the 42d St. and Lexington Ave. zone in New York. . . .

Thousands of refugees crowded the streets. A cold rain fell upon them as they huddled, like stray animals, in doorways, alleyways, the lee of buildings, and in any other shelter that offered.

Upon these miserable humans, who had supposed themselves safe at last in the international area, the snipers suddenly turned their fire.

## U.S. CITIZENS ORDERED FROM HOMES IN ZONE

Feb. 2 — Americans and British, moving with strained and frightened faces, joined the tragic parade of Chinese refugees today. The evacuation of their sumptuous colony of homes, bordering the Rubicon Road, beyond the extreme limits of the French concession, has . . . begun. . . .

All residents of the out-lying portions of the foreign zone were ordered to move to the center. . . .

I have been through a number of crises in Shanghai during the last fourteen years, but this is by far the most serious. . . .

Although the fighting between regular troops moved on today, . . . Shanghai has witnessed no abatement of the horrors of war. The victims of the fighting . . . continue to die, miserably and with pathetic lack of medical and surgical attention. . . .

I visited the Buddhist temple on Bubbling Well Road today, which has been converted into a receiving station for the wounded in last Friday's aerial attack. It is a receiving station, and a mortuary, and no more.

It was mercifully dusk under the venerable roof — raised a thousand years ago by a wandering band of Buddha's disciples, who had found the waters of the Bubbling Well sweet.

In the air heavy with smoldering joss and before altars hung with paper streamers in red and gold, descendants of those priests continued the gentle service. . . .

But the floors were covered with ragged refugees, wounded, dying. . . . They lay, some of them, in pools of blood. . . .

Meanwhile, in the central streets of the International Settlement death moved quietly but remorselessly against the thousands of refugees who huddled there. . . .

They died in their tracks, from hunger, exhaustion and fright.

No one who is unfamiliar with the dense populations of the East can conceive the concentration of humanity.

It is impossible to use the side-walks because of the masses of gray-robed, black-trousered women who move aimlessly about, with their children whimpering at their heels.

## GUNS LOOSE CHAOS ANEW IN SHAMBLES OF SHANGHAI

Feb. 3 — Over the stricken Chapei district war rolled again today, sending thousands of miserable adults and a legion of orphaned and homeless children scurrying like frightened rats into whatever shelter offered. . . .

The scene was one of the utmost desolation. The dead from Saturday's aerial bombardment still lay in streets and alleyways amid heaps of shattered masonry. Some wounded are still in these ruins, unable to escape because of the crossfire of snipers that breaks out intermittently everywhere.

They are cut off from food and water and all possible aid.

But tragic as is the plight of the wounded, still more tragic are the orphaned and homeless children who wander like lost dogs just outside the fighting zone. Pitiful scenes are enacted as they plead for someone to find their parents.

A small blind boy had clung to an iron grating since Saturday. He was crying with hunger and terror, when his small hands were loosened, and he was borne to safety. None can guess his mother's fate.

## JAPANESE START BIG PUSH; 7,000 AMERICANS MAY FLEE

Feb. 20 — While every licensed pilot and all merchant ships stood ready in the river for an immediate attempt to evacuate 7,000 Americans and 18,000 other foreigners from Shanghai, the Japanese turned loose a deluge of shell fire and aerial bombs on the Chinese lines, beginning at noon today. . . .

The whole International Settlement is now ringed with a flaming wall, which stretches ten miles from the Nanking-Shanghai Railway on the southern borders of Chapei to Kiangwan, a Chinese concentration point about midway between the settlement's northern border and the Woosung Forts.

The foreigners, in a condition bordering closely on panic, are wondering how long it will be before the wall of gunfire closes in on the central business district, where they have taken refuge.
. . .

As this dispatch is written, all Shanghai seems to be congregated on rooftops — or else to be hanging breathlessly from windows — watching the battle.

## JAPAN'S INFANTRY STORMS SHELL-RIDDLED DEFENSE

Feb. 21 — Preceded by a furious bombardment, which began at dawn, Japanese shock troops hurled themselves early today upon the Chinese main line of defenses at Kiangwan, to which they had penetrated in a night of machine-gun artillery and tank fighting.

Parts of the village itself changed hands several times and this morning it was under intense bombardment both from Japanese batteries in the field and their airplanes overhead.

Simultaneously, the Japanese naval cannon began another battering of the Woosung forts, into the ruins of which the tireless Chinese had dragged field artillery yesterday, [in order] to shell the enemy warships in the river. . . .

Coffins and corpses flew skyward, with sandbags, masonry and broken tile, all in a swirl of brick-red dust. The repercussion of the Japanese aerial bombs rocked me on my feet.

Unburied dead littered the shell-pitted streets of the No Man's Land around the station. Some, oddly, had been placed in rough boxes, as if they were being prepared for burial, when the fighting broke out afresh.

Overhead, Japanese projectiles screamed through the warm, bright sunshine, and landed with cones of flame and deadening reports upon targets.

Three Japanese planes loitered in the sky. Like careful seamstresses, sewing to a line, they dropped their bombs on the rabbit warrens where the Chinese troops huddled. . . .

As night came on, the International Settlement received a new legion of refugees from the Yangtzepoo mill districts, which had been shelled and set afire by the Japanese during one phase of the day's offensive.

In a seemingly endless stream they came trudging along, in the flapping blue cotton trousers and black coats, carrying bundles and babies on their backs, in their arms, and in creaking wheel-barrows and groaning carts.

In vivid contrast to their anguish was the scene that was then being enacted within the ivory marble walls of the Cathay Hotel, just a hundred yards away. Under beautiful murals and amber lights, crowds of foreigners — their fears relieved by the failure of the Chinese artillery to respond to the Japanese attack — drank cocktails, sipped tea, and listened to splendid music.

On March 3, 1932, the fighting stopped. On March 4, Peggy filed her last story for the *Daily News* from Shanghai. But it was not until May 5 that, as a result of international mediation, the Japanese agreed to vacate the occupied area of Shanghai and Woosung.[20]

Later, Peggy wrote:

The Mexican Border was my West Point. . . . the World War my first active duty. . . . a year with the A.E.F. in Siberia was comparable to a minor Colonial campaign but it was China and her . . . wars which made a veteran out of me.[21]

Though it was the most professionally rewarding reporting she had done and she gloried in the comradeship of the other American reporters[22] on the scene — Floyd Gibbons, Edna Lee Booker, Karl H. von Wiegand, and John Goette — personally the experience was painful for her. The suffering of a people she loved and the destruction in a city that had been her home left her heartsick and shaken, and five years later she wrote to Byron Guise, "I still suffer from the noise and terror. . . . A door slamming violently makes me tremble before I have a chance to remember that it isn't a shell or a bomb. I dread the sound of airplanes overhead and do not believe I will ever get over that feeling."[23]

Because of her experiences with the Japanese military in both Siberia and China, Peggy realized early on that they had dreams of expansion and empire. The troops were "orderly and well disciplined." Furthermore, they had seemed "to enjoy the fighting and the excitement and . . . exhibited their military skill like children with new toys," all of which, she knew, did not bode well for the future of the Far East.[24]

The "war" over, Peggy turned her attention to the original purpose of her trip, securing her divorce from John Kinley. She also purchased furniture and decorations, among them a black teakwood, lacquered bed frame, inset with red and gold carved panels, for the home she and Harvey were soon going to have.[25]

*The scenario writer* had the managing editor fall in love with the girl reporter — something which I've never known to happen in all my years of experience. Once in a while the city editor loses his heart to one of his women workers — and there are always lots of romances between the men and girl reporters, but of course that flight of imagination doesn't spoil the film.

Peggy Hull,
*El Paso Morning Times*

# CHAPTER TWELVE

# Eleanor Deuell, Mistress of Saxton Hall

When Peggy returned from Shanghai to New York to marry Harvey, it seemed like the classic movie ending: tall, handsome, husky, masculine Harvey and short, lovely, vivacious, feminine Peggy — hand in hand, forever together right to the glorious end. At least, that was how Peggy saw it.

> At last, aware that after all the barren, unhappy years we had found each other and in each other the fulfillment our hearts had futilely longed for, a rare and ecstatic emotion bound us. Each poured into the other the unseen but eternal force which gives all life new meaning which gave us an assurance of oneness, indivisible even by death. It is as if we always had been together and always would be. The search was over. We never spoke the words lovers usually speak. There were no moments of towering passion (or its polarity), no periods of indifference. What had happened seemed to be that the soul force of two people had met and joined as rivers meet and flow together to the enfoldment of the sea.[1]

They were a perfect match, adored each other, and had everything the world could give besides; for Harvey, now forty-two, had been phenomenally successful as a newspaperman. Having proved himself as a reporter in Denver, he had gone on to Chicago where he had worked first for the *Examiner* as a copy reader and then, in 1919, the *Chicago Tribune* where in three months he had risen from reporter to night city editor and eventually day city editor. When *Liberty Magazine* was launched in 1924 by the publishers of the *Tribune*, Harvey had been first its Chicago editorial chief, and later its editorial director. Then in

Harvey V. Deuell, third husband of Peggy Hull and managing editor of the *New York Daily News*. *(Peggy Hull Deuell Collection, Kansas Collection, University of Kansas Libraries)*

1927 he had been transferred to New York to become city editor of the *Daily News* and a year and a half later had been appointed assistant managing editor.[2]

The *Daily News* was already the most successful tabloid in the country when Harvey Deuell went to work there. It had been started on June 26, 1919, by Col. Robert McCormick, of the *Tribune,* and Capt. Joseph Medill Patterson with the idea that if it did not make money it could be used as a tax write-off.[3]

To build circulation, the *Daily News* conducted contests with money prizes and concentrated on pictures instead of words. "I learned to read from the News," a satisfied customer wrote. "I like them pictures of the beautiful murdered model, and I tear them out of the paper and hang them on the wall."[4] The paper's staples were sensational divorce cases, sex, and murder. Editorially, it might have been accused of hypocrisy or even cynicism, for "it was strong on piety, patriotism, and prurience."[5] "The *Daily News* was built on legs," Patterson admitted, "but when we got enough circulation we draped them."[6] This aggressive pursuit of readers fit right in with Harvey's philosophy of journalism.

One might have thought that anyone so in command of his career, his public life, would be in command of his private life, too. In Harvey's case, nothing could have been further from the truth. Harvey's home was really his mother's home wherever they were. It seemed to Peggy that he had no more freedom from his mother as an adult than he must have had as a child, and as she got to know Mrs. Deuell she understood only too well why Harvey rarely opposed her, for when opposed, "she became a human generator of a poisonous gas with which she filled her surroundings for hours — it was a frightful condition to combat."[7]

Perhaps until he had met Peggy again, Harvey had wanted it that way. His mother had "protected" him, from unwelcome female attention for one thing, and he had a lot of that. His "bondage" had, however, served to make him overaggressive and dictatorial at work, traits that made him successful if not too popular, especially with J. M. Patterson.

Part of the trouble was two strong characters, and part of it was political. Harvey was fairly conservative while J. M. had in his youth been a socialist, albeit a rich one. Harvey was reticent, intellectually calculating, and hard-driving. J. M. was "impulsive, erratic and impatient, unpredictable, a man who act[ed] and work[ed] on hunches."[8] During the thirties Patterson supported President Franklin Roosevelt which meant that the *Daily News* did, too. So with an almost natural animosity between them, Harvey doubted he would ever be given the ultimate prize, promotion to managing editor. Peggy, with her natural ability for dealing with people, worked on Harvey's attitude and on the way he "handled" the situation.[9] It might have been that Patterson, who was a great respecter of ability and hard work, would have promoted the supercompetent Harvey, anyway. But it certainly did not hurt Harvey's chances for him to be presenting a more reasonable, less irritating demeanor when the position opened up.

By the time Harvey had come to it, the *Daily News* was still as sensational as it had always been, but it was less blatant about it than in its earliest days. An aggressive and hardworking editor, he expected his staff to be aggressive and hardworking, too, but he was not all seriousness and drive; he loved gags and "harmless" practical jokes.

Once when a visiting English newspaperman was due to interview him on the problems of editors in the United States, Harvey got hold of a handgun and a blackjack. As the newspaperman entered his office, Harvey "slapped them down" on his desk and said, "You can't get to first base here without those to start with." Then he fed the gullible reporter a story about "the dire plight of American managing editors."[10]

But even though there was a streak of mischievousness in him, basically he was all business. "The popular view of newspaper life — the city editor a center of romance and the reporter living in an enchanted garden of glamor" was, as far as he was concerned, a myth. "It is a plain and logical business."[11]

And Harvey knew this business. While he was assistant managing editor, the *Daily News* dramatically increased its circulation, for it was Harvey's business to know his readers and he did.

"Self," Harvey contended,

is the crux of the news business. . . .
    You — the reader — are the hero of every news story you read; your words come from the mouths of presidents; you fight the wars of which you read — you are in business, in love, in trouble; . . . If you aren't in this story, it's no good and you won't read it.[12]

This was his basic article of journalistic faith.

He claimed to be opposed to sensationalism, but he advocated what he called "dramatization" of the news, hairsplitting at its finest. His paper was the leading tabloid, and he used all his ingenuity to keep it the leading tabloid. In one notorious instance, a *Daily News* photographer got a picture of murderess Ruth Snyder as she sat strapped in the electric chair at Sing Sing prison. Reporters were forbidden to take cameras with them when they were permitted to watch executions, but Harvey showed the *News* photographer how to get a picture, in circumvention of the rules, using a small camera strapped to his leg.[13]

This was a dramatic example of Harvey's reasoning: that the balance sheet was the arbiter of journalistic morality. To photograph an executed murderer was moral if it increased circulation.

At the same time, it seemed that to participate in setting up a powerful and pompous general for the fun of it was tacky, and Harvey disapproved. For a long time, Peggy had been squeamish about her part in that "Pershing episode," remembering how furious Pershing had been with her as a result of her part in it. Now, because of Harvey's disapprobation, she actively recanted. Later she even came to believe that she had been the victim of the prank instead of one of the perpetrators.[14]

That was not all.

Harvey spent his working time with other newspaper people, but he did not care to spend his leisure time with them; thus, Peggy's new life would have little place in it for her "old" newspaper friends. In fact, she was not even going to be "Peggy" anymore. "Eleanor" was to be her "new" name. Of course it was her actual middle name, but she had rarely used it. The child had been Henrietta, the war correspondent had been Peggy, and now the wife of Harvey Deuell was to be Eleanor; that was what she was now called — at least by Harvey, Harvey's mother, and Harvey's friends.

The transition did not go smoothly from the first.

Knowing that his mother would never approve his marrying Peggy, Harvey persuaded her to take an extended trip to visit relatives. While Mrs. Deuell was gone, they were quietly married. When Mrs. Deuell returned to find her greatest fear a fait accompli, she insisted that they at least have another, proper ceremony.[15] In this remarriage in Brooklyn on June 17, 1933, Peggy used the name "Henrietta" even though the wedding announcement called her "Eleanor." And Eleanor did seem a fitting name for the mistress of what she had named "Saxton Hall" after her paternal grandmother, Ellen Saxton Goodnough.

They had found Saxton Hall, a fourteen-room, pillared mansion, at Cornwall-on-Hudson, a village fifty-six miles north of New York City. Dominated by Storm King Mountain, Cornwall-on-Hudson was only five miles from West Point, a situation that came to be more and more important to her. In February 1933, Harvey purchased the house (built in 1840) along with its ten acres which included a little spring-fed lake, a cook house, a garage, an eight-room "gatehouse" and a small artist's studio-tool shed.[16] He hired local contractor David Taylor to supervise the redecorating and modernizing of the Hall (including the installation of a central heating system) before they moved in.[17] This renovation was a major undertaking and involved some work on almost every room, including three maid's rooms and an observation cupola which

Saxton Hall, the home of Harvey and Eleanor (Peggy Hull) Deuell in Cornwall-on-Hudson, New York. *(Peggy Hull Deuell Collection, Kansas Collection, University of Kansas Libraries)*

sat atop the house. When it was finished, it was a home they could be proud of.[18]

The grounds were as impressive as the mansion. All around the Hall spread lush lawns from which rose giant trees: beech, oak, pine, hemlock, ash, catalpa, and fruit. Lilacs and dogwood abounded; wisteria, clematis, and trumpet vines grew in controlled profusion. But Saxton Hall was the jewel in its picturesque environment. Situated on a slope, it afforded a view of The River. Its access street was Duncan Avenue, to which ran a front drive and a rear road, each with its own gate.

Harvey, tired of apartment living, was delighted with the prospect of this home in such a placid hamlet so far from The City, a place where he could take refuge on the weekends and relax in solitude far from his hectic newspaper office, be with just his wife — and mother, for rooms had been planned and decorated for Mrs. Deuell so she could be with them.

Believing she was ready now to be Eleanor and live a "normal" life, Peggy was delighted to have a house large enough to accommodate

206

furniture like the exotic bed she had brought back from China. For the first time in her life, she had a place where she could have as many dogs and cats as she wanted and be free from worry about them when she was not there because the hired help could always be counted on to look after them.

Mother Deuell did not like Eleanor's pets; though fortunately she was not at Saxton Hall all the time since she traveled and visited a lot, when she was there, the pets were a source of conflict, one of many between them.[19]

Harvey did not expect marriage to change his way of life during the working week; therefore, in New York he rented a penthouse apartment for them near the *Daily News*.

At first, Eleanor enjoyed her new life immensely. For the first time in her life, she had no financial worries, no job pressures, and she had someone eager to indulge her and able to take care of her in a manner quite different from the one to which she was accustomed. She loved the idea of being able to go to any store in New York and buy anything she wanted — expensive clothes, furnishings for their home, whatever struck her fancy. On weekends, when they went out to their beautiful luxurious home on the Hudson, she could play the lady of the manor, presiding over her household, giving elaborate dinner parties with the help of Tei, their Japanese cook and gardener.[20] A good cook herself, she loved to eat well, drink well, and entertain. The reclusively-inclined Harvey indulged her in her entertaining in the beginning; there were times when, to acquaintances, they seemed almost like a sedate, long-married English couple.[21]

But when the new wore off, she found it not so much fun. Although he preferred to have his wife wherever he was, Harvey realized that it was sometimes a dull life for her during the week since he worked at night and slept in the daytime. So he did not object when Eleanor started returning to Saxton Hall in the middle of the week instead of waiting to go when he went on the weekend.

Trying very hard to be the kind of wife he wanted, she worked to have things the way he liked them and to be prepared on the weekends to do the kinds of things he liked to do for relaxation,[22] but it was not easy for her. Although they were soul mates in a way, and they had worked for years in the same profession, they were, of course, very different. This difference had had a lot to do with their attraction for each other, but it was also the source of a lot of their problems.

Everyone could see she adored Harvey. Her kin had remarked that, with her other husbands, you would hardly have guessed she was married from reading her letters. She wrote to them about Harvey, some thought rather too much. If it was obvious that she adored him, it was equally apparent that Harvey loved her. She was the only woman he had ever overruled his mother for. His mother never let him forget it, and for the first three years of their married life, Mother Deuell made life extremely unpleasant for them.[23] Not unrelated, soon after she started staying through the week at Saxton Hall, Eleanor started drinking; because she had a low physical tolerance for alcohol, a moderate amount affected her noticeably.[24]

Never an alcoholic, she had always been a social drinker who could turn even that off when it was in her interest. Her drinking now was a cry for help, a two-by-four with which she tried to get Harvey's undivided attention. He was, tragically, incapable of responding in the way she needed. The problem was that once he had married her, Harvey expected her to be content with just being his wife and to give up the very kinds of activity and behavior which had so attracted him to her in the first place.[25] He could not see that if their marriage was to work, he was going to have to change himself and his life, too.

For her part, Eleanor, though she looked up to him, even idolized him, and did try, found it very hard to remake herself into the kind of person he apparently wanted her to be.[26] She had been a newspaperwoman all her life. Her best friends were newspapermen and women, and she wanted to keep up her contacts with them. But Harvey seemed to disdain people in his profession.[27] Brought up to have a very strong sense of "propriety," he felt that most newspaper people were likely to go to extremes of bad taste — talking too much and too loudly and drinking too much. Harvey was a very temperate man. His wife was not a temperate woman.

Because she wanted so much to please him even though she was not ready to give up her newspaper friends, she arranged their visits to Saxton Hall for weekdays when Harvey was in New York.[28] She also invited "locals" for dinner or for the evening, just to have a little convivial companionship.[29] Then when Harvey was due, all her guests gone, she rushed around getting things the way he liked them: a quiet relaxed atmosphere, meals on time and at regular hours so that he had plenty of time to spend at his hobbies.

Five months after they had been married, Eleanor had a severe gall bladder attack. She was not hospitalized, but she needed personal care, so her doctor arranged for a private nurse, Christine Cummings.[30] Nurse Cummings had just graduated from training. It was her first job, and it lasted a month.

Taking care of a rich woman in a mansion was an impressive beginning to her career, and she was impressed. In some ways it was easy — the principal "medical" task was fixing food and taking it on a tray to the bedroom to which her patient was confined most of the time.

208

In addition, she picked and arranged flowers and helped Tei around the house. Since Harvey stayed in New York City most nights, her main job was to be there in case Eleanor needed her. When he did come home, Nurse Cummings was expected to join him in the dining room for supper. Each sitting at an end of the long table, they were served by the faithful Tei and ate most of the time in silence. After supper Harvey went up to his wife's room where he spent the rest of the evening.

Pleased when Harvey was expected home, Eleanor was excited when Floyd phoned he was coming. "Open the front gate; put on the light; and get everything ready for him," she ordered, obviously feeling better at the mere prospect of his coming.[31] It was always old home week when Floyd was there. Floyd had such energy, such élan, seemed so alive, was so full of fun and stories. But then, he was still working, while Eleanor could not seem to fill her days with anything very satisfying.

Harvey, on the other hand, had a number of serious hobbies, some personal and some aimed at improving his newspaper work. He loved music and had a large record collection. His hi-fi was the latest model and expensive. He often played records for their guests and was obviously irritated that Eleanor could not seem to just sit quietly and listen to his records, but often talked over the music. He had a great interest in radio and photography as they related to news and became a skilled amateur photographer, constantly taking stills of the grounds at Saxton Hall and home movies of anyone he could talk into performing for him.[32]

The Deuells' close neighbors, George and Eleanor Moore, who ran a printing business, were Harvey's closest friends in Cornwall-on-Hudson; the couples spent a lot of time together. Moore, too, was a home movie enthusiast, and the two men loved playing moviemaker, "directing" their wives and any other people who happened to be around like Hollywood directors working with famous stars.

From the Moores, Harvey picked up another enthusiasm: printing. He first tried his hand at it when Eleanor Moore urged him to let her help him set up and print his and his wife's Christmas cards. Before long he was so involved in printing that he bought an old press of his own and set up a little shop in the corner of the garage. He was very serious about it all, a perfectionist, even at his hobbies. Since George Moore was the same kind of person, the men got along wonderfully well.

The only similarity between their wives was that they were both called Eleanor. George's wife, who had worked for years with him in the printing business, made a point of involving herself in all her husband's interests; Harvey's wife did not find the process of printing or the taking of pictures for picture-taking's sake interesting enough hobbies to

take them up for her own, though she was a little jealous of the camaraderie these pastimes engendered between him and the Moores.[33]

Harvey was determined that his wife would have a hobby, too, convinced that it would solve some of her problems; when he pressured
her, she finally turned to needlework for which she had a basic talent,
improved upon during her years in China, and for a time she "embroi-
dered like mad." Harvey was so pleased at the domesticity inherent in
this activity that he fitted up a sewing room with cabinets to hold different kinds and colors of thread and fabric, and when they went to
England, he bought her one of every color of thread that the Farber
company manufactured.[34]

In the late 1920s when everyone else had seemed to be getting rich,
things had been very tight for her financially. Now, with the country
in such an economic mess, she lived in comparative luxury. In her mind
she knew how lucky she was not to have to rustle up some kind, any
kind, of job, as she had so often had to in the old days. It had gotten
harder for her as she had gotten older to get the kind of job she wanted,
perhaps because she was a little less intrepid than she had once been.
However, money, as such, had never been terribly important to her.
When she had little, she made do; when she had a lot, she spent it freely
on herself and everybody else.

Generosity was a trait she and Harvey had in common. Eleanor, with
her feeling for people, was direct in her giving; when she knew of anyone in the town who was having a hard time she opened her pocketbook to them. Harvey, though his giving was done through organizations
instead of in person, was as openhanded to those in real need as she.[35]
In addition to her public giving, Eleanor took a special pride in being
able to continue to send gifts to her Kansas relatives. It was fun for her
to give things to the people she cared about, and she cared about almost
everyone.

These days, when she traveled, instead of boarding a roach-infested
freighter, she could go first class on a passenger ship, which she did in
the spring of 1934 when she and Harvey went to Cuba and Central and
South America.[36]

In October of that year, when she finally had a much-needed gall bladder operation, she could afford the best of care from the best doctors
in the best hospital.

As the wife of the assistant managing editor of the *Daily News* as
well as that paper's former staff correspondent during the battle for
Shanghai, she found herself in the company of rich and powerful people like Patterson, McCormick, W. W. Hawkins, general manager of
Scripps-Howard newspaper syndicate, Cissy Patterson, and Mrs. William Randolph Hearst and was invited to luncheons for notables like

her old China acquaintance, Gen. Tsai Ting-kai.[37] What pleased her most was that Floyd was sometimes at these functions, too.

Now she could afford to hire secretarial help when she started to work again on her book dealing with her experiences as a war correspondent. Many of her newspaper friends were writing about their experiences and getting books published. Her experiences had been just as thrilling as theirs, and especially since she *had* been the first woman to be an accredited war correspondent, it seemed only logical to her that there should be a market for *her* book. Although in general Harvey wanted her to forget about her life before their marriage, he did not seem to mind her working on the book if it kept her occupied and happy and did not interfere with their time together. She hired a young woman from the village, Desirée (Teddy) Hahn, to come to Saxton Hall to type her manuscript as she wrote and rewrote "Beyond This Post."[38]

Quite suddenly, on July 1, 1935, Harvey became managing editor of the *Daily News.* They had been staying in town. That evening when he came back to their apartment, he said to his wife, " 'Well, you were right. Mr. Patterson fired [Frank] Hause today. And I'm the new managing editor.' It was a . . . dizzy experience. Harvey had gone to his office in the afternoon getting $35,000 a year. He came home that evening with a salary and bonus of $145,000."[39]

Harvey's promotion did not change their life style very much. They already had a "good" car, a Cadillac coupé, and Eleanor did not have any interest in the de rigueur mink coat. They did indulge in one extravagance, a boat. Harvey had always pined for a boat, but since his mother had discouraged him from taking part in water activities for fear something might happen to him, it had been his great unfulfilled dream.

Harvey's wife was determined to see that he got what his mother had always denied him, and when the boat show opened that year, Eleanor put a provisional purchase order on the most expensive boat on the floor. She knew Harvey well enough to know that if he wanted it, he would never initiate dealings for anything so expensive that was so "unnecessary," but she also hoped that if she could get his boat fever up, he would at least settle on a small model. When she told him what she had done, he could not conceal his excitement. With her urging him on, he finally picked out a modest-sized Cris-craft cabin cruiser and made arrangements to keep it docked at the Cornwall Yacht Club marina.

On his yacht, Harvey was like a child with a new toy. He and Eleanor packed picnic lunches and cruised up and down the Hudson alone or with friends like the Moores, and he even "drove" it to work occasionally. For his wife, "to see him running his boat was something rare and wonderful."[40]

Now that he was finally at the top, it should have meant that he would have much more time to spend with his wife. But it did not seem to work that way. Instead, it meant more responsibility, more pressure, more time spent on the job instead of less; when he returned from his office, it was either too late or he was too tired for them to do much socially, even if he had been so inclined.

So the beautiful clothes which she had bought were rarely taken off their hangers, and the time she spent in New York became less and less, and the time she spent at Saxton Hall, even when Mother Deuell was there, more and more. Of course, Eleanor and her mother-in-law made it a point to stay out of each other's way. Harvey and Eleanor did have dinner guests, and Harvey liked that as long as the parties involved just the Moores or a few of his other friends.

Her newspaper friends like Floyd usually came to stay only when Harvey was in town, but since most of them were still working, their visits were neither frequent nor long. Sometimes their visits, emphasizing as they did the fact that Eleanor no longer had the freedom she had enjoyed as an independent, self-supporting newspaperwoman, far from picking her up, actively depressed her.[41]

She spent many days at Saxton Hall with Tei, trying to keep busy — and drinking. Those around her knew she drank; it was obvious. Harvey encouraged the help to keep her busy and sober. This responsibility fell especially heavily on Tei who did his best.[42] Since Eleanor, "Missy" he called her, was a very good cook, liked to cook and try new dishes, he taught her Japanese cooking.[43] He also tried to get her involved in the art of gardening, especially rose gardening. Spending so much time with Tei, she became more than fond of him and somewhat psychologically dependent on him. Even so, his influence on her was not strong enough to stop her drinking. All he could do was try to keep her busy.

Under his tutelage she did develop an interest in rose gardening, but it was not a pure pleasure for her, for she was terrified of the bees that loved the roses, too. She once observed to Teddy, now her friend as well as typist, "I've been through all the wars in history and all kinds of guns and ammo, but I can't stand a bee!"[44]

Many days she walked to the post office or to the little store in the village just to find somebody different to talk to. But she found that making friends in the village was not easy. She was isolated by the poorer villagers, who felt there was no future for them socially with people like the Deuells, and the local "patricians," who found it hard to accept any newcomers. Harvey, with his antisocial bent, welcomed their neglect. Eleanor just could not win; she was dismayed by it and desperately lonely.[45]

As provincial as some of its inhabitants were, Cornwall-on-Hudson itself was insular, for though it is verdant and lovely for part of the year, the "long winter months, when Storm King towers bleak and cold above the town and the north wind sweeping off The Hudson cuts and penetrates like a sharp sword,"[46] are damp and bitter. It is beautiful with a kind of beauty which, unless one is used to it, is often hard to live with. The highway, running south past West Point and on toward The City, bends and climbs and descends and, laid over with a glaze of ice or shrouded in fog, is treacherous. Especially when winter holds the village captive, even if for only a day or two, a person used to hordes of people, freedom of movement, and feverish activity might come to feel that it is not so much a haven as a prison, and Peggy Hull/Eleanor Deuell did.

Eleanor Deuell (Peggy Hull) at Saxton Hall. *(Courtesy of Josephine Goodnough Yakich)*

The physical isolation was temporary; the social isolation was not, for as well as "common," she was perceived by some locals to be eccentric. She dressed peculiarly. She wore Russian hats before they were fashionable and slacks before most "nice" women did.[47] She allowed washing to be done and hung out of doors on Sunday. She even did it herself! And, especially horrifying, she was into astrology.

No wonder she found it so easy to believe in. How could she have been anything but a Capricorn, ambitious, undemonstrative, persevering, often down but never completely out. Capricorns could overcome any obstacle by persistence, patience, and single-mindedness, and she had certainly done that. In addition, the secretive, forceful, dignified, shrewd, critical, competitive Harvey, with his love for the water, was definitely a Scorpio. Obviously, one just could not quarrel with astrology.[48]

Filling some of her empty hours with a renewed interest, she had horoscopes worked up for herself, for almost all of her relatives, and for most of her friends. The sheer volume of her astrological mail was a favorite topic of conversation around the town.[49]

But horoscopes and embroidery were no substitutes for the work she loved, the frenetic life she still hungered for. Whenever anything exciting was happening out in The World, she became restless because she was not a part of it. She had lived with excitement for most of her first forty-three years. Uncertainty, political ferment, being around all kinds and conditions of people, this was what life was to her, not day after day, week after week, month after month of the humdrum. Luxury made no difference. She had turned into the wild bird in the gilded cage. She even saw herself that way and clipped a piece which struck this chord out of a newspaper and pasted it in one of her scrapbooks. The piece went:

> Women are not by nature domestic. They do not belong in their homes any more than birds belong in the cages where they have been imprisoned. They are there for the same reason — caught and put in and trained to service some thousands of years ago by men who chose them singly for this purpose. . . . Women have been trained merely to do what is to be done, whichever way they are told to do it.
>
> . . . I do not know if men are to be praised or blamed for this situation. . . .
>
> But I say we, the women, are not what we were made to be. We are merely the trained automatons of an order of things we did not invent.[50]

At first Harvey, caught up in the demands of his job, had not realized what was happening. But small towns being what they are and Cornwall-on-Hudson being no different from any other, it was not long before he started getting reports of her drinking. There was the lonely evening she asked a group of local young people if she could go with them to a dance at a club on Bear Mountain.

She was, they thought, quite stunning in a long emerald green velvet gown. It surprised them because when they had seen her before, she had always been dressed plainly. For Eleanor, with a closet full of lovely

214

gowns, gowns she had thought she would be able to wear when she and Harvey went out together for an evening, it was one of the few times she had an excuse to really dress up in one. During the evening she drank too much; her companions, afraid Harvey (as well as their parents) would be furious with them for taking her in the first place, spent most of the night after they left the club walking her around, trying to sober her up. When he found out about it, which, of course, he was bound to, the humiliated Harvey could do nothing but thank the young people for taking care of her.[51]

Unhappy himself and concerned about her unhappiness, he finally arranged time off for a trip to California as a rest for him and a change of scene and routine for her.

The trip, however, only served to exacerbate their problems. Hearing that they were coming west, William Randolph Hearst invited them for a weekend at San Simeon. Viewing it as the chance of a lifetime, Eleanor was wild to go, but Harvey declined the invitation for them, indicating to her that the reason they were not going was that he did not want her to be exposed to the contaminating influence of Marion Davies, the movie star living there with Hearst. His decision was probably more political than puritanical, since Hearst's wife was a protected member of the Patterson-McCormick circle.

Whatever the reason, Eleanor knew it would have been an exotic, exciting experience. San Simeon was a place of storied opulence, an invitation to be a guest there was a prize, and Harvey had deprived them of it. Eleanor, usually even-tempered, was furious with him.[52]

She did not stay angry with him for long, and when they returned from California, Harvey persuaded her to start again going into New York to stay with him at their apartment at Woodstock Tower during the week, working on her book, going out together to Saxton Hall on weekends. Since he had taken several of her first chapters to a publisher who had shown interest in seeing the whole thing, she worked feverishly to finish her manuscript to meet a deadline of September 1, 1937.[53] Although she realized that Harvey did not like her using "Peggy Hull," she continued to use it literarily because, she said, it was easy to remember. What else could she have used as her nom de plume? The book was about Peggy Hull, not Eleanor Deuell.

With both of them working at it, their marriage did now seem to be going better. Eleanor, who had always had a struggle to keep her weight down, tried watermelon diets and banana diets and finally even signed up for the Elizabeth Arden program, thinking it would please Harvey if she lost some weight. She did succeed in getting down to a size fourteen and bought a whole new wardrobe for her new figure, but in six months she had gained the weight all back again; so she gave away the beautiful clothes she had now outgrown and bought new ones. In fact, it appeared that Harvey did not really care if she was plump. He seemed quite happy with her physically, however that was.[54]

In October Floyd, who was slowing down considerably because his health was deteriorating rapidly, bought a farm near Stroudsburg, Pennsylvania, less than a hundred miles away; though they did not see each other much oftener than they had before, Eleanor found it reassuring to know he was close by.

Just when Eleanor thought things in her life were going so much better, Tei, another of her emotional bulwarks, died. His death left a hole in her life and set back her progress at getting herself straightened out.

To take up Tei's duties, the Deuells hired help from the village, including seventeen-year-old Hilda Connolly.

Hilda and Eleanor took to each other from the start. Hilda adored her and called her "Missy" as Tei had done. Eleanor called her "Little One." Hilda's duties encompassed general house work, except cooking which was left strictly to the cook. Used to the sharp class distinctions of the village, Hilda was captivated by the vivacious personality who did not draw a line between herself and her help. Eleanor asked nothing of others she would not do herself, and more than once when the regular housekeeper got behind in her work, Eleanor and Hilda set up two ironing boards in the sewing room and ironed curtains and then hung them. Eleanor taught her to embroider, and they would sit for hours working together on one of the huge company table cloths to be used on the long table in the dining room.

Sometimes Eleanor took Hilda with her on short trips. In fact, she treated the younger woman much as she would have treated a daughter. She taught her to cut out a pattern and sew up a garment on the sewing machine; when the snow was deep, they had a wonderful time, the seventeen-year-old Hilda and the forty-seven-year-old Eleanor, sliding down the hill on the six-foot Flexible Flyer Eleanor had bought.

Indeed, Hilda was having the time of her life. She was meeting the romantic newspaper people who came out to visit their old friend "Peggy." When Harvey was there, she was sometimes a reluctant performer in his home movies. Later, when he had processed them, he would run the films for her, and they would laugh at her bashful antics.

Usually Hilda found him agreeable company — good-humored, laughing, quite approachable. At other times he was aloof and moody. But he was unfailingly fair to all who worked at Saxton Hall; he seemed, on the whole, much less forbidding than his mother who, though she had been "removed to Kew Gardens, L.I.," the year before, showed up periodically for lengthy and unsettling visits. Hilda thought Mother

Deuell looked like the Queen Mother (Mary) of England and acted as if she thought she were.

During these extended visits, Hilda was impressed with Eleanor's patience and refusal to publicly let Harvey's mother provoke her. She even laughed to Hilda about Mother Deuell's arrogance, suggesting they just try to ignore it, saying that Harvey's mother was just a Tory, as if that explained everything.[55]

Harvey, finally recognizing that their troubles were partly his responsibility, was now taking time off from his work just to be with Eleanor. This was not easy for him. As "Peggy's" had been hers, his work had been his life for as long as he could remember. But now he knew his work was not everything to him. No matter how serious his and Eleanor's problems were, the central fact was that he loved her, and he was willing to do anything he could to keep her, short, of course, of making himself over. That was the real problem: One of them had to change their basic nature. It was turning out to be Eleanor. Unintentionally, Harvey was, as Wilde had put it, "killing the thing he loved."

Eleanor desperately needed a triumph of her own. If she had had it, it might have eased some of the awful, self-imposed pressure she was under. Just when she had begun to think that her book was going to be published, she received a letter from Scribners in November 1938, rejecting the manuscript on the grounds that it was not sufficiently different from other books they had published. This may have been the truth. However, the reason for its rejection may have been more serious. So effective in describing events as they were happening, she seemed unable to bring color and immediacy to them after the fact. One of her friends who read the manuscript said that its style was pedestrian and the book as a whole, unexciting.

Dejected, Eleanor concluded that "the Fates [were] determined that [she should] remain in oblivion."[56] Her article of faith had always been that "intelligence, sincerity, a certain amount of humility, and determination" would lead to success "in spite of all obstacles."[57] Whatever the time, whatever the problems, she had believed that everyone could get whatever they really wanted if they just tried hard enough. She had been living proof of it.

This time she did not persevere, for this time she did not want it quite enough. That, apparently, was Harvey's fault. Some close to the situation thought his "help" had been halfhearted at best and that deep down he was not displeased by the book's setbacks.[58]

When anyone tried to describe Harvey, the one word they always came back to was "private," a very *private* man. He detested publicity, fearing that people might try to use his wife or any scandal connected with her to "get at" him. So if her book were published and became the success she hoped it would, he knew their private lives, not only present but also past, would become public. That was something he could not tolerate.

On a few occasions Harvey did accept an invitation. One of these occasions was a party at the Pattersons'. Eleanor was so excited she had bought a dress especially for that evening. It had a white jacket with a band across the chest to which she pinned her correspondent's insignia and colorful campaign ribbons, proud of them and what they represented. But when Harvey saw it, he was appalled. To display this gaudy regalia was downright déclassé. He himself cared nothing for acclaim or awards. If you were the best, you knew it and so did everyone else. And he was the best. That's why his *base* income was $140,000 a year at a time that $140,000 was a fortune. To his mind you did not *show,* you *were,* and he considered such an exhibit of his wife's "military decorations" to be at least ostentatious and at most monumental bad taste.

Eleanor was terribly hurt, and they had a bitter exchange about it. In the end they did not go to the party.[59]

As upset as she was at his attitude, as usual she tried to resign herself to it. But once again Harvey had managed to make her ashamed of what she had always been so proud of.

In the winter of 1938-39 Harvey came down with a serious case of influenza.[60] Though he finally got over the worst of it, it left him weak and shaken; in the wake of it, he began to think seriously about retiring.[61] He was only forty-eight, but they had plenty of money and good investments. If he retired, he would have time and energy to concentrate on making their marriage the success they both wanted it to be.

In January 1939 they took a Mediterranean cruise, hoping that the sun and sea air would help him regain his strength.[62] When they returned, he worked at getting his financial affairs in order for, as he told her Aunt Ella Haley, visiting them at Saxton Hall, he had concluded that Eleanor would never learn the value of a dollar. Her tendency to spend so freely not just on herself but on others caused him to fear that if anything happened to him, she would soon be destitute.[63] He knew what a soft touch she was and how hard it was for her to turn down anyone who asked for anything. So he had already provided for her security by setting up numerous trust funds through insurance companies. He had also made provision for his mother in case she survived him.[64] It was as if he had a premonition.

Also, in 1939 the Overseas Press Club was organized, and "Peggy Hull" was a founding member. She looked forward to the regular Wednesday luncheons in New York when she could get together with Webb, Hallett

Abend, and Floyd and reminisce about the big stories they had covered.[65] Harvey did not object to her going to the meetings.

In July Eleanor's niece, Eldora Goodnough, whom she had helped financially to get through nurse's training, visited them. It was the summer of the New York World's Fair, and they went to the Fair and into The City to shop, on a tour of Rockefeller Center, to an art gallery, and finally to dinner at the Waldorf. Eldora was overwhelmed by it all: by the famous Waldorf itself, by her aunt's knowing orchestra leader Ben Bernie, by the experience of eating her first raw oysters. For his part Harvey willingly entertained Eldora and took them for cruises in the yacht on the Hudson down past West Point, played records of classical music for her, and explained operas to her late into the night.[66]

Eleanor had hoped that Eldora would decide to settle in New York somewhere near Cornwall-on-Hudson, but Eldora was engaged to John Verburg, a Kansan; when John came after her at the end of the summer, she went home with him.

Harvey and Eleanor planned to take another trip in the fall, this time to Europe. It would be in part another "rest tour" for Harvey. But when war broke out in Europe in September, they postponed the trip. Harvey could not leave the paper in other hands at such a critical time.[67] The vacation was rescheduled for November, and they were making big plans for it.

However, late in September she suffered an emotional blow when Floyd died of heart trouble at his farm at the age of fifty-two.[68] He had had such a life force; it had run out so soon. Now the old days were really over for her.

But she had Harvey and a lifetime of peace and security and love ahead of her. Or so it seemed. Harvey, however, had suffered more ill effects from the flu than anyone had realized and had worked too hard afterward. On October 29, 1939,

> Harvey V. Deuell, managing editor of The News, was fatally stricken with a heart attack shortly after 3 p.m. . . . on Route 4 in Teaneck, N. J., while driving to The News office. His heavy coupe, out of control, smashed into a cable fence, ripped up six metal posts and ran down a 10-foot embankment before it stopped without overturning.
>
> By striking coincidence, the first to reach Deuell as he lay trapped were two employees of The News — photoengravers also driving into New York City.
>
> The men, Richard Bozian and Warren Peters, leaped from their car into the six-foot wide ditch to aid the imprisoned driver.

They found that the car had ploughed along the ditch for about 200 yards. Deuell, inert in the driver's seat, was gasping for breath, unconscious. The motor was idling and the car was undamaged.
. . .

Deuell was dead when he arrived at the hospital. . . .
[He] would have been 49 on Nov. 20.[69]

The description of his end, in its attention to graphic detail, epitomized the *Daily News* style.

The great and near great trooped to the funeral (conducted by the Reverend W. A. Burner, Presbyterian minister in Cornwall-on-Hudson) in Campbell's Funeral Chapel on Madison Avenue and to the final rites at Saxton Hall and burial in Woodlawn Cemetery in New Windsor. Mayor Fiorello La Guardia, who called himself Harvey's personal friend, and J.M. Patterson were among the honorary pallbearers. The city gave its most famous editor a royal send-off.[70]

Almost lost in all the pomp and circumstance, tribute and eulogy, was his widow.

Completely stunned, Eleanor, who had found it hard to adjust to her life with him, suddenly found herself forced to adjust to life without him.

*She recalled* with a chill the night she . . . dreamed about her grandmother. That lusty, gay-hearted pioneer, who sang like a lark, strummed her guitar to keep her six children quiet, lay in the tall grass on her stomach — then big with child — while she and her husband guarded their horses and cattle from thieves. . . . Her grandmother had stood up in her grave and told her she would never in this world find what she wanted. . . . She [was] never . . . able to forget it or the sorrow on the handsome face.

Peggy Hull,
Unpublished manuscript

## CHAPTER THIRTEEN

# Peggy Again

If there was ever a sadly classic example of *sic transit gloria mundi,* it was Harvey Deuell's. Thought "by many [to have been] the greatest managing editor of all time,"[1] he sank leaving hardly a trace, his most audacious journalistic stunts credited to someone else, usually Frank Hause who had preceded him as managing editor of the *Daily News.*[2]

It was largely his own fault, of course. In life he had done little to endear himself to his acquaintances and coworkers. Yet, he had had an endearing side, if few had ever seen it: His wife, his mother, his wife's niece, and his "hired girl" all testified to it.

As for his widow, even after his death she was trying to please him, to live up to the expectations he had had of her. Ever conscious of "the proper thing," conduct he would have approved of, she wore black in public, but made no public spectacle of her grief.[3] That, she kept private. Most remarkably, she invited Harvey's mother to come back to Saxton Hall to live with her. But then Mary Deuell was not the same woman who had been "removed to Kew Gardens" two years before. When her son died, a radical change had come over her virtually overnight. Never before had she come face to face with her innermost self "squarely and honestly."

> She [had] sailed right through life thinking herself to be the most wonderful mother — the best wife. . . . Harvey's sudden death brought her the awakening. It was a ghastly thing to witness. At last she stood naked[,] unable to escape the full reality of her long selfish existence. And what was worse — it was too late to make amends.[4]

Now the competition, the long-time conflict were gone. Harvey's mother and Harvey's widow were finally drawn together by their common loss.

To her credit, Mary Deuell declined Peggy's offer, and even graciously, realizing they had nothing in common but memories of Harvey, memories that hovered, ghost-like, over Saxton Hall.

In the weeks immediately after Harvey's death, some of Peggy's friends rallied round: Doris Fleeson, a fellow Kansan and well-known political columnist; another friend who stayed with her for several weeks; and even the Pattersons, who invited her to dine with them. For once she had a pleasant and relaxed time with "J. M." She no longer had to worry about what Harvey would think of her behavior or that something she said or did might reflect badly on him or affect his position. Patterson responded with a generosity and warmth that surprised her.

Harvey's efforts to leave his wife well provided for were apparent in his final will, drawn up in February 1938. He left to her the bulk of his estate in the form of earnings from investments. He also made nominal bequests to his two aunts, an uncle, and his cousin to whom he had been fairly close, Georgine Walsh.

To his mother, whom he had already taken care of financially, he left items of sentimental poignancy: the watch and chain that had been his father's, any article of "personal adornment" of his that she wanted, and any of the pictures (during her lifetime) she wanted that his father, an amateur artist, had painted. It was his testamentary hope that ultimately the paintings would be sold and the proceeds given to the Metropolitan Museum of Art in his father's name.

He also stipulated that if Peggy died intestate, the whole estate was to be divided in two equal parts between his living relatives and Peggy's brother Edward (or his daughters); if his relatives were no longer living, it was all to go to Edward (or his daughters).

In an unusual but characteristically practical article, he had directed that $15,000 be set aside and held for two years, this sum to be used by his wife, if she so desired, to remodel Saxton Hall to turn it into a hotel or boarding house to make it income-producing for her.[5] They may have discussed this possibility; but if Harvey knew her at all, he knew that to pursue such a course would have been quite unlike his wife, as, of course, it was, and she did not. What she did do was immediately open up Saxton Hall to her friends, hoping they would come and spend time with her. Several of them did the best they could, but their time was not as free as Peggy's; most of them were still working journalists.

The first thing that happened was that "Eleanor" became "Peggy" again, and she made it clear to her friends that was what she wanted to be called from then on.

But she never really *was* "Peggy" again. By his death Harvey had made her his wife in a way he had never been able to during their married life. Though she was "Peggy" to her friends, to the outside world she continued to be Mrs. Harvey Deuell or Mrs. Eleanor Deuell; she still used those names formally, in memory of the one real chance she felt she had had at married happiness, a chance which had finally eluded her.

There were other drastic changes in her life. Since Hilda Connolly had been married shortly before Harvey's death, she was no longer available as either a part-time companion or "hired girl,"[6] so Peggy hired other local people to do the kinds of housework that Hilda had done. She found a new companion, this time not an impressionable young "disciple," but a twenty-nine-year-old struggling writer, Hobert Skidmore.

Their meeting was inevitable since he and his wife, actress Mildred Todd, had been renting the charming four-room converted Greenhouse immediately adjacent to Peggy's estate.[7]

Skidmore had a twin brother, Hubert, also a writer. When Peggy first met them, Hubert had had five novels published, all fairly successful. Hobert's plays and stories, however, had earned him only a mountain of rejection slips, and he was reduced to reading other people's novels and plays, looking for movie possibilities for 20th Century-Fox to earn a living.

The Skidmore twins had been born in the hill country of West Virginia. Their mother realized early on that they were of extraordinary intelligence, and so she engineered the family move into Clarksburg, a town she felt was large enough to offer them decent educational opportunities. The twins were, from the beginning, excellent students; ultimately both graduated from the University of Michigan where each won an Avery and Jule Hopwood Award for his writing.[8] It was only natural then that they had both decided to become professional writers.

Although Peggy knew Hobert had been living in the Greenhouse, that Mildred had recently moved out and Hubert subsequently moved in, she had had little contact with them until one evening in early 1940 when she happened on Hobert down by her little lake. He was wandering alone, depressed about his separation from his wife, a separation he knew was going to end in divorce. When their eyes first met, Peggy had a premonition, a psychic warning that it would be wise just to nod and walk on.[9] Ignoring it, she joined him and was soon encouraging him to talk about his problems; when she sympathized and consoled him, he, in turn, encouraged her to talk about her loneliness and unhappiness and gave her badly needed attention and understanding. The outcome was inevitable. Soon they were friends and then constant companions. That Hobert was homosexual did not matter to her. Peggy had always taken people as they were; she, of all people, certainly understood how he could be depressed about the dissolution of a marriage, though it was one which should never even have taken place. However, his homosexuality did bother Hobert and the people in the village who knew about it.[10]

But the thing the villagers were most scandalized by was his assuming of the role of master of Saxton Hall. Peggy, as usual, ignored the gossip and began, with his encouragement, even help, to indulge in the social life she had sorely missed during her marriage to Harvey. Even some of those villagers who were most outspoken in their criticism of them eagerly accepted invitations to the parties at Saxton Hall. Cheered on by Hobert and his brother, she began working again on her book, sure once more that eventually she would find a publisher for it.

About the time she met Hobert she also met Dr. Richard A. Smith and his wife, Leonore. Smith taught at New York University and was an inventor of considerable success and renown, best known for his invention of the bubble light. The Smiths were occasional weekend guests and their friendship became increasingly important to Peggy. She even told the Smiths, "In some mystic way you are my 'children.'" In fact, she said, "Dick seems like Harvey's son to me." Then as an odd disclaimer she added, "Not my son but the son Harvey might have had."[11]

Peggy still had not abandoned her hope that one of her nieces would come to live, if not with her, at least near her. Having faced the fact that Eldora was lost to her, she tried again with her brother's second daughter, Frances, inviting her for an extended stay in the summer of 1940.[12] The activities of that summer were in sharp contrast to those Eldora had taken part in just one year earlier when Harvey had been alive.

While Peggy did not go into The City very often during this time, she kept up her contacts, especially with those she knew from the *Daily News,* like Al Binder, columnist Danton Walker, and Doris Fleeson. Though duly in awe of Fleeson, Frances Goodnough was most impressed with a red-haired police court reporter friend of her aunt's. When they met the friend's train with a banner they had made, reading "Welcome Julia," Julia's obviously inebriated condition testified she had already started her own private celebration; she continued to "celebrate" throughout the weekend of her stay. Julia, it developed, was inordinately fond of the rhumba and determined to teach it to everyone in the house. Those who did not care to learn had to figure out routes through the house which avoided the library where she was entrenched, practicing, because whenever she heard someone coming down the hall, she lurked by the door, reached out and yanked the hapless passerby into the room to be her partner.

Frances might not have been eager to do the rhumba with Julia, but she was delighted by an invitation, issued on the strength of Peggy's friendship with officers at West Point, to a dance for the plebes and was thrilled to find herself a much sought-after partner there. Even realizing that her popularity was due, at least in part, to a shortage of women did not dampen her spirits or keep her from having a wonderful time.

Though Frances's feelings for the ever-present Hobert were colored by jealousy, she had a hard time maintaining her ill will after he turned his considerable charm on her and went out of his way to amuse her and ingratiate himself with her. They even shared a sort of conspiratorial merriment one day when a general, whom Peggy had known since their El Paso days, came to lunch. Frances and Hobert found it hilarious that the general inadvertently kept getting his foot on the bell under the table which summoned a servant from the kitchen. His mounting embarrassment each time the servant appeared made it even funnier to them. Peggy, however, did not find him laughable; after dinner they had several drinks together and then danced, as they had in the old days on the Border, to music on Harvey's hi-fi.

Frances was also amused at her aunt's occasionally playing the grande dame for the benefit of guests. She was never quite sure if Peggy was "putting on" or not when she called her "Frahncess," but she found it amusing either way.

Frances liked the social life and helping the cook when there were a lot of guests to be fed at the Hall, but she was not wild about the singing and violin lessons which Peggy arranged for her. She was pleasantly surprised though, when her aunt invited her fiancé, John Atkins, to come for a visit. This worked out well, for while he was there, John made himself useful by typing manuscripts for Hubert. Peggy had no doubt hoped that John would take one look at the area and want to settle there with Frances. This strategem did not work; at the end of the summer Frances and John went home to Kansas as Eldora and her John had done the year before.[13] Peggy had not exhausted all the possibilities: There was still Edward's youngest daughter, Josephine. However, at thirteen, she was obviously not an immediate candidate for resettlement.

In spite of all the entertaining Peggy did, she managed to find time to work on several short pieces of writing based on her foreign experiences, and hers were the lead articles in both of the Overseas Press Club's books published in 1940. "Open Grave in Shanghai," for *Eye Witness,* was about her brush with death in the 1932 Shanghai war and the other article, "Twenty Died at Dawn," for *The Inside Story,* about Villa's raid on Columbus, New Mexico. The editor of the books, Robert Spiers Benjamin, came out to Saxton Hall to consult with her on the articles. She was also, on occasion, doing some writing with Edna Lee (Booker) Potter whose teenage son, John, was spending the summer at Saxton Hall.[14]

Peggy's friendship with the Skidmore twins brought her in contact with other young people, many of whom were also writers. Impressed when they learned of her accomplishments, they accorded her the admiration she was starved for. Indeed, she derived a kind of ego nourishment from young, creative people. One to whom she became especially attached was Maritta Wolff.

Like the Skidmores, Maritta Wolff was a graduate of the University of Michigan where she had won the major Avery and Jule Hopwood Award for fiction for her novel, *Whistle Stop*. When it was published by Random House in 1941, reviewers characterized it as a "realistic and sordid picture of the seamy side of American small-town life" and likened it to the works of Steinbeck and Caldwell.[15] The book was already in its fifth printing by the time Maritta met Peggy that year. She was first brought out to Saxton Hall by Hubert and subsequently returned for fairly frequent visits at Peggy's urging. Though not normally an early riser, when she was at the Hall, Maritta got up at dawn to breakfast with Peggy who was at her best over her morning coffee and newspaper, making perceptive and humorous comments about what she found in the news.[16]

Most energetic in the morning during this period of her life, Peggy seemed to run down as the day wore on.[17] This may have been the result of a dependence on sleeping pills a doctor had given her to help her over the bad and sleepless times following Harvey's death.[18]

Though she felt that her Overseas Press Club articles served to reinforce her standing with her young friends, none of these writing efforts proved to be lucrative. This was unfortunate because Saxton Hall was becoming too expensive to operate on the funds from the trust left by Harvey, especially since she had assumed the considerable financial responsibility for Hobert on whom she lavished gifts to an extent disturbing to friends concerned about her own financial well-being.

But it was not only Hobert. Her generosity was legendary. She would give anyone she liked anything she had if they showed the slightest proprietary interest in it. Far from admiring this quality, a lot of people took advantage of it, borrowed things they never returned or even just carried her possessions off, knowing she would not make any trouble about it.[19]

The consequences of this openhandedness caught up with her in May 1941, and she was forced to list the estate with the National Real Estate Clearing House, offering all of it for sale for $40,000, or, excluding the cottage which she would occupy, for rent at $2,400 per year.[20]

She could not find a buyer even at that price, but in spite of the fact that she was having such money difficulties, she continued to entertain extravagantly, and on July 13 hosted the annual meeting of the Overseas Press Club.[21] The club was terribly important to her and she wanted to impress her fellow members, so she planned a variety of entertainments and laid out a lavish picnic lunch. More than fifty people attended.

The early afternoon amusements were surprisingly unsophisticated: a tug-of-war, a hog-calling contest, a wheel-barrow race, drinking and pretzel-eating contests. Since Peggy loved to dance, she had had an outdoor pavilion erected (with special dance floor) near her little lake, and throughout the afternoon she and her guests danced to recorded music.

In the late afternoon they all went back up to the house and watched movies, after which there was a light supper; by the time it was dark, most people had left for home.[22] The few who remained formed a new party, a much more rollicking one. In fact, what went on at "that party" was the subject of gossip around the town for weeks afterward, for judged by the standards of the outwardly straitlaced Cornwall-on-Hudson, it was perceived to have been a full-fledged bacchanalia.[23]

Of course, everything that went on at Saxton Hall was perceived in a most sensational light. Rumor was rampant: There was unseemly carousing; people slept where they pleased with whom they pleased. Peggy found this gossip more amusing than annoying, usually. It even seemed sometimes as if her attitude was that if they were going to talk, she would give them something to talk about!

Following Harvey's death, she had swung back and forth between grieving for him and trying to forget him with frantic social activity. On the anniversary of his death, she had put on her "widow's weeds" and withdrawn into a period of mourning and depression.[24] Unable to get a hold on her life, she had seemed adrift, her mornings offering hope, her evenings filled with despair.

It was this bad time that Hobert and Hubert and Maritta helped her get through. They, especially Hobert, gave her a reason to get up in the morning. Never mind that he drank too much and was a difficult and destructive drunk;[25] never mind that his homosexuality got him, and consequently Peggy, into trouble;[26] he admired her, loved her, and needed her at a time that she desperately needed to be admired and loved and needed. A remarkable bond developed between them.

Even while she had been struggling with the turmoil in her personal life, Peggy had been only too well aware of the international events which were leading slowly but inexorably toward U.S. involvement in another war. When France fell in June 1940, she wept.

Now, as the American preparedness program got under way, since it looked as if, at fifty, she were too old to report this war, she found a new interest: helping the families of young (and poor) officers from West Point to find housing which they could afford in the area. The generosity she had first lavished on the indigent of Cornwall-on-Hudson, a constant stream of guests, and struggling young writers like Hobert was now also directed to those like Dorothy Sutherland, wife of a career soldier then at West Point, and her three little daughters who rented a small house on Peggy's property. With her usual disregard of any idea of class or social status, Peggy personally cleaned the house and washed its windows in preparation for the Sutherlands' moving in. This display of unselfconsciousness astounded the insecure young army wife used to the strictures of rank at the Point.[27]

Later, the Sutherland family was transferred briefly to Newfoundland; but Dorothy and her daughters returned to New York after Pearl Harbor when her husband was ordered overseas. Dorothy, left to shift for herself and her children and with almost no money, reluctantly faced the prospect of having to move in with some of her family near Hancock, but when she stopped by Saxton Hall to see Peggy on her way "home," Peggy offered her the tenancy of the cottage again, and Dorothy gratefully accepted.[28]

Yet another young friend Peggy found at this time, one who became a part of what Maritta called Peggy's "pseudo family," was a shy English girl, Sheila Foote, a painter fresh from art school. Archaeologist Giles Healey, who owned property in Cornwall, brought her to Saxton Hall to see if one of Peggy's cottages was available for rent for a studio/home for Sheila. They made a colorful entrance in Giles's Hispano-Suiza, a monster of a car with enormous wheels and a "boat" body of wood. The vehicle, which had once belonged to the duke of Alba, seemed almost to float through the gate and up the drive. The attraction between Sheila and Peggy was instantaneous; Peggy made arrangements to sublet the Greenhouse to her.[29]

There were those in the Cornwall community who did not approve of Peggy's interest in young people. Some even saw her, with her free-living, free-spending ways, as a corrupter of their youth; she was the victim of several unpleasant "incidents," one of which resulted in her suing the local police chief. According to the *Cornwall Local,* one summer's night, well after midnight, the chief was making his rounds when he ran into a West Point athletic coach, who was greatly perturbed because his daughter was spending the night at Saxton Hall. Eventually (at 3:30 A.M.) the chief and the coach stormed out to Saxton Hall and forcibly removed the coach's daughter from the premises. That she was twenty-one years old and therefore an adult made no difference to them. Peggy, furious, charged the chief with boisterous conduct and menacing behavior. The case was heard by the village board and subsequently dismissed,[30] but Peggy had indicated that she did not intend to sit still for what she no doubt considered to be overt harassment.

The entry of the U.S. into World War II and her brother's death of bone cancer two days before Christmas made 1941 one of Peggy's most unhappy years. She did not go to Kansas for her brother's funeral, pleading illness. Perhaps this was just another indication of how troubled her life was at this time.

But 1942 presented the national emergency sharp and clear. Determined to do her part, she looked around for ways to actively aid in the war effort. One of her first attempts centered on a scheme to cut down on the cost of having the extensive lawns of Saxton Hall mowed. Following the example of President Woodrow Wilson who had pastured sheep on the White House lawn for a short time in the spring of 1918 during World War I, she bought a flock of sheep, thinking they would not only keep the grass eaten off, but would also produce a money crop of wool. The sheep she bought were long past their prime and, worse, not, it turned out, overly fond of grass, especially when their diet was supplemented by their mistress with delicacies like peaches and watermelons. They left droppings all over the drive and oily smears on the house where they rubbed up against the walls. Undaunted, Peggy hired a boy to sweep up the dung and a painter to periodically touch up the paint.[31]

Indeed, she threw herself into this new project, personally undertaking the herding of her little flock. Unable to herd them twenty-four hours a day and lacking fences to keep them at home, she soon lost control, and when the sheep ran over other people's property, eating their corn and garden crops and leaving masses of manure in their yards and flower beds, her neighbors became vocal in their irritation.[32] So she sold the sheep to another estate owner in the region.

It was hard for her to part with them, for she had grown fond of them as pets. They were individuals. Each had a name. In fact, her emotional attachment to them was strong enough that when a dilapidated old truck showed up to collect them, she could not let them go in such a questionable vehicle and hired, at her own expense, an "elegant" horse van to deliver them to their new home.[33] All in all, what had started out as an economy measure turned into a costly experience, as many of her ventures seemed to.

Furthermore, she was finding that staying at home tending sheep and young military wives, interesting as these occupations might have been to most women her age, were totally unsatisfying to her. What really mattered was what was going on on the battlefields. Like the cliché fire horse, she smelled the smoke, and she made up her mind that, whatever the obstacles, nothing was going to keep her from going to this war.

*There will be no scoops,* no prize awards, no Purple Hearts or memories of desperate hours well shared with brave Americans. I am a woman and as a woman am not permitted to experience the hazards of real war reporting. After a long and varied experience in the first World War, on the Mexican border, in France, Siberia, and China, these restrictions have laid a heavy hand upon my dreams. But I have found work to do.

Peggy Hull,
*Cleveland Plain Dealer*

## CHAPTER FOURTEEN

# Peggy's Last War — World War II

"The Sunday bombs did more than start a war," Gwenfread Allen wrote of Pearl Harbor, "they changed a way of life."[1] Certainly the old way of life at Saxton Hall was gone forever.

Hubert, now linked romantically with Maritta, enlisted first and was sent to Officers' Candidate School at Fort Monmouth, New Jersey. Then on September 1, 1942, Hobert left for the service,[2] and Peggy started her drive to get back into uniform. She knew it would not be anything like the same. She was the only one of the old bunch left to carry on, and she felt less alive than she once had, for it seemed to her that a piece of her had died with each of them: Floyd, Ring, Webb. Webb had been the first correspondent to die in this war. He had been only forty-eight.

Probably no one would ever know if it really had been just an accident. They had found his body beside the railroad tracks thirty feet from the Clapham Junction station in southwest London. The German news agency had immediately accused British intelligence of having murdered him.[3]

He had been a trouble to them. He was one of the very few who believed almost nothing they put out as news, and his public comments like "the Germans will go through that line like crap through a little tin horn"[4] had made him unpopular with them.

On the other hand, it was no secret that he was a heavy drinker. It had been night. He had been covering debates in Parliament — thirsty work. He had been lonely — his wife and son had returned to the U.S. the month before. It was quite possible that he had opened the carriage door and, in the pitch dark of the blackout, thinking that his train compartment was opposite the station platform, he had stepped out and fallen to the roadbed. Such a fall might well have been enough to injure him fatally. It had probably been the accident the coroner had ruled it was.[5] Still, there were those who wondered long afterward.

She missed Webb and Ring and especially Floyd. Even when she had not seen them very often, just to know they were there —

Well, they were not there anymore, but she was; she was going off to war again, alone this time, but going nevertheless.

First, of course, she had to have a sponsor; so she began the old struggle to find a paper that would send her. Finally, in July 1943 she turned to the *Cleveland Plain Dealer* which had carried her early Border stories and where Paul Bellamy, who had been city editor at the time, was now managing editor. After Peggy marshaled all her powers of persuasion, played on auld lang syne, entreated, and cajoled, Bellamy agreed to take her on as *one* of the *Plain Dealer's* accredited correspondents; and with this support and that of the North American Newspaper Alliance which followed, the first part of her battle was over.[6]

Next, she got her affairs in order and went to Washington, D.C., to get her accreditation from the War Department. She had assumed that all the experience she had had would make it relatively easy for her; she soon found that the attitude toward women correspondents had not changed much since her first war reporting.

The first officer she encountered told her "there were some commanding generals who did not like war correspondents — especially women war correspondents." This was not news to her. Now she also faced discrimination because of her age. Others made it plain that as far as they were concerned she was too old. They even told her she would not be able to stand the rigors of field duty anymore, that she should be home — on her front porch — in a rocking chair![7] On the Border with Pershing, in World War I, Siberia, China, they had said she was too young — or not robust enough — or the "wrong" sex. Now she was too old. Well, too old or not, her name was going to be on the big board with the rest of the accredited correspondents. If they thought they could get her to roll over, they did not know Peggy Hull! The only thing about her that was old was the fire burning inside her.

Staying with Maritta who now lived in Falls Church, Virginia, Peggy went into Washington every day to argue, plead, or just sit waiting.[8] Then, one sweet day, a defeated Lt. Col. Marshall E. Newton handed her the official application.[9]

It was a considerable victory.

All those years she had spent in the Far East could surely be made to count for something now, she reasoned; she requested permission to join Lt. Gen. Joseph Stilwell's command, sure that she was as good as on her way.

Peggy Hull Deuell, Hobert Skidmore, and Maritta Wolff, author of WHISTLE STOP, flanked by unidentified soldiers, Atlantic City, N.J., 1943. *(In authors' possession, courtesy of Raymond A. Ruffino)*

The weeks and then months dragged by with no reply. It was as if her request had been "tucked into an old brown bottle, floated across the Atlantic and Indian Oceans to Bombay where it [had gone] by pack pony over the Himalayas to Chungking." When the answer had finally come from Stilwell, "it was [a] definite and impressive 'no.'"[10]

Although she was deeply disappointed at not getting assigned to China, she had no intention of giving up. There were other commands she could ask to visit. She might better be able to reach the Pacific area of war indirectly, she decided, so she requested permission to join Lt. Gen. Robert C. Richardson's command in Hawaii. Since it had taken General Stilwell's command four months to turn her down, she figured that she should not hear from the central Pacific until well after Christmas, but within five days of her request, she received permission to go to Hawaii.[11]

On Thanksgiving Day 1943, Maritta and Hubert, now a lieutenant in the signal corps, were married in the chapel at Fort Myer, Virginia, with Peggy as matron of honor and Chaplain Wilbur N. Pike, whose father had succeeded Peggy's grandfather as rector on the Oneida Indian Reservation, conducting the Episcopalian service.[12]

237

Peggy had gotten her problems with alcohol under control as soon as she became determined to go off to the wars again. Indeed, one of her greatest strengths was that she could exercise total self-discipline when she had a strong enough motivation to do so.

Having received her pass November 19, 1943, and gotten Maritta and Hubert married, her next step was to secure a proper correspondent's uniform. Women correspondents wore WAC officers' uniforms to which they added the official brassard, a green cloth band four inches wide with the word "Correspondent" in white letters on it, but without any insignia or grade or arm of service. She had been assured that the uniforms could be found in any Washington department store; however, three days of searching had not turned up any, so as she had done on earlier occasions, she looked to a tailor for help.

As soon as her uniform was ready, she put it on and, as a sentimental gesture, reported to her friend from her El Paso days, Allen Gullion, now a general, for inspection. After he had redone her necktie, adjusted her overseas cap to a suitably rakish angle, and shortened the sleeves of her khaki shirt with rubber bands, she gave him the best salute she "could muster after two decades of disuse" and said good-by to him and his staff,[13] then boarded the train for San Francisco.

In San Francisco she went to the Navy Public Relations Bureau on December 18, 1943, to make arrangements for the trip to Hawaii. She immediately ran into unexpected problems and the usual government-issue runaround. Her basic pass, which accredited her to the army, did not entitle her to transportation by the navy. Therefore, since she did not have a navy pass, she was sent to the superintendent of transportation at Fort Mason to ask the army to arrange for her trip.[14]

But there, since she was the first woman correspondent they had seen on the West Coast and they had not received any authority from Washington to validate her army pass, they not only did not help her, but even took her pass to hold until such authorization arrived. When she protested that the only thing she had to wear was her uniform and that she could be arrested for wearing it if she did not have her pass, no one seemed very concerned about her problem. They kept saying she would simply have to wait until they heard from Washington.[15]

She spent the next two weeks and her fifty-fourth birthday in her hotel room in bed with influenza. On the first day she was beginning to feel better, New Year's Day, the superintendent of transportation telephoned her. Her status had been satisfactorily established, and she was to report to his office immediately with her luggage.

Although not fully recovered from the flu, she was out of bed like a shot, packed, and at his office within half an hour to pick up her pass, a navy card, and written permission to embark. Only a few hours later she found herself on board a navy transport, with no tropical uniform, no dog tag, serial number, or APO address. Obviously, no particular orders had come for her, but by now she knew better than to ask any questions.[16]

She later expressed surprise at finding herself at her "first stop on the way to Tokyo," but she had reason to believe from her first decision to seek accreditation that in the end she would get it, for so many of the colonels, majors, and generals in whose hands the decision lay remembered her as an adventuresome, romantic young reporter who had a way of getting what she wanted in 1916 and 1917 and 1918; and they could not say "no" to her now, twenty-five years later.

Her first assignment was to Honolulu; from there she sent her first stories to the *Plain Dealer* starting in January 1944, using the byline "Peggy Hull Deuell." Only the second woman accredited to the area (the first was Lorraine Stumm of the *London Daily Mirror;* there were at least 100 accredited men),[17] Peggy was soon in for a hassle reminiscent of her World War I reporting days. Adm. Chester Nimitz "had a 'thing' about women in the war theaters. He simply did not want women around, and the Navy nurses were the one exception he could not control. He would not accredit women correspondents to the fleet," and he revoked the card Peggy had received, which meant that she was restricted to Hawaii.[18] She still hoped to eventually get permission to go to the South Pacific and the China-Burma theater. But for the time being she tried to accept the limitations philosophically. She realized that it was a minor miracle that she had gotten this far and that she had not been shipped back to the mainland after her navy card had been revoked. Promising to "be a good girl and write only about the army . . . [and] in general . . . be a very fine character," she was permitted to stay.[19]

During the time that she was restricted to Hawaii, her reports were made up of stories told to her by men who had been in combat areas and were now in the Islands for rest and recuperation, stories written to her by soldiers who were still in the forward areas, and some personal experiences. Since she was not allowed to be in any area close to the action, in her old resourceful way she made the most of what she could get. As a result, some of her stories dealt with the everyday problems of the American forces, such as how to get along without starch for the soldiers' uniforms which tended to wilt without it; or, since clothespins were unobtainable, how to make do by substituting safety pins. Her articles were humorous, detailing the "perils" of torn or bunched-up clothing arising from such shortages.

Once again she was one of a handful of women surrounded by men; now, rather than a romantic, dashing young reporter, she was a mother figure to the young soldiers. She accepted her new role gracefully —

always ready to lend a sympathetic ear to their stories or to wield her needle to mend or to sew on buttons for them.[20]

The real difference age made came home to her when a three-star British general stopped at the base and the young captain from Oklahoma assigned to him prevailed upon her to entertain the general on the grounds that no one but she could understand his jokes and laugh at the right time. It did not take her long to see that the real reason the captain asked for her help was so that he would be free for a date with a young blond.[21] The realization that in the old days she would have been the blond may have given her a pang, but she never showed it. She accepted this task, and any others, willingly.

Every so often something would put her in mind of "the old days," like a balmy April afternoon she wrote about that she had been with a group of young GI's at a luau. They were singing the old war songs; as she listened, a sense of melancholy swept over her, for they were the same songs soldiers had sung on the Mexican border around the campfire and in France in 1917 "in village bars and along the weary roads to the front." "Mad'-moisell from Armentieres," "Santy Anna," "Bon Soir, Ma Cherie." Soldiers had sung those songs in Siberia

> in the frozen streets of Vladivostok and Spasskoe and in a railroad car by the side of a bridge where some 1918 G.I.'s were on guard — a railroad car which . . . the boys of that other American Army had magically made into a home. It had been painted white inside; there were tiny yellow curtains, and the pin-up girls were Mary Pickford and Norma Talmadge.[22]

Now here in a new war, in 1944, even these new soldiers were singing the old songs.

Another article grew out of an invitation to spend a day with a small antiaircraft outfit in an isolated section of the Islands. She found that the area was overrun with rodents which had made their nests in the low, thickly-branched trees. A mouse dropping in her hair on an evening stroll or a rat landing on her shoulder during a blackout was not something she could contemplate with enthusiasm, and she found that the GI's did not like those prospects any more than she did in spite of the old myths about only girls being afraid of mice.

Then there were the flies. "Flies may appear as inconsequential things in comparison to the steel and explosives which are flying around at this time, but given enough flies a G.I.'s life can become almost unendurable." Telling her about an island infested with flies, a soldier said, "It must have been a rather pretty place once upon a time, . . . but it is a sorry place now and we don't make it look any better in the [woolen

240

gloves and headnets] we have to wear [because of] the fly situation. . . . When we dive for a foxhole in our fatigues, . . . headnets and gloves we look like something dreamed up by . . . [Salvador] Dali."[23]

One of the tales that especially delighted her concerned an incident at a base hospital when Brig. Gen. Joseph L. Ready was making the rounds pinning on Purple Hearts. When he got to a young private first class and asked him the usual question of where (meaning in what battle) he had been wounded, the soldier, misunderstanding, blurted out, "In the butt, sir." Those who had been there had been particularly amused that Ready, who had a reputation for toughness, had been shocked at this reply.[24]

Most of her stories about hospitals were far from humorous. For the first time since the Japanese attack on Shanghai in 1932, she was where she was seeing horribly wounded men as they came off the battlefields before they were patched up or even bandaged, and her emotions sometimes showed so clearly on her face that she found herself being reassured by those she had sought to comfort. On other occasions her heart ached when a soldier would tell her that when she came into the room to see him, it was as if his mother were coming through the doorway.

Although she spent a lot of time visiting the wounded, she found it hard to write about them: They were all so terribly young and so uncomplaining. She described the awful and commonplace scene:

> The public address system stabs the dark, star-studded night with sound: "All stretcher bearers report to the receiving station immediately." . . . Up on the hill the long platform in front of the quonset hut is brightly lighted and lined with litters. Gray blankets cover the quiet figures. Medical officers kneel beside the wounded. . . . You look at the next litter, and the pallor even in the deceiving night light, carries a significant warning. The pallor and the resignation, as if death had already been accepted.[25]
> . . . The mangled bodies of boys who were so young and virile a short time before . . . now mutilated, some beaten for life. . . .
> It was agony to see them go; worse to see them come back.[26]

She noted that one effect of the war on the attitudes of many young men was to make them more religious, in a nonsectarian sense. Their faith seemed to be a simple and eclectic one, like that of a soldier who talked to her about the belief in reincarnation which he had come to accept as a part of his faith. He was convinced he could not have learned so much about soldiering in so short a time if he had not fought before, perhaps with Roman legions during an earlier life.

While most of her contacts were with men, she had great admiration for the women in the service. She was impressed with the skill of those in the Women's Air Raid Defense who operated the plotting board at the Air Defense Command Post, and she had praise for the many Red Cross workers who did their best to entertain and cheer up men who were recovering from wounds.

Her greatest admiration was for the nurses, especially those who volunteered to take "commando" training. These women, "combat nurses," were landed as soon after the beachheads were secured as the commanding officer considered reasonably safe and practical. There was an obvious tinge of envy in Peggy's report of the first nurses to be sent to Saipan after that island had been taken from the Japanese. She wrote:

> For months these nurses had learned to wriggle themselves through barbed wire, crawl along the ground under live gunfire, hike under a suffocating sun or in a steady downpour with a field pack on their backs; to bathe in cold water and to sleep where and when a shelter tent could be pitched. They knew the taste of field rations and they had been taught how to defend themselves in the event a Japanese infiltrated into their area. They were in every sense of the word, young, hardy brave soldiers perfectly competent to look after themselves.[27]

To a woman who had sometimes thought that she wanted more than anything else to be a soldier, these young women were to be envied. She was as thrilled as they when word came that Congress had finally passed legislation making them real officers with real rank instead of the "relative rank" they had held before.

At the same time, she shared their reluctance to go by the book, especially when it came to refraining from being friendly with the enlisted men, whom they regarded as buddies and brothers; for while she had officer status as an accredited war correspondent, her closest friendships during this war were not with officers, but with homesick GI's.

> The army, the medical corps, the Red Cross and the special services have succeeded in thinking up something to do for all the problems and ailments of the soldier except his homesickness. They haven't been able to do anything about that. . . . Spring has been particularly hard on the farm boys at this base. Of course, the only way they know it is spring is by the date on the calendar, for the weather is the same the year around out here.[28]

In all the military action she had covered, she had found that homesickness was the unceasing companion of the soldier in combat. Fear was only sometimes; homesickness was constant. One night "sitting on the beach with a group of soldiers watching the moon come up over [a] long, jagged mountain," she listened to them talk about one they had all known whom they called "Chief." Chief's great dread had been that he would be killed and "'burried out here on one of these ash heaps' 10,000 miles from New York. . . . 'I don't ever want to be planted in one of these places,'" he had said. He longed for the subways, the tenements, the crowded lower east side of New York City. But in the end he had been killed and buried on a lonely island where no grass, no shrubs, no palms, even, grew. It was the worst fate any of them could imagine.[29]

Food seemed to be on her mind a good deal, for many of her articles described the "chow" available to American forces. At the same time, she admitted that she really should be on a diet, but that it was nice to be in her fifties and no longer have to worry about her weight. In fact, the active life she now led made hearty meals a necessity, for she never turned down an assignment, even a fairly strenuous one.

For example, in Hawaii she and other reporters were taken to observe a practice of the Air Defense Command. After they had watched the operations that activated the interception system at the first approach of planes, she wrote:

> We ran out of the tunnel and jumped into jeeps and headed for another observation post. I had the wildest ride of my life. There is nothing to hang onto in a jeep. You hold your seat by sheer wishful thinking and at the wheel of my jeep was as fearless a driver as ever drove a racing car.
>
> The roads to the observation post were made for mules and pack trains and we slithered along ledges with a nice drop of 100 feet or more straight down. We went as far as the jeeps could take us and then scrambled up a hill through cactus and barbed wire.[30]

A major source for reports from the "front" while she was in Honolulu was Hobert Skidmore. Though his brother had been commissioned and sent to Europe, Hobert declined assignment to OCS, preferring to remain with the rank and file, the "common" soldiers. Starting at the bottom, he worked his way up the noncommissioned ladder to staff sergeant and served as a waist gunner on a B-24 in the Gilbert, Mariana, and Marshall islands. Among other things, Hobert wrote to her about "Ireland's well" around which he and a group of other men had had long discussions about the war, life before the war, and what they hoped life would be like after the war.

The lack of a good water supply on the atolls made it necessary for the GI's on them to dig wells; they were very competitive about it. "Ireland's well," dug by S. Sgt. Romeo Ireland of Cache, Illinois, was one of the most popular wells in the area. It was built up with beautiful white coral rock and equipped with a brilliant blue bucket made from a GI can suspended from a bamboo pole. Ireland had also laid a terrace a few feet wide all around the well, and this made it a natural meeting place for soldiers at twilight. Here they drank their beer rations, played guitars, or just talked. In the moonlight, it was "like a movie set of a Moslem oasis in the Near East Desert."[31]

Most of the conversation, though, was not of a romantic nature. Some of the men looked back on the struggle they had had just trying to find jobs before the war, and they wondered "what the hell" they were fighting for, in the end. Hobert argued that it was pointless to try to see the future by looking backward. He believed they were victims of an era, and that only if they learned from their war experience would they make progress in living. He had come to know, he said, that there could be and "should be dignity and pride in living," and he felt that "for the first time [he] was beginning to live."[32]

His optimistic outpouring of introspection led Peggy to believe that Hobert was solving the problems that had been responsible for his drinking so heavily before the war, that he would give up the torment he seemed almost to cultivate and after the war try to find peace and happiness. Her belief that his outlook had changed freed her from the worry she had had about his future.

And when she learned that he had dedicated his book, *Valley of the Sky*, written while he was with a B-24 crew and published by Houghton Mifflin, "For Peggy Hull Deuell, war correspondent, who taught us the meaning of service," she was overwhelmed with pleasure, especially when she had just come to accept something herself — the fact that there would be

no scoops, no prize awards, no Purple Hearts or memories of desperate hours well shared with brave Americans. I am a woman and as a woman am not permitted to experience the hazards of real war reporting. After a long and varied experience in the first World War, on the Mexican border, in France, Siberia, and China, these restrictions have laid a heavy hand upon my dreams. But I have found work to do. There [are] the little stories to write — the small, unimportant story which [means] so much to the G.I., but for which no editor [will] use his wire service and which no "spot news" correspondent [has] time to seek out and write.[33]

But evidence that Peggy was not accepting her situation as philosophically as it might have appeared was revealed in a conversation she had with Col. Georges Orselli, governor of Tahiti, who stopped in Honolulu on his way south in October 1944. In response to the colonel's contention that American women were free to do what they pleased, but were not happy even so, Peggy said,

> Our freedom is ephemeral. Our presence in various fields is bitterly resented by the men we compete with. Overwhelming obstacles are frequently set up to prevent us from working and yet, odd though it may seem, women must live.
>
> . . . The majority of American girls face the necessity of earning their living as soon as they have reached their teens. They also find it compulsory to contribute to the family.[34]

These were not idle observations on her part but were descriptive of her personal experience.

Though she chafed under the restrictions the army and navy imposed on her, there were compensations. The soldiers appreciated her "little stories" about them. "You will never realize what those yarns of yours on Staff Sergt. Romeo Ireland's coral well with its blue bucket did to this gang," Hobert wrote to her from Makin. "Nothing but a 30-day furlough or a shipload of beer could have topped the lift they got. You made them know they weren't forgotten."[35] After such a boost to her morale, it is no wonder that Peggy felt closer than ever to him.

Having been the "good girl" she had promised to be, she was rewarded with the return of her navy card in November 1944 and received authorization on January 26, 1945, to go to "Guam, Saipan, Tinian, Guadalcanal, New Hebrides, Angaur, Peleliu, Christmas, Funafuti, Samoa, Tongatabu, Ulithi, Tarawa, Makin, Apamama and other . . . points in the POA."[36] Two other women also received accreditation to the Pacific fleet at this time — Barbara Finch, Reuters correspondent, and Patricia Lochridge of the *Woman's Home Companion*.[37]

Since women correspondents were now permitted to follow soon after nurses were landed, she sometimes found herself on islands which were supposedly pacified, but where, in fact, Japanese soldiers were still hiding in caves and carrying out sniping attacks and Japanese planes made frequent bombing raids.

This was impressed on her on February 11, 1945, the first night she spent at an Air Transport Command Transient Camp in the Marianas. She occupied one of the tents which stood in "orderly rows looking like small pyramids in the soft moonlight." Her foxhole had been dug within easy sprinting distance of her tent, and she suddenly realized that this

Peggy Hull Deuell with a group of Gilbert Islanders, Spring, 1945. *(Peggy Hull Deuell Collection, Kansas Collection, University of Kansas Libraries)*

"soft moonlight" was a "bomber's moon" and as such, bad news. Since she had not been asleep for forty hours, she did not stay awake worrying about air attacks; it seemed only minutes after she had gone to bed that she was awakened by the sound of reveille being played by a bugler standing in the center of the camp. It had a sweet, clear, genuine sound, qualities that were lost when it was played over a loudspeaker system as it was in the rear bases, and it brought back a flood of memories to her.[38]

The night had been clear, but by morning it was raining, and after she returned from her long walk to the shower room where she had to bathe and dress in the dark because she had forgotten her flashlight, she started her half-mile walk to the mess hall for breakfast, resigned to being soaked by the time she got there. She was pleased when a truckload of soldiers stopped to pick her up, but not so pleased when the driver told her that a Japanese soldier had been killed in the night not more than a hundred yards from where she was sleeping. He had then gone on to "reassure" her that it was not an unusual occurrence.

The danger of snipers and air raids was something one had to accept if she was going to function. Peggy always had adjusted to the unchangeable, and she did now. When the air raid alert sounded in the middle of the night, she tumbled out of her cot, put on a bathrobe, pulled on her boots, grabbed her helmet, and ran with the rest of the soldiers to "the long narrow slit which resembled nothing so much as an open grave."

When Peggy and Hobert met again, in the Marianas in February 1945, he was on a tour of the Pacific Ocean areas as a member of Lt. Gen. Robert C. Richardson's first information and historical section.[39] From this time, Hobert accompanied her on many of her trips "to obtain the best stories from the enlisted men."[40]

As far as Peggy's writing from the Pacific during World War II is concerned, she did the best she could under the circumstances. She found at the very beginning that, partly because of her sex and partly because of her age, her activities were to be very carefully circumscribed. Although she chafed under the restrictions, she again proved herself a good reporter and specialized in the kind of human interest stories that would be eagerly read by the families of the servicemen and women whose lives and activities she was describing. They were the same general kind of stories that Ernie Pyle became so famous for, but they had been her forte long before he had come to war reporting.[41]

At the same time that she realized, considering her age and sex, how lucky she was to be doing war reporting of any kind anywhere, she could not help agreeing with soldiers in the Pacific who wished they were in Italy or England. "In the army it is natural to think that the best part of the war, the exciting and interesting part, is some place you [are] not."[42]

Even so, she conducted herself in such a way as to draw praise from those who tended to be critical of women war correspondents and thus made the way smoother for later women correspondents. She did not complain about hardships, and she made only an occasional reference to the discrimination against female reporters.

Very early on, she had become popular with the men, so popular that sometimes she found herself being interviewed by soldiers she had intended to interview. However, it was not Peggy the war correspondent they were interested in so much as Peggy their friend, one who would treat their complaints and concerns with wisdom, understanding, and sympathy. They asked her such questions as "Why do we have civilian workers in jobs at this base which WACs could fill?" and "Why are strikes tolerated? Why is it that some of the American people can do exactly as they please while we have to do what we are told whether we like it or not?" And they "deplored racial prejudice and the various ways in which it was manifested."

These soldiers who had fought at Attu and Kwajalein were emphatic about their belief that an American-Japanese should be given as much opportunity to demonstrate his loyalty as a German-American. They deplored the action of the people at Great Meadow, N.J., where a farmer was forced to send away the five Japanese who were working for him. "We are not fighting to inherit a world full of hatred and suspicion and when the people at home stage a scene like that we feel betrayed. Why can't they let us do the fighting out here where it belongs? We are unhappy and home-sick and worried and what we hear from the States doesn't make us feel any better. . . . Sometimes we wonder what we will be going back to."[43]

These were things that worried her, too; while she could not reassure these men, she could and did make it very clear to them and to her readers back home that she understood and sympathized with the frustration of the soldiers about some of the deplorable things going on stateside.

Peggy Hull Deuell in the Central Pacific, 1944-45. (In authors' possession, courtesy of Raymond A. Ruffino)

One of the ways the GI's showed their affection for her was by presenting her with the patches from their outfits, patches they expected her to display on her beret. The beret had been designed for her as being more becoming than an overseas cap, and the colorful emblems sewed to it served to relieve its plainness.

The first patch had been given to her by Pfc. Frederick White of Wellington, Ohio, who had later been killed on Leyte. At the time, they had both been in Honolulu, he on a pass and she waiting for her orders to move out to the war zone. One day in the spring of 1944 they had been walking along Waikiki Beach when "he suddenly reached up and ripped his division badge from his sleeve.

"'You seem to like our outfit,' he said, shyly. 'We thought you might not mind being adopted.'

"'You mean the whole division's adopting me?'" she asked, "holding the beautiful black and red patch as if it might disintegrate before [her] eyes."

Fred had smiled at her. "'This is just the beginning. You wait and see.'"[44]

He had been right. By the end of the war, she had seven berets and fifty patches, patches presented to her by men ranging in rank from private to general.

She had an indication of what the berets had come to mean to the soldiers when she was meeting the planes bringing back the wounded from Iwo Jima.

A . . . soldier smile[d] up at me from a . . . litter. His young blue eyes [were] bright. "Say, haven't I seen you before?" he ask[ed]. "Didn't I see you in Honolulu? I'd know that hat anywhere."

"Yes, I was there." I straighten[ed] my beret so he [could] see all the bright-colored insignia of the army and air force divisions. . . .

"You've got the wrong patches," the marine [told] me.

"The wrong ones?" . . .

"Sure," he talk[ed] with difficulty for his throat [was] encased in a vise-like cast. A bullet had gone through his mouth, taken out some of his teeth and broken his neck. . . . "Sure — you ought to have the Third Marines," he pulled at the blanket, "you ought to have the Fifth —" and then as if he had just thought of it and it made him feel good, . . . "say — you ought to have a hat with only marine patches." . . .

"I'll make up a hat," I promise[d], "and it will be just for the marines and you."

"That's swell — put the Third Marines right in front." I touch[ed] his hand as his litter [was] carried away.[45]

In some of her columns she made herself the focus of her story. One such report showed how her usual fastidiousness about her clothes as well as her love of uniforms interfered with her appreciation of a briefing at the Seventh American Air Force Fighter Command she had looked forward to with eagerness.

The morning she was to report for the briefing at a place about ten miles from where she was billeted, she was so excited she could hardly eat breakfast. Then, only a mile and a half into the trip, the cab she hired had a flat tire, and the native driver had no spare. There was nothing for her to do but start walking. It was much hotter than she had realized, and soon her clean shirt was soaked with perspiration. After the damage had been done, her clothing wet and wrinkled, she finally caught a ride with two other correspondents; she arrived on time at least but was uncomfortable about her appearance.

When Col. Ernest Moore came in to give the briefing, she became so interested in observing every detail of his uniform that what he said was almost wasted on her. She wrote:

It was the best-looking outfit I've seen out here, and I discovered there and then what has been the matter with me. If I could get some uniforms like Mickey Moores's — uniforms which fit in the right places — I think I'd sleep in them, I'd be so happy. There is no use arguing, a uniform can build a woman up or tear her down, and mine are doing a lot of tearing down.[46]

At times like these when the sun boiled down and she was sweltering and soaked with sweat, she would think of her home on the Hudson.

There would be snow around it and the old trees would proudly lift their bare branches to the winter sky. In the living room, there would be a fire in the grate. The big range in the kitchen would be glowing. Someone in the house would be taking off soon for the village tobacco shop to pick up the newspapers. . . .

Here under the first hot rays of the Mariana sun, with the air full of bronze dust, with the bulldozers and caterpillars backing and groaning, turning and screeching across the road, my home seemed very far away.

The soldiers who passed me on the road turned thoughtful faces to me as they returned my greeting. They, too, were thinking of home.[47]

One of her last reports from the Marianas reflected Peggy's usual eagerness to learn about the native people wherever she was and to pass on to her readers what she had discovered. In order to visit some native villages, one day she rode eighty miles in a jeep over rutted paths through the jungle. She wrote:

We passed cave after cave where our men had fought bitterly. . . .

The first village was down by the sea. . . . There were rock foundations and wooden walls and a tiled roof or two. The yards were scrupulously clean. Closely woven straw mats laid out in the sun were covered with quantities of corn. . . .

[The Japanese occupation had been] a bitter experience for [these] gentle, lovable, smiling [people]. Their "Uncle Sam" . . . had always been kind and generous. . . . Then the Japanese came. . . . Their lands were confiscated and became the property of the imperial government. They were sent to the fields to work like slaves and their food was rationed to them in small, inadequate amounts. They were beaten and beheaded and shot because they did not know the intricate and senseless routine of Japanese manners. They were tortured for information which they did not have.[48]

In the spring and summer of 1945 she visited an American camp in the Fijis. She was especially fascinated by these people, commenting that she did not believe she had "read a paragraph about Fiji since [she] left the eighth grade," where she had gotten the impression that it was inhabited by "awesome" black men with enormous heads of bushy hair who carried spears and enjoyed human flesh.

On her arrival at Suva, she was struck by the contrast the islands presented to the barren coral atolls she had just left. As she described it,

> The sky was full of showery clouds, and delicate white mist hung in the range of thickly-wooded mountains to the west. . . . The deep green fields, the great glistening trees, the acres of bright green turf, the sweetness of the cool moist air were all joys I had almost forgotten . . . and I wondered if I would ever want to go away.[49]

During her stay, she was the guest of the British governor's wife for afternoon tea at the governor's mansion. Other guests were the wife of the bishop of Polynesia and, of course, Hobert.

On another occasion, she attended a cocktail party given by the bishop's wife where she was amused to find that the English guests "were a trifle aghast that a woman of [her] years should undertake war corresponding."[50]

Peggy made the greatest impression on the native Fijians. She knew people were staring at her, but she did not know just how she appeared to the local gentry in her khaki uniform and her khaki beret with its bright patches until she came upon an old man sunning himself in a doorway. She reported, "He looked up as I moved along the sidewalk, incredulity and surprise spread across his face. When I came opposite him, he half arose and exclaimed, 'My God, what is that?' "[51] It was a reaction she had suffered in other places, during other wars.

In welcome contrast, the Fijian women were delighted with her and especially loved her hat with the American patches in their brilliant blues, yellows, and reds. In return, she found the native women the most beautiful of any she had seen in the Pacific, of regal bearing and graceful walk, with their bushy hair sometimes dyed a "fetching brick red . . . oddly enough . . . not unbecoming." She was appalled at their clothing, for which she blamed past missionaries who had taken away

> their native covering made from grass and the bark of trees and dressed them in mother hubbards, high necked, long sleeved, and ankle length. In the intervening years this has changed to a tight fitting jacket of bright color and a long sarong-like skirt with about four inches of an ugly petticoat showing. Surrounded as they are

with all the exotic products of a tropical climate, they seem to have no sense of color and will put together colors and materials which cry out in protest.[52]

She thought the Fijian men's westernized clothing much more becoming than the women's and was much taken with the police uniforms which had a theatrical look to them. "Barefooted, dressed in white scalloped hemmed skirts and tightly fitting dark blue jackets, lobe sleeved, piped in scarlet and fastened with brightly polished brass buttons, policemen look like something thought up by the ballet master of the Radio City Music Hall."[53]

When Peggy commented on the extraordinary musical ability of the natives, the British adjutant told her that he had formed a band of native soldiers before the war which had become good enough that he wanted to take it on a world tour. Unfortunately, his superiors in the colonial government decided this would be unwise because the Fijian musicians might be subjected to temptations that would not be good for them, that they

> would be flattered and lionized and might become enamored of the great wonderful world outside their own little paradise and this was unthinkable. The government reasoned that the world was getting along very well without Fijian band music and that the natives themselves were happy. Why ask for trouble.[54]

There was obviously a monumental inconsistency in this fear of ruining them, for the British did not hesitate to train the Fijian men as soldiers, and as one English woman commented, "They can be sent away to fight and die but not to give people happiness."

Peggy wrote frequently and approvingly about most of the food found in abundance in the Fijis. One item that she detested was boiled taro which, she said, tasted "like nothing but a boiled sponge." The GI's disagreed with her; they thought it tasted like soured potatoes.

While she was in the Fijis, the news came that President Franklin Roosevelt had died. She reported on the shock and confusion of the Americans at Suva, who referred to the president as their assurance that the things at home for which they were fighting would not change while they were away. Men and women of other nationalities stopped her and Hobert on the street to tell them how bad they felt about the president's death.

While they were all shocked and grieved at Roosevelt's passing, they were soon buoyed up by the report of the end of the war in Europe. Some American soldiers she knew had been in the Pacific for thirty-eight months, and although they feared there would still be a lot of fighting before Japan was defeated, they felt that they would at last receive more help in their region than they had had with the Allied concentration on defeating Hitler first.

Peggy had hoped that her war reporting would finally take her all the way to Japan (she said she wanted to laugh at Admiral Nomura who, years before in Shanghai, had taunted her, saying Americans could not fight), but she did not make it. When the war in the Pacific ended in August 1945, after the dropping of the second atomic bomb on Japan, she returned to the United States. She did not intend to stay. "I'm not coming back to New York to live," she had said. "The climate is too bad. I'm going to settle down . . . on one of [the Pacific islands, maybe Fiji or even Hawaii again] in a small house with a big view — sea and mountains — raise flowers and have birds and pleasant days all the year round."[55] Failing a Pacific island, she thought she might be satisfied to settle in California.

In April 1946 she received a special commendation signed by Rear Adm. H. A. Miller and Secretary of the Navy James Forrestal, awarded "For Outstanding Performance and Service Rendered to the United States at War, As an Accredited Navy War Correspondent."[56]

Her friend from early days, Carroll Michener, had written her on August 11, 1944:

> I saw the story about you in a recent issue of Editor & Publisher. What a train of recollections it stirred up! I wallowed in them for days. The combination of you and Hawaii was too much for me. The picture presents certain changes, but you are essentially the same. I have not, of course, changed in any respect. I even deny that I am somewhat bald. I don't deny, however, that today I am 59 years of age. . . .
>
> Do you remember Allensworth? He was an old Duluth newspaper buddy who came out to see me at Denver. We three spent a New Year's eve together — or, rather, since I had to work, you two did. He always speaks of you when we meet, which is about a couple of times a year. . . . You can imagine how a couple of old gaffers like us would romanticize!
>
> Got out a kodak album the other day to see how you looked when you saw me off on the S.S. China for the Far East in 1912. You looked romantic. You *were* a romance![57]

In spite of the assertion in her reply to Michener's letter that she had never "enjoyed each day" as much as she did her days in the Central Pacific, there was a marked contrast between Peggy's experiences in

World War I and World War II. During the earlier war, as in El Paso at the time of Pershing's expedition into Mexico, she had been young and vigorous; now she was tired and, at least she thought, old. In addition, in that earlier war, the "war" stories she had written had not been based on what she had seen but on what someone else had told her, except for what she had observed in the training camps in France and there she had not seen what really happens in all-out war. Her story of the imagined bombing of El Paso in December 1917 was not based on anything she had witnessed.

During this war, even though her movements had been restricted, her contact with American boys who had recently been in battle and her visits to the maimed and dying in military hospitals brought home to her what war was really all about. Even the real war in Shanghai in 1932 had not been painful like this, though it had come close. But the boys she saw now, their bodies torn and bleeding, were *her* boys, and she was devastated by their suffering. In 1917 she had returned from France to El Paso to be welcomed as a heroine by an enthusiastic population, and she was in demand to speak to groups about her interesting, sometimes humorous, "war" adventures. But somehow her experiences in 1944-1945 had not quite been what she had hoped they would be. They were not "fun" as her earlier experiences had been, and she did not return from World War II full of stories to tell, even if she was asked. The suffering of her soldiers was hard for her to write about at the time. Now, reliving it must have been more than she could bear.

At last she understood what war was really all about and the romance was gone. If she had once been a war lover, that war lover was now dead.

There are men who cannot, must not age; ... *a cavalier is always young.*

Catherine Drinker Bowen,
*Biography: The Craft and the Calling*

# CHAPTER FIFTEEN

# "Whatever Happened to Peggy Hull?"

Peggy's life after the end of World War II was primarily the story of her alliance with Hobert Skidmore, the last man in her life.

All they had been through, good and bad, in the Pacific, had strengthened the remarkable bond between them.

After being demobilized in 1945, she, Hobert, and a friend of his started on an odyssey across the country. Hobert, who had had several stories published in the *Saturday Evening Post* during the war, was now on assignment for the *Post* to write a series of articles on the rehabilitation of returning war veterans. He was traveling to cities in various parts of the country to find out what was being done to help those veterans who were having difficulties making the transition to civilian life.[1]

On the way east, they stopped briefly at Oketo, Kansas, to visit Peggy's aunt and uncle, the Wrights.[2] In Marysville they were interviewed by the editor of the *Marshall County News,* Byron Guise, and his wife, Eulalia Weber Guise. Eulalia had followed Peggy's fortunes through her relatives at Marysville and Oketo ever since that meeting twenty-five years before.

Later, Eulalia could not help contrasting the Peggy she had first met in 1920, "the epitome of adventure and glamour — a trim figure in black, which enhanced her short, fluffy blonde hair and large luminous eyes," and the Peggy who had returned from the Pacific overweight, "careworn and weary." Eulalia was still "enamored with [Peggy's] mentality and personality, as when she started talking she fairly glowed."[3]

Subsequently, in an interview in Elmira, New York, Peggy was asked if she was going to write a book about her latest experiences as a war correspondent. She replied, "I didn't after the first war and I'm not going to now."[4] She had, of course, started working on a book after her return

Peggy Hull Deuell and Hobert Skidmore, April 1945. (Marshall County News *photo,*
*Peggy Hull Deuell Collection, Kansas Collection, University of Kansas Libraries*)

from France in December 1917. Though Floyd had jokingly suggested
that she call it "I Slept with a Million Men," her first working title had
been "How Peggy Got to Paris." Over the years, as she changed the
emphasis, the title changed to "Mlle. La Guerre" and then, by 1937,
to "Beyond This Post." These changes made no difference. It remained
unpublished.

She believed she might be able now to make a success of writing short
pieces in the same style as her war writing, and she made big plans to
go back to the Pacific as a roving reporter, covering Guam, Okinawa,
India, Burma, China, and the occupation of Japan. Gen. Robert L.
Eichelberger had encouraged her to do it, assuring her, "I shall be happy
to have you join my command."[5] She intended to take on this one last
writing task and then retire to her tropical island paradise or live in
California "on the side of a hill with a beautiful view."[6] Hobert was planning to continue his career as a roving reporter.[7] He was also hard at
work on his third book. (His second, *More Lives Than One,* published
in 1945, had been dedicated to "Major John Philip Bird, Great Friend,
Greater Oklahoman and again . . . Peggy Hull Deuell, War Correspondent, Who Stood By When the Spirit Wavered.")

As strong as the bond between them was, they seemed to be making plans to go on with their lives separately.

In February 1946, something happened that changed all their plans: Hubert Skidmore burned to death in a farmhouse fire in Pennsylvania.[8] It was a blow from which Hobert never recovered.

Gone were all the noble resolutions he had made around "Ireland's well." He sank once more into his old self-destructive self-pity. He did not stop working, but he stopped hoping.

Hobert had always been mystical about his relationship to his twin, feeling that he and his brother were only halves of the same whole. Whether it had really been that way or not, he saw the two of them as having been a fortress against the hostile world. In a thinly disguised autobiographical novel, *The Years Are Even,* published six years later, he attempted to work through his sense of loss and grief by reliving their times together. It was not a success. Some reviewers found it morbid and unpleasant.

Peggy, who seemed to understand what his twinness had meant to Hobert, became his refuge. After the funeral, when she came home to Saxton Hall, he came with her.

Soon Saxton Hall was full of visiting friends and relatives once more.[9]

Though on the surface Peggy seemed the same, she was one of those "returning veterans" who was having trouble adjusting to "civilian" life. She lost the sense of purpose she had felt during the war. Abandoned were her plans to take off for the Far East to join Eichelberger's command, to find her island, to live in peace. She was surrounded by people but, as in the old days after Harvey's death, she was depressed and lonely.

Disturbed by her unhappiness, her friends and family tried to help her (her Aunt Myrtle had come for an "extended" visit, and Maritta was planning to spend the summer with her[10]), but her problems seemed beyond them. And her chief problem, as her family saw it, was her attachment to Hobert.[11]

Peggy herself knew that she would be much better off without him. In June, when Hobert decided to go to Hollywood to "write for the movies,"[12] she was relieved.

In July 1946 she finally faced the fact that she could no longer handle Saxton Hall financially, and she sold it to Richard and Leonore Smith.[13]

When she left Saxton Hall and moved into the Gatehouse,[14] Peggy left the only luxurious home she had ever had. Though she had spent the exciting part of her life in hotels and barracks and tents and she was at least better off now financially than she had been in the days of living from paycheck to paycheck, the move was a comedown for her. Saxton Hall had been a stabilizing force in her life. In addition, she had always taken enormous pride in the place. It was roomy, comfortable, impressive: a tangible symbol of success. However, Saxton Hall had been going little by little, anyway, for she had been selling off her furniture piece by piece.

Harvey's cousin, Georgine, with whom Peggy had always been friendly, retired in September and moved into a nearby house on Duncan Avenue to lend her company and support.[15] Peggy also kept an apartment in New York City and spent a lot of her time there. Her Aunt Myrtle, feeling that with Hobert gone, Peggy was now going to be all right, went back to Kansas.

When, however, the movie writing did not work out, Hobert came "home" and started working on a new novel.

In March 1947 Harvey's mother died. Peggy arranged for her funeral to be held at the Gatehouse and for her burial near Harvey in the cemetery at New Windsor.[16]

Hobert back and things back to an unfortunate "normal," Peggy's Aunt Myrtle returned, hoping to use her influence to free Peggy from the hold he seemed to have on her. Peggy was becoming annoyed by the situation in which she found herself. As she wrote to the Smiths,

> Gosh, I feel like an old rag doll being pulled apart by [a] half dozen children. Aunt Myrtle pulls me this way and Hobe pulls me that way and Georgine is out there pulling too and I know she wishes they would go away and leave [me] alone and that I would come and stay with her — why don't people hate me? It would be very convenient at times![17]

Though she knew the life they had fallen into was disaster for both her and Hobert (she even copied into a personal notebook a short comment on the devastating effects of alcohol in excess: "In a home, love, affection, loyalty all go. It is tragic how patient people can be when you're visibly smashed[ — ]a broken back or something[ — ]and what a nuisance you become if your broken soul is stumbling about before their eyes"),[18] she was becoming less inclined to tolerate anything she viewed as interference in her life, even from the most favored members of her family.

In July Byron and Eulalia Guise, as part of their lengthy trip east that year, stopped in New York to see her. They were first entertained by Peggy, Myrtle, Georgine, and Hobert at Peggy's penthouse apartment in The City. Hobert, whose novel, *Disturb Not Our Dreams,* had just come out in hard cover, took them on a tour of bookstores where it was on display.[19] The book had been well received, and Hobert, always at his best when he was enjoying success, was at his most charming. In fact, they found what many before them had, that when he wanted to be, there were few people as charming as Hobert; even those who had reservations about him had to admit he was enormously attractive.[20]

Peggy returned to Cornwall-on-Hudson after making arrangements for the Guises to come out later that day. When they arrived, they saw that she had already started on the pitcher of martinis she had prepared for them.[21] They were surprised by her drinking. They could not know how insecure she had become, how apprehensive about their visit, how fearful she must have been that all the glamour had worn off and now in obviously "reduced circumstances," she was not living up to Eulalia's longtime image of her. The means she took to bolster herself was, as usual, counterproductive, for it resulted in their getting the very impression she no doubt wished to avoid giving.

During these years another of their problems was that while Hobert was successful with his writing, he had a tendency to spend his money, on others as well as himself, as fast as he got it.[22] Since Peggy shared this weakness, their financial position had grown worse and worse. That, coupled with their weakness for alcohol, was making for some pretty painful times for them.

The Guises could see that, whatever their problems, there was something very deep between Peggy and the usually pleasant, friendly Hobert. She was obviously very proud of his success,[23] and he quite openly admired her for her achievements as a war correspondent, an admiration she needed, and he encouraged her to continue her writing. From time to time she made lists of possible titles for stories: "Go West Young Woman if You Would Marry," "A Hot Time in Cold Siberia," "Sinister Shanghai," "I Married My Husband," "Does Divorce Pay?"[24] They seemed a sad sort of outline of her life. She even completed several stories based on her personal experiences, but they all remained unpublished.

In December 1947 Peggy's father died, and one of the last constants in her life was gone. Now that she had lost both of her parents, suddenly she felt a lot older as part of the oldest generation in her immediate family. All of these realities undoubtedly added fuel to the periods of depression she frequently fell into.

In April 1949 Hobert's novel, *O Careless Love,* was published to excellent reviews, and in the summer Peggy went to California to visit Maritta, now remarried, and Sheila Foote and Giles Healey, now married.[25] She hoped to find some relief from the strain of Hobert and his problems. She had barely arrived when Hobert called her. It was 6:30 in the morning and he was obviously very drunk. A couple of days later she got word from a friend that Hobert had been so drunk and destructive that day, the friend had had to call the police. Peggy was beginning to feel there was no escape from him, and she "was scared to death as usual that something terrible would happen" when he was on one of his violent binges.[26]

The situation did not improve after she returned from California, and she began the search for a new home in earnest. But almost a year passed before she saw a real estate advertisement that captured her imagination. The ad offered "attractively furnished secluded houses in beautiful country place."[27] The place was Guemes Island off the coast of Washington, not far from Seattle. It seemed to be just what she had dreamed about.

In the fall of 1950, Peggy went west to Guemes. At first she loved it, the peace, the quiet, the closeness to untrammeled nature. As she wrote in an article, "I Ran Away from Home at 60," published in *Family Circle* in December 1955,

> I find that country life is kind to us older ones. All around us are age-old forests, rocks, mountains, and sea.[28]

It was such a relief to her to get away from the frustrations and loneliness which she had often felt in New York. Though most of her life she had not been given to introspection, now, in a fit of regret, trying to figure out where it had all gone wrong, she conducted a solitary inquest into the causes of the unhappiness of her last marriage and decided, not unreasonably, that a lot of credit belonged to "Mother" Deuell.

> I loved Harvey as much as it is possible to love but I did not want to surrender this freedom to his mother — for him I could have . . . gone anywhere — lived in a tent on the desert because we belonged to each other — but the presence of his mother who was determined there was to be no happiness for us put such a terrible price on our union that I know I did not go into it with the complete surrender which I should have made. In my efforts to rise above the ensuing difficulties which came thick and fast when we moved into Saxton Hall, I pushed my resentment deeper and deeper into the subconscious.[29]

From this distance she could see that in Cornwall-on-Hudson she had been living with "dead dreams" and "a dead Harvey."

> Here Harvey is alive and vital — he does not hold me in tight cold hands, *he is free too.* . . . In Cornwall the name Deuell reproached

me — I [felt] I was not able to rise to the height of spiritual perfection which Harvey deserved.[30]

Her belated self-examination led her to the conclusion that her "revolting extravagance — [her] psychotic desire to get rid of every cent which Harvey had left — [her] distaste for money" had grown out of a deepseated, long-standing lack of self-confidence. She had been "as afraid of [herself] as a little child [is] . . . of a bogey man."[31] She had never known what she "was going to do or how disastrous an undertaking [she] might indulge in." Now she felt she was getting it all sorted out. She no longer drank to excess when she felt she could not cope.

She was full of ideas for business ventures — mail-order sales, glassmaking factories, a revolutionary kind of "cat toilet" — for her friends to initiate that would make them all millionaires.

She reveled in the friendliness of the Island. Here they, for Hobert had joined her almost immediately, were being given a fresh start. Hobert loved it and it was a great relief to Peggy to see that everyone liked him, too. "There is none of that resentment which I always sensed around Cornwall," she wrote.[32] Because he seemed so content and had a new friend in Seattle, she hoped he would make the Island his permanent home.

Unfortunately, the euphoria did not last. The Island was too quiet, too remote, too far from her friends. She started to experience fits of her old depression again. One day she was "full of energy — good health — and zim"; the next she was overtaken by a "sudden and terrible fatigue . . . an odd drowsiness."[33] Guemes was not her paradise, after all. At sixty she had "run away from home"; at sixty-one she ran back to "civilization" and Cornwall-on-Hudson.

During the summer of 1952 she went to California again. It was looking better and better to her as the place to start a new life, or at least a different one.[34]

Finally, in 1953, she gave in to California's siren call, the appeal of being closer to Maritta and Sheila, and Hobert's urging (he had not stayed on Guemes, after all), packed her camel's hair shawl, Harvey's bathing suit, her uniforms, an Indian rug, Harvey's dress clothes, and her few remaining treasures, poignant mementos of a life of romance, excitement — and love. She gave her Chinese bed to the Smiths; in May she and Hobert moved to Capistrano Palisades, then a desolate, semiabandoned housing development of many streets and few houses.[35] Theirs was, she thought, a "pleasant, rambling, white and blue house with a fine view of the ocean."[36] Four cats shared the house with them, and to Peggy's delight a small skunk took up temporary residence in their garage.

Now in her sixties, Peggy still dreamed about romantic adventures; she told a reporter who interviewed her for the *San Clemente Post,* "There's a trip my grandfather didn't make, around Cape Horn. I think he was sorry he hadn't, and he wanted me to do it for him. There's a place on the Straits of Magellan — Punta Arenas — where nobody ever goes. I think I might look into it."[37]

The trip was another of her unrealized dreams, but she did not cease to dream, to make elaborate plans for her friends and herself even when she knew the plans would probably fall through. She did enjoy a triumph: "I Ran Away from Home at 60" brought her welcome attention and admiring letters from readers who identified with the situation. Under the influence of this precious celebrity, she started making big plans for new writing projects. She was going to write a biography of Harvey and rewrite her own "in episodes" so that her agent could sell it "as excerpts." She was going to finish a piece on Billy Mitchell, one on Patton and one on Pershing and then "go on from there."[38]

That same year, 1955, the year of her last successful writing, she moved from the Palisades because it had suddenly come alive and was being overbuilt. "I took," she wrote Dorothy Sutherland, "as usual — a $5,000 loss on the place."[39]

She did not go to Punta Arenas but north to Carmel Valley, a little community twelve miles inland from Carmel-by-the-Sea, where Hobert had found and rented a neat little green wood bungalow she called La Rancheria. A charming house, La Rancheria boasted a huge fireplace/bookcase wall on one side of the living room, on another a great expanse of glass facing the mountains on the other side of the valley, and a protected patio.

Hobert and the cats, of course, moved to La Rancheria with her. Even here she found a retired general who had been "a beau of [hers] on the Mexican border."

Now sometimes when things became particularly difficult for her, her thoughts would turn to Tei,

> the most devoted, best friend I ever had — Tei came to me at Saxton Hall out of a blue sky — he stayed until he died and almost his last words were that he would always "take care of you Missy" — I had many manifestations of that but there was a long time that it seemed as if Tei had gone on to some other part of the Universe.[40]

One of these manifestations was the appearance of Henri Ernst Marchon, a Swiss native who was a waiter and bartender in San Francisco.

Hobert Skidmore, Peggy Hull Deuell, and Henri Ernst Marchon at La Rancheria, Carmel Valley, California. *(In authors' possession, courtesy of Raymond A. Ruffino)*

Everybody loved the sweet, gentle, always smiling Ernie. In the beginning he had been Hobert's friend, but as Hobert became more and more of a problem, their mutual bondage to him forged a tie between Ernie and Peggy, and he became the friend she could count on and confide in and receive help from.

Maritta and Sheila kept in touch with her and tried to help, too; but they both had families and careers to be concerned about (Maritta's sixth novel, *Buttonwood*, was published in 1962), and so Peggy did her best to cope with Hobert with the help of Ernie who came down from San Francisco almost every weekend.[41]

During the last decade of her life, much to the dismay of her Kansas relatives, Peggy was gradually turning away from them.[42] They blamed Hobert, but there is evidence that he was not entirely (at least directly) to blame. Peggy resented her relatives' efforts, however well intentioned, to "rescue" her from the toils of Hobert. She knew that all her relatives were aware of his homosexuality. She had always accepted it, and she was in no mood to suffer their disapproval of it. Admittedly, his drinking was a never-ending problem, one which caused her pain and resulted in almost reclusive periods for her because, as she admitted to friends, "I can't encourage any social life because I never know when Hobe will be in a bad condition."[43]

Peggy in the 1960s with one of her cats. *(In authors' possession, courtesy of Raymond A. Ruffino)*

It was this situation that made her thankful that Hobert was in the village when her cousin, Doris, and her husband arrived, unannounced, on her doorstep one day. Since Hobert did not return while they were there, Doris's most vivid impression was of Peggy's cats.

"She loved those cats," Doris said. "They had a life!"[44]

Peggy herself realized that "if it hadn't been for [the various cats she had had over the years, she] could have operated with more sense but," she said, "I do love them and they gave me comfort at a time when I so sorely needed it."[45]

265

There was something besides Hobert that caused Peggy to avoid her family. Her health was poor now[46] and, having given up any attempt to control her weight, she was very heavy. Whatever she might have said about accepting it gracefully, her vanity recoiled from the realization. The correspondents on the Mexican border in 1916 had had the saying long before Gen. Douglas MacArthur had adapted it: "Old war correspondents never die; they merely fade away."[47] Peggy was fading away. "Women live too damned long," she said. "I know I have."[48] She could not bear to have her relatives, particularly her nieces, whom she wanted to remember her as the dashing, romantic aunt they had known, see her now as fat and old; and so the aunt who had been so generous and friendly now withdrew from them. There were even times that, when they telephoned to find out how she was, she was cross with them; since they were sincerely concerned about her and still loved her, they were terribly hurt.[49]

Having cut herself off from any close ties with relatives, she leaned more and more on Ernie who gave her strength and on Hobert, the weakest of reeds. On several occasions, Hobert walked out and went on lengthy binges, but he always came back. He was, in truth, the child she had never borne; though he often caused her almost unendurable pain, while he was there, she was not alone.

Finally she realized that he would never get control of his life. She blamed herself, knowing that many times, instead of helping him become independent, she had encouraged his weaknesses to tie him to her. She poured out her feelings to a few friends:

> Hobe is still a problem and I think will be as long as he lives or I live — I can't seem to shed the shackles — . . . He has so many psychological problems in connection with his alcoholism. . . . He is so pathetic — . . . he wants friends and he wants to be loved and yet he destroys every chance of friendship. . . .
>
> I know that the first inclination is to blame this poor, lost soul — I can't. . . .
>
> [Now] I keep telling myself and hoping and praying that somehow it will end and I will be able to make a little contentment before it is too late.[50]

At her wits' end, searching for something to give her peace, she began to think about the reassurance and rest the church seemed to offer. Ernie was a devout Catholic and felt that his church ties gave him strength and consolation. Hilda, happy, always able to cope, Hilda was a Catholic, too.

In this frame of mind, she fell under the spell of the local priest, young, handsome Juan Oronoz; despite having believed in astrology most of her life and toyed with supernaturalism and Rosicrucianism, she succumbed at last to the powerful appeal of Catholicism. On January 31, 1965, she was baptized with Ernie Marchon and Lucille Erdle, a local friend, as her sponsors.[51]

Near the end she must sometimes have wondered if any of it had mattered, after all; if she had mattered. No one even knew her name anymore. They remembered Floyd and Ernie Pyle and Marguerite Higgins, but Peggy Hull was just a paragraph in articles about women war correspondents and a line or two in standard journalism texts, a by-the-way or an-interesting-sidelight or the-first-woman-officially.

She had not been a lightweight. What she had done had been important. She had a navy commendation as tangible evidence that she had served her country well and faithfully. The top brass — Morton, March, Eichelberger, even Pershing — had taken her seriously, had helped her, some had become her friends.

So why was she being forgotten when others, like Pyle, had done no more than she? It was not that she was covetous of his fame or the fame of any of them. She had never begrudged anybody else their good fortune. But surely she must have had a hard time understanding why people could not have remembered her, too.

The happiest times of her life had been the years she was on the Border and in France during World War I. She was unable to recall, in 1965, where she had been on VJ Day of World War II, while she could remember vividly that at the time of the Armistice in 1918 she was on "a rusty Russian, cock roach filled old steamer on [her] way to Vladivostok."[52] Her pride was that she had once — a lifetime ago — been a dashing war correspondent.

To be sure, she had not found happiness in her marriages — well, maybe a little with Harvey, a very little, but a little, and maybe if Harvey had lived — but Harvey had died. She had lived, and now she was, at last, too weak to fight anymore.

And she had a new worry, a pain in her left breast that would not go away. She tried to ignore it, no doubt suspecting what it meant. Finally, she told Hobert about it and he took her to a doctor. The doctor confirmed her fears: It was cancer.

Always so fiercely independent, so apparently in charge of her own destiny, she began to wonder now if she ever really had been in fact. Perhaps after all,

you don't choose a life — Life does the choosing for you — you don't really make a decision with a capital D — Life is a series

267

of pressures — influences exerting pressures from various directions. You ultimately succumb to the greatest pressure.[53]

All her life, she had felt compelled to play a part she thought she had chosen for herself, a role of dashing romantic, heroic SOMEBODY. Now she was tired and sick and searching for rest.

She grew more and more dependent on Hobert who, finally realizing he was going to lose her, became gentle and loving, taking care of her when she was ill, teasing her, and driving her around the peninsula in their old Ford.[54]

In May 1967 he wrote to Frances and her second husband, Alan Rankin:

> For sometime [Peggy] concealed a pain in her breast and . . . when I discovered it, I took her to the doctor and he found she had cancer. . . . [Now] a small place has also been found cancerous in the shin of her left leg. I am trying to prepare for whatever happens . . .
>
> We have many friends and neighbors and between us, we keep her as happy and cheerful as possible. Her morale is high, her mind as lucid and sharp as ever. . . .
>
> My friendship with Peggy, almost thirty years now, is the proudest part of my life. I do not know anyone else who has had such a rewarding friendship based on mutual respect, admiration and affection. It has been a purpose for me. . . .
>
> Peggy has been content with her life and, I am sure with the way it will end. . . .
>
> I am devoting the months ahead to Peggy's condition, and welfare, and everything possible will be done for her. She has always love[d] you, and been so very proud of you, and she always will be.[55]

This letter, which would have made all the difference to her bewildered and heartsick niece, was misplaced in Hobert's anguish over Peggy's rapidly worsening condition and was not ever mailed.

Peggy had never been a complainer, and she was not one now. She was seventy-seven years old and had had, taken whole, an eventful, even wonderful life. She would take what came as she always had.

She had long been an insomniac, but now she accepted that, too, and lay in her bed with the window open so that the cats, her solace, could come in and go out as they pleased. When she would see the lights of her neighbors, Frieda and Lew Harbin, come on, signaling the start of a new day, she would be grateful that she had survived another night.

She sometimes talked to Frieda about all the places she had been, the things she had done.[56]

By the time she was forced to enter the Monterey hospital, it was obvious to Maritta and Sheila and the other friends who went to see her that she did not have long to live.

The cancer had so altered her appearance that the afternoon of the day before she died, when Frieda visited her, she said, "Oh, Frieda, I didn't want you to see me like this."[57] It was a brave echo of her old fierce personal pride.

Of course if, just passing by, you had looked into the room, and if you had seen her lying on the antiseptic bed waiting for the disease to eat away what little was left of her life, if you had not known, you would have thought she was just an ordinary seventy-seven-year-old woman.

But you would have been wrong.

She was the brown-eyed, khaki-clad plucky Yankee girl reporter who had won her spurs in France and run with "Dad" Whiffen in pursuit of a scoop in Vladivostok, who had roamed the deck of an England-bound ship, scanning the sea for torpedoes, the girl with whom all of El Paso had fallen in love.

She was the girl in the picture in the *El Paso Morning Times*, riding in front of a general leading her troops out of Mexico.

## Death and Funeral Notices

DEUELL — Eleanor Goodnough Deuell, June 19, 1967. A resident of the Monterey Peninsula 14 years. A native of Bennington, Kansas. Age 76 years. Beloved wife of the late Harvey V. Deuell. First Woman War Correspondent. A member of the Overseas Press Club of America, Our Lady of Mount Carmel Sodality, and the North American Newspaper [Alliance]. Private prayers for the departed and Recitation of the Rosary will be held tomorrow, Tuesday, at 8 p.m. in the Mission Mortuary. Interment, Woodlawn Cemetery, New Windsor, New York. Mission Mortuary in charge of local arrangements.

*Monterey Peninsula Herald*

Hobert Douglas Skidmore died twenty-two and a half months later in the Veterans Administration Hospital at Palo Alto of "multiple liver abscesses."

He was fifty-nine years old.[58]

# NOTES

## INTRODUCTION

1. Mary P. Ryan, *Womanhood in America,* 3d ed. (New York: Franklin Watts, 1983), 212.

2. Sophonisba P. Breckinridge, *Women in the Twentieth Century: A Study of Their Political, Social and Economic Activities* (New York: McGraw-Hill Book Co., Inc., 1933), 99, 158, 172, 176, 188-90.

3. Carroll W. Pursell, Jr., *Technology in America: A History of Individuals and Ideas* (Cambridge, Mass.: MIT Press, 1981), 4.

4. Laurence Houseman, "What is WOMANLY?" *Good Housekeeping* 64 (Jan. 1917): 53, 118.

5. Peggy Hull Deuell to Carroll K. Michener, Feb. 22, 1945, Carroll K. Michener and Family Papers, Minnesota Historical Society, St. Paul, Minn.

6. *Ibid.*

7. Irene Corbally Kuhn, "Peggy Hull Deuell: Correspondent on Four Fronts," Overseas Press Club *Bulletin,* July 15, 1967, 4.

8. William Broyles, Jr., "Why Men Love War," *Esquire* 102, no. 5 (Nov. 1984): 55-65. This is a fascinating and enlightening article on war's seductive appeal to men (and women).

9. "First Accredited Woman War Correspondent Describes Death and Beauty on Pacific Atolls," *Park East Magazine,* Nov. 1945, 7, Box 1, Folder no. 10, Peggy Hull Deuell Collection, Kansas Collection, University of Kansas Libraries, Lawrence, Kans.; hereafter cited as PHDC.

10. Peggy Hull to Byron E. Guise, July 1, 1937.

11. Ernest J. Simmons, *Leo Tolstoy,* 2 vols. (New York: Vintage Books, 1960), 1:xiii.

## CHAPTER ONE
### Growing Up in Kansas

1. Deuell to Michener.

2. Carroll K. Michener to Peggy Hull Deuell, Aug. 11, 1944, Box 1, Folder no. 8, PHDC.

3. Deuell to Michener.

4. *Minneapolis* (Kans.) *Commercial,* Jan. 1, 1890.

5. *Seventh Biennial Report of the Kansas State Board of Agriculture . . ., 1889-1890* (Topeka: Kansas Publishing House, 1891), 189.

6. James L. Ehernberger and Francis G. Gschwind, *Smoke Above the Plains* (Calaway, Neb.: E & G Publications, 1965), 14.

7. Mildred (Kephart) Rake, interview with authors, Salina, Kans., Dec. 7, 1979.

8. Alice (Goodnough) Reissig, interview with authors, Salina, Kans., Dec. 1, 1979.

9. J. K. Bloomfield, *The Oneidas* (New York: Alden Brothers Publishers, 1907), 243.

10. *Ibid.,* 240-88.

11. Alice (Goodnough) Reissig to authors, Feb. 6, 1988.

12. *Ibid.*

13. Doris (Haley) Briney, interview with authors, Bennington, Kans., Dec. 1, 1979.

14. Frances (Goodnough) Rankin, interview with authors, Terre Haute, Ind., Dec. 14, 1979.

15. Minnie E. Goodnough, plaintiff, v. Edwy Goodnough, defendant, District Court of Ottawa County, Kans., Oct. 30, 1894 (Case no. 2970).

16. *Goodnough v. Goodnough,* Answer and Cross Petition, Dec. 10, 1894.

17. Rankin interview.

18. *Goodnough v. Goodnough,* Final Decree, Feb. 21, 1895 (Case no. 2970).

19. *Kansas State Decennial Census, 1895, Richland Township, Ottawa County,* Microfilm, reel no. 116, Fort Hays State University, Hays, Kans.

20. Briney interview; *Ottawa County Democrat* (Bennington, Kans.), Apr. 3, 1896.

21. *Ibid.,* Apr. 2, 1897.

22. Hull to Guise.

23. *Ibid.*

24. "Notes for Naked on a Limb," MS, Notebooks, C31, vol. 1, PHDC.

25. *Ibid.*

26. *Ottawa County Democrat,* Mar. 30, 1900; June 8, 1900; May 10, 1901.

27. Briney interview.

28. *Ottawa County Democrat,* Nov. 28, 1902; Dec. 26, 1902.

29. *Ibid.,* Mar. 6, 1903.

30. *Ibid.,* June 12, 1903; Mar. 10, 1905.

31. *Ibid.,* Nov. 01 [*sic*], 1905; July 21, 1905; Dec. 29, 1905.

32. Rake interview.

33. *Ibid.*

34. Rankin interview.

35. *Ottawa County Democrat,* Aug. 22, 1907.

36. *Ibid.,* "Social Events," Feb. 20, 1908.

37. Byron E. Guise, "Peggy Hull, Remembered Here As An Ambitious Girl, First Accredited Woman War Correspondent, Again Reports the War," *Marshall County News* (Marysville, Kans.), Feb. 10, 1944.

38. "The Post Goes Visiting — Peggy Hull Deuell — First Woman War Correspondent," *San Clemente* (Calif.) *Post,* Aug. 6, 1953, Box 1, Folder no. 9, PHDC.

39. Harry J. Lambeth, "Distant War Fronts Are Peggy Hull's Beat," *Editor & Publisher,* May 6, 1944, 58.

40. *Junction City* (Kans.) *Sentinel,* July 22, 1909; Aug. 13, 1908; July 1, 1908.

## CHAPTER TWO
### Go West, Young Woman

General information about Hawaii, 1912-1914, came from the *Honolulu Star-Bulletin* (Territory of Hawaii), 1912-1914; the *Pacific Commercial Advertiser,* Honolulu, 1912-1914; the *Hawaiian Star,* Honolulu, 1912-1914; the *Evening Bulletin,* Honolulu, 1912-1914; Joseph Feher, *Hawaii: A Pictorial History,* Bernice P. Bishop Museum Special Publication No. 58 (Honolulu: Bishop Museum Press, 1969); William Simonds, *The Hawaiian Telephone Story* (Honolulu: Hawaiian Telephone Co., 1958).

1. "The Post Goes Visiting."

2. *Ibid.*

3. *Junction City Sentinel,* Aug. 5, 1909.

4. *Denver City Directory* (Denver: Ballenger & Richards, 1910), 618.

5. *Salina* (Kans.) *Daily Union,* Oct. 28, 1910.

6. *Ibid.*

7. *Ibid.,* Sept. 15, 1910.

8. *Ibid.,* Oct. 28, 1910.

9. L. D. Avery, city editor, "To City Editors," Denver, Colo., [n.d.], Scrapbooks, vol. 2, PHDC.

10. *Hawaiian Star,* Apr. 16, 1912; "The Post Goes Visiting."

11. Michener to Deuell; *Hawaiian Star,* May 31, 1912.

12. *Pacific Commercial Advertiser,* Oct. 4, 1913.

13. *Evening Bulletin,* Apr. 17, 1912.

14. Henrietta Goodnough Hull, "My Impressions of Hawaii," *Ocean Travel,* Scrapbooks, vol. 1, PHDC.

15. "The Post Goes Visiting."

16. *Pacific Commercial Advertiser,* Oct. 28, 1912.

17. *Sunday Advertiser,* Nov. 17, 1912.

18. *Ibid.,* Aug. 9, 1912.

19. *Ibid.*

20. Guise, "Peggy Hull Remembered."

21. Reissig interview.

22. *Pacific Commercial Advertiser,* Sept. 1, 1912, Feature section.

23. *Evening Bulletin,* June 18, 1912.

24. *Honolulu Star-Bulletin,* Oct. 1, 1913.

25. Guise, "Peggy Hull Remembered."

26. *Ibid.*

27. Barbara Belford, *Brilliant Bylines: A Biographical Anthology of Notable Newspaper Women in America* (New York: Columbia University Press, 1986), 191.

28. *Pacific Commercial Advertiser,* Dec. 14, 1913.

29. Henrietta Goodnough Hull, "Laupahoehoe, Its Beauty and the Grandeur of the Leisurely Trip Across Country from Hilo," Scrapbooks, vol. 1, PHDC.

30. *Pacific Commercial Advertiser,* Feb. 14, 1914.

31. *Ibid.,* Mar. 8, 1914.

32. "Peggy Writes of Escape from Mexicans," Scrapbooks, vol. 2, PHDC.

33. Stanley Walker, *City Editor* (New York: Blue Ribbon Books, Inc., 1940), 41.

34. "Harvey Deuell, Managing Editor of News Dies," *New York Daily News,* Oct. 30, 1939.

35. *Ibid.*

36. *New York Times,* Oct. 30, 1939.

37. *New York Daily News,* Oct. 30, 1939.

38. Desirée (Teddy Hahn) Godfrey, interview with authors, Cornwall-on-Hudson, N.Y., May 15, 1980; Deuell to Michener.

39. *El Paso* (Tex.) *Morning Times,* Feb. 17, 1918.

40. Maritta (Wolff) Stegman, interview with authors, Los Angeles, Calif., Apr. 7, 1980.

41. "The Post Goes Visiting."

42. *Minneapolis* (Minn.) *Daily News,* Scrapbooks, vol. 1, PHDC.

43. Deuell to Michener.

## CHAPTER THREE
### "I'm a Soldier Now!"

1. George Juergens, *Joseph Pulitzer and the New York World* (Princeton, N.J.: Princeton University Press, 1966), 133.

2. *Ibid.,* 132-33.

3. Frank Luther Mott, *American Journalism, A History: 1690-1960,* 3d ed. (New York: MacMillan Co., 1962), 599.

4. Juergens, 16n.

5. *Cleveland* (Ohio) *Press,* Feb. 23, 1916.

6. *Ibid.,* Mar. 1, 1916.

7. "Girl Writes Clever Stories," *Editor & Publisher And The Journalist,* Apr. 8, 1916, 1361.

8. "Let Peggy Shop for You," Box 1, Folder no. 1, PHDC.

9. *Cleveland* (Ohio) *Plain Dealer,* May 3, 1916.

10. *Ibid.*

11. "Peggy Returns from Hike to Be Honor Guest at Gyro City," Box 1, Folder no. 1, PHDC.

12. Michael C. Meyer and William L. Sherman, *The Course of Mexican History,* 3d ed. (New York: Oxford University Press, 1987), 539.

13. *Ibid.*

14. *Ibid.,* 540.

15. Haldeen Braddy, *Pershing's Mission in Mexico,* 2d ed. (El Paso, Tex.: Texas Western Press, 1972), 8.

16. *Cleveland Plain Dealer,* Apr. 5, 1916.

17. *Ibid.*

18. *Ibid.,* Apr. 19, 1916.

19. *Ibid.*

20. "The Post Goes Visiting."

21. Alfred Mewett, *A Brief History of Troop A, 107th Regiment of Cavalry, Ohio National Guard[:] The Black Horse Troop For Many Years Known As the First City Troop of Cleveland* (Cleveland, Ohio, 1923), 97.

22. *Columbus* (Ohio) *Dispatch,* July 9, 1916.

23. *Ibid.*

24. *Cleveland Plain Dealer,* July 14, 1916.

25. Briney interview.

26. "Peggy Will Go to Mexico to Write War News," Scrapbooks, vol. 2, PHDC.

27. *Ibid.*

28. *Ibid.*

## CHAPTER FOUR
### With Pershing on the Mexican Border

General information in this chapter came from the *Cleveland* (Ohio) *Plain Dealer,* 1916; the *El Paso* (Tex.) *Herald,* 1916; the *El Paso* (Tex.) *Morning Times,* 1916-1917; and Alfred Mewett, *A Brief History of Troop A, 107th Regiment of Cavalry, Ohio National Guard[:] The Black Horse Troop For Many Years Known As The First City Troop of Cleveland* (Cleveland, Ohio, 1923).

1. *Cleveland Plain Dealer,* Aug. 24, 1916.

2. *Ibid.*

3. Braddy, *Pershing's Mission in Mexico,* 62.

4. *Cleveland Plain Dealer,* Aug. 24, 1916.

5. "Girl Will Fly to Vera Cruz," Scrapbooks, vol. 2, PHDC.

6. *Ibid.*

7. *Cleveland Plain Dealer,* Sept. 21, 1916.

8. "Book Notes," Notebooks, B28, vol. 2, PHDC.

9. *El Paso Morning Times,* Aug. 19, 1917.

10. *Cleveland Plain Dealer,* Sept. 21, 1916.

11. *Social Hygiene,* Apr. 1917, 207.

12. Braddy, *Pershing's Mission in Mexico,* 61.

13. *Social Hygiene,* 210.

14. "The Undesirables," Scrapbooks, vol. 2, PHDC.

15. Mewett, *A Brief History of Troop A,* 99. It was at Camp Pershing that "dog tags" were first used.

16. Edward Gibbons, *Floyd Gibbons: Your Headline Hunter* (New York: Exposition Press, 1953), 57; *El Paso Morning Times,* Jan. 31, 1917.

17. *Marysville* (Kans.) *Advocate Democrat,* May 1, 1919.

18. *Sunday News* (Charleston, S.C.), Oct. 22, 1916. We could find no similar story in El Paso newspapers. A comment in her *Herald* column (Sept. 23-24) has led us to question whether the extent and duration of her participation in the march were as extensive as this article portrayed them; however, she was changing jobs from the *Herald* to the *Morning Times* at this time, which might account for the lack of a report in either of these papers.

19. *Ibid.*

20. *Marysville Advocate Democrat,* May 1, 1919.

21. *Ibid.*

22. *Sunday News,* Oct. 22, 1916. She had a "pink fixation." To her the color seemed to symbolize all that she should be, but not necessarily what she wanted to be. She may have experienced what researchers have lately found evidence of: that pink has a calming, even enervating effect on people. Perhaps in Peggy's case, it soothed her, gave her rest after her khaki-colored "military" exertions.

23. *El Paso Herald,* weekend edition, Sept. 23-24, 1916.

24. *El Paso Morning Times,* Nov. 12, 1916; *Cleveland Plain Dealer,* July 28, 1916.

25. *El Paso Morning Times,* Nov. 5, 1916.

26. *Ibid.,* Dec. 10, 1916.

27. *Ibid.,* Dec. 17, 1916.

28. *Ibid.,* Feb. 4, 1917.

29. *Ibid.,* Aug. 19, 1917.

30. *Ibid.*

31. Herbert Mason, *The Great Pursuit* (New York: Random House, 1970), 231-32.

32. "Peggy Watches Homeless Horde of Starving Mexicans Enter United States at Columbus, New Mexico," Scrapbooks, vol. 2, PHDC.

33. *Ibid.*

34. *El Paso Morning Times,* Feb. 6, 1917.

35. Kalton C. Lahue, ed., *Motion Picture Pioneer: The Selig Polyscope Company* (New York: A. S. Barnes & Co., 1973).

36. Irene Corbally Kuhn, "Peggy Hull Deuell," 5.

37. Frank. E. Vandiver, *Illustrious Americans: John J. Pershing* (Morristown, N.J.: Silver Burdett Co., 1967), 191.

38. Braddy, *Pershing's Mission in Mexico*, 61-62.

39. Vandiver, *Illustrious Americans*, 191.

40. John J. Pershing, *My Experiences in the World War*, 2 vols. (New York: Frederick A. Stokes Co., 1931), 1:10.

## CHAPTER FIVE
### How Peggy Got to Paris

1. W. C. McCormick to "Miss Peggy," *El Paso Morning Times*, Apr. 1, 1917.

2. *El Paso Morning Times*, Apr. 8, 1917.

3. *Ibid.*, May 20, 1917.

4. *Ibid.*, June 2, 1917.

5. "Plucky Yankee Girl Reporter First War Correspondent to Win British Censor's Praise," Box 1, Folder no. 3, PHDC.

6. *Ibid.*

7. *El Paso Morning Times*, June 16, 1917.

8. *Ibid.*

9. Historical Division, Dept. of the Army, *United States Army in the World War, 1917-1919: Reports of Commander in Chief, A.E.F. Staff Sections and Services*, pt. 2, 116-17, and *Bulletins, G.H.Q., A.E.F.*, 73-74 (Washington, D.C.: GPO, 1948); Burnel Hershey, "Sons o'Guns of August," in *Dateline 1966: Covering War* (New York: Overseas Press Club of America, 1966), 44.

10. *El Paso Morning Times*, Aug. 8, 1917.

11. *Ibid.*, June 2, 1917.

12. *Ibid.*, June 17, 1917.

13. *Ibid.*, June 16, 1917.

14. *Ibid.*

15. *Ibid.*

16. "Plucky Yankee Girl Reporter."

17. *El Paso Morning Times*, July 18, 1917.

18. *Ibid.*

19. *Ibid.*

20. *Ibid.*

21. *Ibid.*

22. *Ibid.*, July 24, 1917.

23. *Ibid.*, July 23, 1917.

24. *Ibid.*

25. *Ibid.*

26. *Ibid.*, July 31, 1917.

27. *Ibid.*

28. Phillip Knightley, *The First Casualty from the Crimea to Vietnam: The War Correspondent as Hero, Propagandist, and Myth Maker* (New York & London: Harcourt Brace Jovanovich, 1975), 85.

29. *El Paso Morning Times*, Jan. 26, 1918.

30. *Ibid.*, July 31, 1917.

CHAPTER SIX

A War Correspondent Without Accreditation

1. *El Paso Morning Times,* July 31, 1917.

2. *Chicago Tribune,* Army edition (Paris, France), Aug. 18, 1917.

3. *El Paso Morning Times,* Aug. 9, 1917.

4. Frank E. Vandiver, *Black Jack: The Life and Times of John J. Pershing,* 2 vols. (College Station, Tex.: Texas A & M University Press, 1977), 2:618.

5. Emmet Crozier, *American Correspondents on the Western Front, 1914-1918* (New York: Oxford University Press, 1959), 151.

6. Alfred E. Cornebise, *The Stars and Stripes: Doughboy Journalism in World War I* (Westport, Conn.: Greenwood Press, 1984), no. 37, *Contributions in Military History,* 4. The *New York Herald* had been publishing a Paris edition for some time. The *Stars and Stripes,* which did not appear until February 1918, was created because servicemen complained that "there was no reliable news from home and no indication of what the nation was doing or thinking [and the] . . . *Tribune* and . . . *Herald* did not suffice."

7. Clipping [no title], Scrapbooks, vol. 2, PHDC.

8. *Chicago Tribune,* Army edition, Aug. 18, 1917.

9. *El Paso Morning Times,* Aug. 15, 1917.

10. *Ibid.*

11. *Ibid.,* Aug. 30, 1917.

12. *Ibid.*

13. *El Paso Morning Times,* Sept. 11, 1917.

14. *Ibid.,* Aug. 15, 1917.

15. *Ibid.*

16. *Ibid.,* Sept. 16, 1917.

17. *Ibid.,* Sept. 18, 1917.

18. *Ibid.,* Sept. 2, 1917.

19. *Ibid.,* Oct. 16, 1917.

20. *New York Times,* Mar. 11, 1915.

21. *El Paso Morning Times,* Oct. 16, 1917.

22. *Ibid.*

23. *Chicago Sunday Tribune,* Nov. 4, 1917, pt. 1. Peggy herself was not deceived that this was necessarily the case. Carolyn Wilson, also an *un*accredited correspondent (for the *Chicago Tribune*), wrote that one night when a group of them had been at a Paris café, they had watched several ambulance corpsmen, whom they knew to be married, drinking, carousing, and generally "carrying on." Peggy had looked at her, "a pained little smile on her face. . . . 'I wonder why it is,' [she] said, 'that so many of the men who are over here as volunteers are married men.'"

24. Crozier, *American Reporters,* 153-55.

25. Floyd Gibbons, *And They Thought We Wouldn't Fight* (New York: George H. Doran Co., 1918), 98. Gen. Peyton C. March, a colorful figure, U.S. Grant-like with his "stubby-pointed beard" and teeth clamped "on the butt end of a cigar . . ., frequently [wore] the $11.50 regulation issue uniform of the enlisted men," and was often seen in "rubber boots standing hip deep in the mud of the gun pits, talking to the men like a . . . kindly, yet stern father."

26. Crozier, *American Reporters,* 153-55.

27. *El Paso Morning Times,* Oct. 24, 1917.

28. *Ibid.*

29. *Chicago Tribune,* Army edition, Oct. 3, 1917.

30. *El Paso Morning Times,* Jan. 26, 1918.

31. *Ibid.,* Nov. 8, 1917.

32. *Ibid.*

33. *Ibid.,* Dec. 14, 1917.

34. *Ibid.,* Jan. 26, 1918.

35. *Marysville Advocate-Democrat,* May 1, 1919.

36. Gibbons, *And They Thought,* 115.

37. Note attached to spur, Box 2, PHDC.

38. Crozier, *American Reporters,* 151-55.

39. "By Peggy Hull in the China Press," Box 1, Folder no. 5, PHDC.

40. *El Paso Morning Times,* Aug. 19, 1917.

41. *Ibid.,* Dec. 13, 1917.

42. *Ibid.*

43. "The Post Goes Visiting."

44. "Dear Officers and so;diers [*sic*] of the A.E.F. /) [*sic*]," MS, Box 1, Folder no. 3, PHDC.

### CHAPTER SEVEN
#### The Heroine Returns to El Paso

1. *El Paso Morning Times,* Dec. 30, 1917.

2. *Ibid.*

3. *Ibid.,* Jan. 20, 1918.

4. *Ibid.,* Jan. 6, 1918.

5. *Ibid.,* Dec. 24, 1917; *Los Angeles Times,* May 13, 1918, Scrapbooks, vol. 2, PHDC.

6. *Chicago Tribune,* Army edition, Dec. 24, 1917.

7. *El Paso Morning Times,* Dec. 17, 1917.

8. *Ibid.,* Dec. 18, 1917.

9. *Ibid.*

10. *Chicago Tribune,* Dec. 22, 1917.

11. *El Paso Morning Times,* Dec. 21, 1942. Peggy's triumphant return to El Paso was remembered twenty-five years later by Ollie P. Lansden. "Peggy Hull came home. This was a great event with bands playing, speech making and so on. Peggy, a young reporter on The El Paso Times, had gone overseas as a war correspondent and her travels were watched by all El Paso."

12. *Ibid.,* Dec. 24, 1917.

13. *Ibid.*

14. *Ibid.,* Jan. 6, 1918.

15. *Ibid.,* Annual Prosperity and Industrial edition, New Mexico section, Oct. 25, 1917. Northwest of Deming, New Mexico, this training camp was 3.4 miles long and 2.5 miles wide, and was made up of hundreds of buildings and tents and 35,000 to 40,000 men. The *New Mexico Blue Book,* describing its advantages, read more like an ad for a vacation spot than an army camp. "In September . . . the climate of the Mimbres valley is matchless. The extreme heat of summer, the high winds and the season of thunder storms

will have passed, and the soldiers will have the experience of living in a land of cloudless days, with a temperature warm enough but not too warm for comfort — in short, an ideal climate for outdoor life, with plenty of the purest water on the American continent!"

16. *Ibid.,* Dec. 25 and 26, 1917.

17. Ross Evans Paulson, *Women's Suffrage and Prohibition: A Comparative Study of Equality and Social Control* (Glenview, Ill.: Scott, Foresman and Co., 1973), 161.

18. *El Paso Morning Times,* Jan. 2, 1918.

19. *Ibid.,* Jan. 3, 1918.

20. *Ibid.*

21. *Ibid.,* Dec. 27, 1917.

22. *Ibid.,* Jan. 8, 1918.

23. *Ibid.,* Jan. 27, 1918.

24. *Ibid.,* Jan. 18, 1918.

25. *Ibid.,* Jan. 11, 1918.

26. *Ibid.,* Jan. 17, 1918.

27. *Ibid.,* Jan. 7, 1918.

28. General March observed that at Le Valdahon, "the percentage of venereal disease was larger in the Y.M.C.A. than in any unit of my command." Peyton C. March, *The Nation at War* (Garden City, N.Y.: Doubleday Doran, 1932), 212-13.

29. *El Paso Morning Times,* Jan. 7, 1918.

30. *Ibid.,* Jan. 26, 1918.

31. *Ibid.,* Jan. 18, 1918.

32. Webb Miller to Peggy Hull, Dec. 29, 1917, Box 1, Folder no. 8, PHDC.

33. *El Paso Morning Times,* Feb. 17, 1918.

34. *Ibid.,* Jan. 20, 1918.

35. *Ibid.,* Feb. 3, 1918.

36. For an interesting article on this colorful war photographer see David Mould's "Donald Thompson: Photographer at War," *Kansas History: A Journal of the Central Plains* 5 (Autumn 1982): 154-67.

37. *El Paso Morning Times,* Feb. 5, 1918.

38. *Ibid.,* Feb. 17, 1918.

39. *Deming* (N.M.) *Graphic,* Mar. 1, 1918.

40. *Chicago Tribune,* Scrapbooks, vol. 3, PHDC.

41. *El Paso Morning Times,* special section, May 26, 1918.

42. *Ibid.,* June 16, 1918.

43. *Ibid.,* May 26, 1918.

CHAPTER EIGHT

Accreditation at Last — to Siberia

1. Jack O'Donnell, "Peggy Hull," *The Ladies Home Journal* 37, no. 4 (April 1920): 83.

2. Eulalia (Weber) Guise and Byron E. Guise, interview with authors, Marysville, Kans., Dec. 6, 1979.

3. O'Donnell, "Peggy Hull."

4. *Ibid.*

5. "Book Notes," Notebooks, B28, vol. 2, PHDC. Some of the other women who had gone to France to do "war reporting" had been confident that they would easily be

accredited, but it did not happen; when they learned that Peggy finally had been, she became the object of snide speculation as to just how she had accomplished it. She had frequently felt that she was the subject of unfair gossip, feeling as if she could not "go any place with soldiers [without] people . . . worrying" that she was behind the bushes with them. She resented it bitterly. In fact, there is every reason to believe that she did not "carry on" with the men she came in contact with in the military. If she had, she would not have enjoyed the high regard she did with both the officers and the men.

6. Correspondent's pass (photocopy), Box 2, Folder no. 8, PHDC.

7. Hull to Guise.

8. Peggy (Henrietta G.) Hull, United States passport, Washington, D.C., Sept. 26, 1918. (In authors' possession)

9. Edward M. Coffman, *The Hilt of the Sword: The Career of Peyton C. March* (Madison: University of Wisconsin Press, 1966), 101.

10. March, *The Nation at War,* 128.

11. Robert J. Maddox, *The Unknown War with Russia: Wilson's Siberian Intervention* (San Rafael, Calif.: Presidio Press, 1977), 61.

12. William S. Graves, *America's Siberian Adventure, 1918-1920* (New York: Arno Press and the New York Times, 1971), 56.

13. Knightley, *The First Casualty,* 155-56.

14. *Ibid.,* 162-63.

15. Peggy Hull to Alice Goodnough, Aug. 17, 1919.

16. *Cleveland Press,* Jan. 3, 1919.

17. "U.S. Honor Impaired Due to Lax Discipline of Troops in Siberia," NEA (Newspaper Enterprise Association) Press Release, Box 1, Folder no. 4, PHDC.

18. *Cleveland Press,* Jan. 3, 1919.

19. Hull to Goodnough.

20. "The Post Goes Visiting."

21. "U.S. Honor Impaired."

22. *Ibid.*

23. *Cleveland Press,* Mar. 6, 1919.

24. *Ibid.,* Jan. 8, 1919.

25. "U.S. Honor Impaired."

26. Maddox, *The Unknown War,* 70.

27. "U.S. Nurses 9 in Room in Vladivostok," Scrapbooks, vol. 3, PHDC.

28. *Ibid.*

29. *Ibid.*

30. "Soldiers Marooned in Filthy Siberia Are All Homesick," NEA Press Release, Cleveland, Ohio, June 20, 1919.

31. *Cleveland Press,* Mar. 6, 1919. These workers did little more than "live in barracks and go hunting. Every effort to repair the railroad [was] blocked by the Japanese."

32. *Ibid.,* Feb. 27, 1919.

33. Graves, *America's Siberian Adventure,* 108.

34. *Ibid.*

35. Gen. Peyton C. March to Gen. William S. Graves, May 18, 1919, Container no. 22, Peyton C. March Papers, Library of Congress.

36. *Topeka* (Kans.) *Daily Capital,* June 23, 1919.

37. *Ibid.*

38. "Peggy Finds Fighting Men Better Company Than Gossiping Foreign Colony in Vladivostok," NEA Press Release.

39. Peggy Hull, "The Land of Roaring Rumor," *Leslie's Illustrated Weekly,* Apr. 10, 1920, 445.

40. *Ibid.,* 445, 446, 464.

41. *Ibid.,* 464, 465.

42. *Ibid.,* 465.

43. *Cleveland Press,* Jan. 22, 1919.

44. "Soldiers Marooned in Filthy Siberia."

45. *Cleveland Press,* Jan. 28, 1919.

46. Graves, *America's Siberian Adventure,* 341, 347, 354.

## CHAPTER NINE
### Capt. John Taylor Kinley and the Shanghai Years

1. Harry J. Lambeth, "Distant War Fronts Are Peggy Hull's Beat," *Editor and Publisher,* May 6, 1944, 58.

2. Edna Lee Booker, *News Is My Job: A Correspondent in War-Torn China* (New York: MacMillan Co., 1940), 15. Booker paints an interesting and informative picture of life in China in the 1920s and 1930s.

3. *Ibid.,* 25-26.

4. *Ibid.,* 26.

5. *Ibid.,* 19, 46.

6. *Ibid.,* 24.

7. Peggy Hull, "United China Demands Her Rights," *Leslie's Illustrated Weekly,* July 26, 1919, 156.

8. Hull to Goodnough. In this letter there was this tantalizing bit: "As I don't feel well my doctor-husband thinks the heat would be bad for me." Since she never mentioned him again, it would seem that this "marriage" was aborted, extralegal, or chimerical.

9. Guise interview.

10. *Oketo* (Kans.) *Eagle,* Apr. 7, 1920; C. G. Morton to Peggy Hull, July 6, 1920. (In authors' possession)

11. *Current Biography,* 1946, 313.

12. Kuhn, "Peggy Hull Deuell."

13. Irene Kuhn, *Assigned to Adventure* (Philadelphia & New York: J. B. Lippincott Co., 1938), 160. See this work for more about Peggy and Irene and for the charming and witty account of their trip as well as Kuhn's own remarkable story.

14. *Ibid.,* 169-70.

15. *Ibid.,* 176.

16. *Ibid.,* 172.

17. *Ibid.,* 180.

18. *Ibid.,* 188.

19. *Ibid.,* 189-90; Clipping [no title], Scrapbooks, vol. 3, PHDC.

20. "War Correspondent Now a Bride," Scrapbooks, vol. 3, PHDC.

21. Rankin interview.

22. "War Correspondent Now a Bride"; "Prominent Woman Correspondent Is Alhambra Visitor," *Star News* (Alhambra, Calif.), Scrapbooks, vol. 3, PHDC.

23. *Current Biography,* 1946, 314.

24. Briney interview.

25. Eldora (Goodnough) Verburg, interview with authors, Lawrence, Kans., Nov. 30, 1979. From France, Peggy had sent a rather unusual present, hair restorer salve, to her little niece, Eldora, who had lost her hair as a result of influenza. Soon after the treatments with it began, Eldora's hair started to grow back in.

26. Kuhn, *Assigned to Adventure,* 208.

27. *San Francisco Examiner,* Jan. 25, 1924; "Seafarer Weds Miss Peggy Hull," *Chicago Tribune,* Box 1, Folder no. 10, PHDC.

28. Kuhn, *Assigned to Adventure,* 218.

29. Booker, *News Is My Job,* 163.

30. *Ibid.,* 164.

31. *Montreal Daily Star,* Oct. 18, 1924, Shanghai and other misc. clippings, PHDC.

32. Kuhn, *Assigned to Adventure,* 216.

33. "Tching Mai Takes Missy to the Fair," Scrapbooks, vol. 3, PHDC.

34. *Shanghai Times,* June 15, 1924, Scrapbooks, vol. 3, PHDC.

35. "Western Drama in Chinese," and "Shanghai As Hollywood of the Orient," Scrapbooks, vol. 3, PHDC.

36. *Ibid.*

37. *Montreal Daily Star,* July 17, 1926, Shanghai and other misc. clippings, PHDC.

38. "U.S. Tourist Party Stops Off at Shanghai," Scrapbooks, vol. 3, PHDC.

39. *Ibid.*

40. *Ibid.*

41. "Shroffs and Chits," Shanghai and other misc. clippings, PHDC.

42. "Shanghai Sub-Deb's Letters," Scrapbooks, vol. 3, PHDC.

43. "By Peggy Hull in the China Press," Box 1, Folder no. 5, PHDC.

44. "First of Her Kind," Box 1, Folder no. 10, PHDC.

## CHAPTER TEN
### Peggy Hull Kinley, Alien

1. *Chicago Tribune,* July 1, 1927.

2. *New York World,* Feb. 27, 1926.

3. *New York Times,* Feb. 27, 1926.

4. *Chicago Tribune,* July 1, 1927.

5. *New York Times,* Feb. 27, 1926.

6. *New York World,* Feb. 27, 1926.

7. Emma Wold, "American Women and the Immigration Law," Box 1, Folder no. 6, PHDC.

8. *Life,* May 20, 1926, 14.

9. *New York World,* July 24, 1927.

10. *Ibid.*

11. *Ibid.,* July 26, 1927.

12. "Sherwood Sued for Idea 'Theft,'" Box 1, Folder no. 10, PHDC.

13. *New York Daily News,* Oct. 30, 1939.

14. "Sherwood Sued for Idea 'Theft.'"

15. *New York World Telegram,* May 23, 1931.

16. *Salina* (Kans.) *Journal,* July 16, 1929.

17. Briney interview.

18. Rankin interview.

19. Peggy Hull Deuell to Richard and Leonore Smith, early 1951.

20. *The Congressional Digest,* Nov., 1930, 262. A March 3, 1931, "perfecting amendment" finally granted equality of citizenship to women.

21. Notarized statement of Edwy Goodnough, Oct. 22, 1930, Salina, Kans. (Photostat in authors' possession)

22. *New York American,* May 21, 1931; *New York World-Telegram,* May 23, 1931; *New York Times,* May 24, 1931.

23. *Time,* Feb. 22, 1932.

24. *Literary Digest,* May 3, 1930, 6.

25. Reissig interview.

26. Deuell to Michener.

27. Stegman interview.

## CHAPTER ELEVEN
### "The Battle for Shanghai" by Peggy Hull

1. "Only Woman War Correspondent Is Shanghai Visitor," Box 1, Folder no. 5, PHDC.

2. Immanuel Chung-Yueh Hsu, *The Rise of Modern China* (New York & London: Oxford University Press, 1970), 648; *New York Daily News,* Jan. 31, 1932.

3. Stegman interview.

4. "The Post Goes Visiting."

5. Booker, *News Is My Job,* 262.

6. Lambeth, "Distant War Fronts Are Peggy Hull's Beat."

7. *Chicago Tribune,* Jan. 29, 1932.

8. *New York Daily News,* Feb. 5, 1932.

9. Guise, "Peggy Hull Remembered." Nomura was subsequently Japanese ambassador to the United States at the time of Pearl Harbor.

10. Peggy Hull, "Open Grave in Shanghai," *Eye Witness,* ed. Robert Spiers Benjamin (New York: Alliance Book Corp., 1940), 8.

11. *Ibid.,* 5.

12. *Ibid.,* 4-5.

13. *Ibid.,* 6.

14. *Ibid.,* 8.

15. *Ibid.*

16. *Ibid.,* 15.

17. *Ibid.,* 12-13.

18. *New York Daily News,* Feb. 25, 1932.

19. *Newburgh* (N.Y.) *News,* Sept. 8, 1934. (This picture is in the Peggy Hull Deuell Collection.)

20. Hsu, *The Rise of Modern China,* 648.

21. Peggy Hull, "The Last Crusade, 1918 A.D.," *The Pointer* (West Point, N.Y.: U.S. Corps of Cadets, United States Military Academy), Dec. 2, 1935, 16.

22. M. L. Stein, *Under Fire: The Story of American War Correspondents* (New York: Julien Messner, 1968), 228.

23. Hull to Guise. Byron Guise was the husband of Eulalia Weber, who, as a teenager, had been forever marked by her meeting with Peggy.

24. *Chicago Tribune,* Jan. 29, 1932.

25. Stegman interview.

## CHAPTER TWELVE
### Eleanor Deuell, Mistress of Saxton Hall

1. "Harvey," Notebooks, C31, vol. 2, PHDC.

2. *Newburgh News,* Oct. 30, 1939.

3. Silas Bent, *Ballyhoo: The Voice of the Press* (New York: Horace Liveright, 1927), 186.

4. Helen McGill Hughes, *News and the Human Interest Story* (Chicago: University of Chicago Press, 1940), 220.

5. Bent, *Ballyhoo,* 187.

6. Hughes, *News and the Human Interest Story,* 224.

7. Deuell to Michener.

8. John Tebbel, *An American Dynasty* (Garden City, N.Y.: Doubleday & Co., Inc., 1947), 296.

9. Deuell to Michener.

10. Tom Cassidy, "In Memoriam," Box 1, Folder no. 11, PHDC.

11. *Chicago Tribune,* Apr. 20, 1923.

12. *Ibid.*

13. *New York Daily News,* Oct. 30, 1939.

14. Hilda (Connolly) Ochsen, interview with authors, Cornwall-on-Hudson, N.Y., May 10, 1980.

15. Deuell to Michener.

16. "Beautiful Saxton Hall, Cornwall-on-Hudson, New York, Country Home of The Late Harvey V. Deuell, Managing Editor of the New York Daily News," Brochure. (In authors' possession)

17. David Taylor, interview with authors, Cornwall-on-Hudson, N.Y., May 10, 1980.

18. "Beautiful Saxton Hall."

19. Stegman interview.

20. Hull to Guise.

21. Taylor interview.

22. Ochsen and Dorothy Sutherland, interview with authors, Cornwall-on-Hudson, N.Y., May 10, 1980.

23. Deuell to Michener

24. D. Reeve Ketcham, interview with authors, Cornwall-on-Hudson, N.Y., May 14, 1980; Taylor interview; Christine (Cummings) Bates, interview with authors, New Windsor, N.Y., May 25, 1981; Eleanor Moore, interview with authors, Cornwall-on-Hudson, N.Y., May 15, 1980.

25. Ochsen and Sutherland interview.

26. Briney interview; Ochsen and Sutherland interview.

27. Godfrey interview.

28. Ochsen interview.

29. Ketcham interview.

30. Bates interview.

31. *Ibid.*

32. Moore interview.

33. *Ibid.*

34. Briney interview.

35. Ochsen interview; *Newburgh News,* Oct. 30, 1939.

36. *Newburgh News,* Sept. 8, 1934.

37. *Ibid.*

38. Godfrey interview.

39. Deuell to Michener.

40. *Ibid.*

41. Godfrey interview.

42. Moore interview.

43. Ochsen interview.

44. Godfrey interview.

45. *Ibid.*

46. "Spring in Cornwall," *Cornwall Local,* May 5, 1949.

47. Ochsen interview.

48. Fred Gettings, *Dictionary of Astrology* (London: Routledge & Kegan Paul, 1985), 53, 281.

49. Godfrey interview.

50. Clipping [no title], Scrapbooks, vol. 1, PHDC.

51. Ketcham interview.

52. Godfrey interview.

53. Hull to Guise.

54. Ochsen interview.

55. *Ibid.*

56. Eleanor Deuell to Hilda Connolly, Nov. 1, 1938.

57. Hull to Guise.

58. Ochsen interview.

59. *Ibid.*

60. *New York Daily News,* Oct. 30, 1939.

61. *Newburgh News,* Oct. 30, 1939.

62. *Cornwall Local,* Feb. 2, 1939.

63. Briney interview.

64. "Harvey V. Deuell Will Leaves Estate to Widow," and "Wills for Probate," Box 1, Folder no. 11, PHDC. According to the *Cornwall Local* of March 27, 1941, the gross value of the estate was $259,044.

65. *Cornwall Local,* Aug. 3, 1939.

66. Verburg interview.

67. *New York Herald-Tribune,* Oct. 30, 1939, Box 1, Folder no. 11, PHDC.

68. Robert Livingston Schuyler, ed., *Dictionary of American Biography,* vol. 11, pt. 2 (New York: Charles Scribner's Sons, 1958): 231.

69. *New York Daily News,* Oct. 30, 1939, Box 1, Folder no. 11, PHDC.

70. *Ibid.; Ibid.,* Nov. 1, 1939.

## CHAPTER THIRTEEN
### Peggy Again

1. Tebbel, *An American Dynasty,* 304.

2. *Ibid.,* 257.

3. Godfrey interview.

4. Deuell to Michener.

5. Exhibit "B," Last Will and Testament of Harvey V. Deuell, Feb. 5, 1938. (Photocopy in authors' possession)

6. Ochsen interview.

7. (Dr.) Richard and Leonore Smith, interview with authors (Saxton Hall), Cornwall-on-Hudson, N.Y., May 25, 1981.

8. *Saturday Evening Post,* June 16, 1945, 4.

9. Peggy Hull Deuell to Richard and Leonore Smith, Oct. 26, 1949.

10. Sutherland interview.

11. Deuell to Smiths.

12. Rankin interview.

13. *Ibid.*

14. *Ibid.*

15. *Current Biography,* 1941, 932; *Twentieth Century Authors,* First suppl., 1955, 1103.

16. Stegman interview.

17. *Ibid.*

18. Sutherland interview.

19. Taylor interview; Smith interview.

20. Real Estate Brochure, Box 1, Folder no. 10, PHDC.

21. *Cornwall Local,* July 17, 1941; *Newburgh News,* July 14, 1941.

22. *Ibid.*

23. Moore interview; Taylor interview.

24. Sutherland interview.

25. Taylor interview.

26. Sutherland interview.

27. *Ibid.*

28. *Ibid.*

29. Stegman interview.

30. *Cornwall Local,* Aug. 13, 1942; Aug. 27, 1942; Sept. 3, 1942; Sept. 10, 1942; Sept. 17, 1942.

31. Stegman interview.

32. Moore interview.

33. Stegman interview.

## CHAPTER FOURTEEN
### Peggy's Last War — World War II

1. Gwenfread Allen, *Hawaii's War Years, 1941-1945,* Reprint ed. (Westport, Conn.: Greenwood Press, Publishers, 1950), 57.

2. *Cornwall Local,* Aug. 20, 1942.

3. *New York Times,* May 9, 1940.

4. Knightley, *The First Casualty,* 223.

5. *Ibid.; New York Times,* May 9, 10, 1940.

6. Lambeth, "Distant War Fronts Are Peggy Hull's Beat." Peggy paid for a subscription to the *Plain Dealer* for her father so that he would be sure to see all her articles.

7. *Cleveland Plain Dealer,* Feb. 29, 1944.

8. Stegman interview.

9. *Cleveland Plain Dealer,* Feb. 29, 1944.

10. *Ibid.,* Mar. 1, 1944.

11. *Ibid.*

12. *Cornwall Local,* Dec. 2, 1943.

13. *Cleveland Plain Dealer,* Mar. 3, 1944.

14. *Ibid.,* Mar. 6, 1944.

15. *Ibid.,* Mar. 7, 1944.

16. *Ibid.*

17. "Only Two Women War Correspondents in Pacific Areas," Box 1, Folder no. 7, PHDC.

18. Edwin P. Hoyt, *How They Won the War in the Pacific: Nimitz and His Admirals* (New York: Weybright & Talley, 1970), 355.

19. "First Accredited Woman War Correspondent," 36.

20. *Cleveland Plain Dealer,* Sept. 27, 1945.

21. *Ibid.,* Apr. 17, 1944.

22. *Ibid.,* Apr. 14, 1944.

23. *Ibid.,* Feb. 15, 1944.

24. *Ibid.,* Mar. 23, 1944.

25. *Ibid.,* Apr. 6, 1945.

26. "First Accredited Woman War Correspondent," 36.

27. *Cleveland Plain Dealer,* Nov. 13, 1944.

28. *Ibid.,* May 6, 1944.

29. *Ibid.,* Aug. 8, 1944.

30. *Ibid.,* May 24, 1944.

31. *Ibid.,* Mar. 27, 1944.

32. *Ibid.,* May 2, 1944.

33. *Ibid.,* Aug. 20, 1944.

34. *Ibid.,* Oct. 3, 1944.

35. *Ibid.,* Aug. 20, 1944.

36. Headquarters United States Army Forces, Pacific Ocean Areas, Office of the Commanding General, Travel orders, Mrs. Peggy Hull Deuell, Jan. 26, 1945. (In authors' possession)

37. "First Woman Reporter Files from Pacific Area by Telephone to the New York Times," Box 1, Folder no. 7, PHDC.

38. *Cleveland Plain Dealer,* Feb. 12, 1945.

39. *Ibid.,* Feb. 23, 1945.

40. *Marshall County News,* Nov. 8, 1945.

41. Knightley, *The First Casualty,* 327. "In the Pacific, the military went to great lengths to protect him [Ernie Pyle], and, since his appeal depended so much on mixing with the ordinary fighting man, his writing lost its quality." During most of her career, Peggy was forced to operate under this kind of stifling protection.

42. *Cleveland Plain Dealer,* Aug. 4, 1944.

43. *Ibid.,* May 9, 1944.

44. *Ibid.,* July 9, 1945.

45. *Ibid.,* Apr. 6, 1945.

46. *Ibid.,* May 20, 1944.

47. *Ibid.,* Feb. 23, 1945.

48. *Ibid.,* Mar. 14, 1945.

49. *Ibid.,* May 28, 1945.

50. *Ibid.,* June 25, 1945.

51. *Ibid.,* May 31, 1945.

52. *Ibid.*

53. *Ibid.*

54. *Ibid.,* June 30, 1945.

55. Ben Gross, "Listening In," *New York Daily News,* Jan. 20, 1945.

56. Commendation, United States Navy, Executive Office of the Secretary, April 11, 1946. (In authors' possession)

57. Michener to Deuell.

CHAPTER FIFTEEN

"Whatever Happened to Peggy Hull?"

Much general information in this chapter came from the *Cornwall* (N.Y.) *Local,* 1945-1953.

1. *Marshall County News,* Nov. 8, 1945.

2. *Ibid*

3. Eulalia Guise to authors, Oct. 28, 1985; Guise to authors, Aug. 15, 1989.

4. Alice M. Dennis, "Veteran Woman Correspondent Who Covered Two World Wars Visits Writer's Home Here," Box 1, Folder no. 10, PHDC.

5. "First Accredited Woman War Correspondent," 36.

6. *Ibid.*

7. *Marshall County News,* Nov. 8, 1945.

8. *Cornwall Local,* Feb. 7, 1946.

9. *Ibid.,* Feb. 14, 1946; *Ibid.,* Apr. 18, 1946.

10. *Cornwall Local,* June 6, 1946. The *Cornwall Local* ad (May 30, 1946) for the movie running at the Storm King Theater said, "THE NOVEL 'WHISTLE STOP' BY MARITTA M. WOLF, YOUR FRIEND AND FORMER NEIGHBOR, IS NOW A PICTURE." Her visits to Saxton Hall hardly qualified her for a down-home description like "neighbor," and her name (Wolff) was misspelled.

11. Verburg interview.

12. *Cornwall Local,* June 6, 1946.

13. Smith interview; *Cornwall Local,* July 18, 1946.

14. *Cornwall Local,* Mar. 13, 1947; *New York Times,* Feb. 2, 1947, Real Estate section.

15. *Cornwall Local,* Sept. 19, 1946.

16. *Ibid.,* Mar. 13, 1947.

17. Peggy Hull Deuell to Richard and Leonore Smith, Aug. 7, [1947].

18. Comment on effects of alcohol, Notebooks, C31, vol. 2, PHDC.

19. *Marysville* (Kans.) *Advocate,* Aug. 7, 1947.

20. Taylor interview.

21. Guise interview.

22. *Ibid.*

23. *Ibid.*

24. Lists of titles, Notebooks, B28, vols. 2 and 3, PHDC.

25. *Cornwall Local,* Sept. 1, 1949.

26. Peggy Hull Deuell to Richard and Leonore Smith, Sept. 11, 1949.

27. Peggy Hull Deuell, "I Ran Away from Home at 60," *Family Circle,* Dec., 1955, 6.

28. *Ibid.*

29. Peggy Hull Deuell to Richard and Leonore Smith, [1951].

30. *Ibid.* After his death, Harvey became something of a saint in Peggy's mind.

31. *Ibid.*

32. Peggy Hull Deuell to Richard and Leonore Smith, Mar. 20, 1951.

33. Peggy Hull Deuell to Richard and Leonore Smith, Mar. 27, 1951.

34. *Cornwall Local,* Sept. 11, 1952.

35. Stegman interview. On February 2, 1953, George Hull died in Los Angeles of coronary arteriosclerotic heart disease. (Certificate of Death, Office of State Registrar of Vital Statistics, Department of Health Services, State of California, no. 53-018628)

36. "The Post Goes Visiting."

37. *Ibid.*

38. Peggy Hull Deuell to Dorothy Sutherland, Dec. 11, 1955.

39. *Ibid.*

40. *Ibid.*

41. Frieda Harbin, interview with authors, Apr. 10, 1980, Carmel Valley, Calif.

42. Verburg interview.

43. Deuell to Sutherland.

44. Briney interview.

45. Deuell to Smiths, Mar. 20, 1951.

46. Peggy Hull Deuell to John B. and Mrs. Adams, June 30, 1965 (rough draft), Box 1, Folder no. 6, PHDC. In this reply to a letter from the Adamses asking for information about her World War II activities, she apologized for her delayed response and wrote, "I'm just home from a long hospital seige [*sic*] and a couple of major operations."

47. Webb Miller, "Webb Miller Tells of Hardships of Newsmen in Ethiopia," *Editor & Publisher,* Nov. 9, 1935, 11.

48. Peggy Hull Deuell to Richard and Leonore Smith, Mar. 10, 1957.

49. Verburg interview.

50. Deuell to Sutherland.

51. Records of The Baptism, Our Lady of Mt. Carmel Church, Carmel Valley, Calif., Jan. 31, 1965.

52. Deuell to Adams.

53. Quotation attributed to Mrs. Thomas Dewey, Notebooks, B28, vol. 2, PHDC.

54. Harbin interview.

55. Hobert Skidmore to Frances and Alan Rankin, May 26, 1967. (In authors' possession)

56. Harbin interview.

57. *Ibid.*

58. *Monterey* (Calif.) *Herald,* Apr. 3, 1969; Hobert D. Skidmore, Certificate of Death, Office of the State Registrar of Vital Statistics, Department of Health Services, State of California, no. 69-041312. Peggy's will, dated March 22, 1966, left one dollar to each of her "heirs and distributees" (her nieces) and everything else, including the remnants of the trust Harvey had set up, to Hobert Skidmore. Hobert's heirs (he, also, left the token dollar each to his close relatives) were his sister and Ernie Marchon. For many years, Ernie was a respected waiter at the Del Monte Lodge in Pebble Beach and the French Poodle Restaurant in Carmel. It was he who gave Peggy's papers to the University of Kansas. Ernie died in September 1979. His heir was Raymond A. Ruffino.

# INDEX

*The Wars of Peggy Hull*

# PEGGY HULL

The text pages of this book are printed on
60 lb. recycled, acid-free
*Cross Pointe Halopaque Cream White Vellum;*
the text type face is
*Sabon,*
the display type is
*Zapf Chancery.*

Typesetting and printing by the
UTEP Printing Division.

Jacket and Book design by
Rebecca Quiñones.

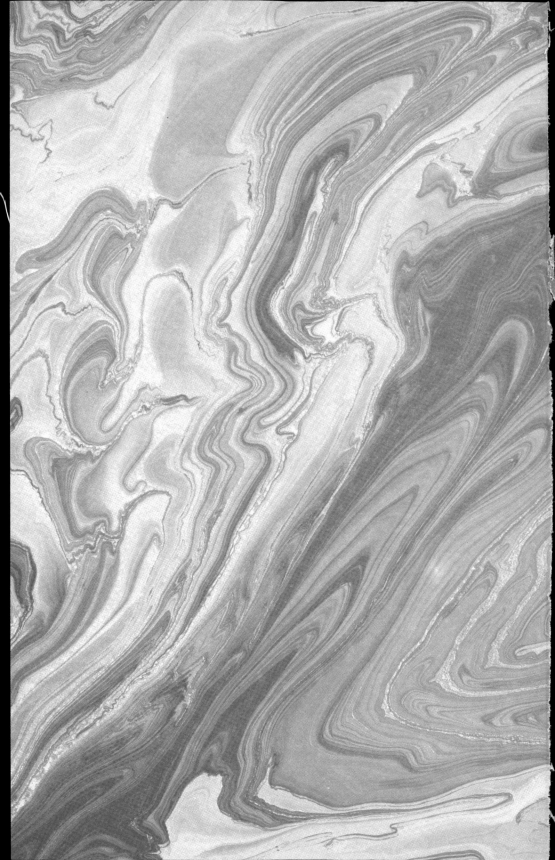